The Country Church Visitors' Handbook 1995

A Guide to the Country Churches of
Hereford and Worcester,
South Shropshire and South - West Warwickshire.

Compiled
by Sandy Marchant
on behalf of the churches involved with
Through the Church Door

A Through the Church Door Publication.

This guide has been compiled from information supplied and checked by the churches themselves. Every effort has been made to ensure that the information is accurate but mistakes can arise and you are advised to check the information , where possible, before setting off for a visit. No liability for any errors or omissions is accepted.

© Through The Church Door 1994

ISBN 0 9524866 0 1

Published by : Through the Church Door

The Hay Loft, The Old Vicarage, Stoulton,

Worcester WR7 4RE

Front Cover : Bridget Dowty

Illustrations : Les Ashton

Bridget Dowty and a great many others

Historic Maps : John Clifton

Typing : Joanna Bryant

Printed and bound by Severnside Printers

Bridge House, Upton - upon- Severn, Worcester WR8 0HG

CONTENTS

Introduction:

Our Christian Heritage
The Anglo-Saxons - when the Normans came:

The Anglo-Saxon Legacy:

Gazetteer with Dates for Your Diary

In the Steps of St. Wulfstan: June 3rd 1995

It is entirely fitting that the Through the Church Door project should be launched to coincide with the celebrations to mark the 900th anniversary of the death of St. Wulfstan of Worcester.

Wulfstan was a Bishop whose Diocese stretched south as far as Bristol and east to Warwick. He was a man whose life was rooted and grounded in his faith. As he travelled around this huge area he would stop to pray in each of the churches he passed. He mixed with all classes of society and was accepted by them. He saw the salvation of all to be their relationship to God and did all in his power to develop that relationship with his preaching, church building and example. He built churches on his estates and encouraged other landowners to do likewise. Not many of the churches known to the Anglo-Saxon Wulfstan survive today but each living church we can see is a part of the legacy of the Anglo-Saxons.

Churches all over the ancient Diocese and beyond are preparing to piece together parts of a jigsaw that together make up the story of St. Wulfstan. They invite you to construct your own jigsaw on June 3rd by visiting as many of these churches as you can. St Wulfstan was a monk, he was obedient to the Rule of St Benedict and would pray in each of the churches he entered. He prayed that people would live together in peace. We invite you to join us in this prayer on June 3rd.

Worcestershire
Worcester Cathedral

Alfrick	St Mary Magdalene
Bengeworth	St Peter
Blakedown	St James the Great
Broadway	St Michael and All Angels
Church Lench	All Saints
Churchill in Halfshire	St James the Great
Cowleigh (Malvern)	St Peter
Cropthorne	St Michael
Crowle	St John the Baptist
Defford	St James
Drakes Broughton	St Barnabas
Eckington	Holy Trinity
Evesham	All Saints
Grimley	St Bartholomew
Hanbury	St Mary the Virgin
Hartlebury	St James the Apostle
Harvington	St James
Hindlip	St James the Great
Inkberrow	St Peter
Kidderminster	St Mary and All Saints
Knightwick	St Mary
Leigh	St Edburga
Lower Broadheath	Christchurch
Malvern Link	Church of the Ascension
Malvern Link	Saint Matthias'
Norton	St James the Great
Pershore	Abbey Church of Holy Cross
Pirton	St Peter
Powick	St Peter's
Romsley	St Kenelm
Rous Lench	St Peter
Salwarpe	St Michael
Sedgeberrow	St Mary the Virgin
Stoulton	St Edmund King and Martyr
Warndon Villages (Worcester)	St Nicholas
Wribbenhall	All Saints'

Herefordshire
Hereford cathedral

Acton Beauchamp	St Giles
Dorstone	St Faith's
Eye (Morton)	St Peter and St Paul
Kilpeck	St Mary and St David
Little Dewchurch	St David
Peterchurch	St Peter
Putley	Christchurch
Vowchurch	St Bartholomew

Shropshire

Bishop's Castle	St John the Baptist
Cound	St Peter
Dorrington	St Edward the Confessor
Highley	St Mary
Hopesay	St Mary
Quatford	St Mary Magdalene
Stokesay	St John the Baptist

Warwickshire

Coughton	St Peter
Long Itchington	Holy Trinity
Norton Lindsey	The Holy Trinity
Ratley	St Peter ad Vincula
Salford Priors	St Matthew
Tysoe	The Assumption of the Blessed Virgin Mary
Wellesbourne	St Peter
Whatcote	St Peter

Gloucestershire
Gloucester Cathedral

Tewkesbury Abbey	St Mary
Bishops Cleeve	St Michael
Deerhurst	St Mary
Odda's Chapel	
Dymock	St Mary
Hawkesbury	St Mary
Longney on Severn	St Lawrence

and all the ancient churches between Cheltenham and Cirencester

From the Bishop of Worcester

I have great pleasure in introducing this imaginative project entitled, "Through the Church Door". I hope that in spite of the general need for security against vandals, people will in fact be enabled to spend time inside our churches in the Diocese of Worcester, as well as see their exterior, so much a part of our landscape and townscape.

This project, the origin of which we owe to Sandy Marchant, will enable us all to take a new look at our churches. It will enable them to speak to us of our history but, above all, of our faith. This coincides with celebrations in the Diocese of Worcester to mark the nine hundredth anniversary of the death of one of our greatest bishops namely, Wulfstan. He began his ministry in Anglo-Saxon England and continued it in the reign of the Norman King William the Conqueror. It was an active ministry of sixty years!

I have asked all parishes and diocesan boards and councils to take a step forward in mission during 1995. My guess is that each parish or diocesan body will choose different projects forming an enormous variety across the diocese.

Without a doubt, both in Hereford and Worcester, **Through the Church Door** will assist us to understand the Christian tradition into which we enter and pose for us the question, "What is required of us today?" It was an immense vitality which caused Christian believers in Anglo-Saxon and medieval England to build so extensively and so gloriously. How should such a vital faith find its outlets in our contemporary and utterly different world?

First, however, study The Country Church Visitors' Handbook 1995. It is the essential guide to the exciting possibilities which you can discover, "Through the Church Door".

+Philip Worcester

WHAT IS THROUGH THE CHURCH DOOR?

Through the Church Door is the name of a three year project which aims to help places of worship in the countryside to be open and to welcome visitors. The people who are charged with the upkeep of village churches are ordinary people, often with no particular expertise, with a deep affection for the buildings in their care. They also have an appreciation of all that has happened in them and an awareness of the place they have in the local community. They want to pass them on to their children and grandchildren, not as museums of the past, but as living, breathing entities doing what they have always done; offering a place for renewal and refreshment, a place for worship and communion with Almighty God.

They want to share this with you.

We live in a time of great change. It is to the countryside that many of us look for rest and restoration. What sort of images of the countryside do we carry with us as we ramble along country footpaths, past farmyards and into villages where the most obvious building is the village church? How much do we really know about the communities we are visiting? What do they know or understand about us and the places where we live? The Through the Church Door Project is about sharing and learning to understand. Each of the churches listed in the Gazetteer has opted to staff its church on the days listed in the 'Dates for your Diary' sections of this book. These are not necessarily the only days when the churches are open but they are dates that you can rely on to plan your visits. Use them to find out more about the architecture and history of the church buildings and the communities who have laughed and cried in them and who still use the building as a place where the deepest of emotions can be expressed and where you are still welcome to pause to pray.

The network of churches involved in the project is growing. In this our first year we have learned and are learning a lot. We are grateful to all those who have so freely given their time to help us find out and better understand the things we can see in our buildings. We still have a lot to learn. We would welcome your comments and experiences and encourage you to contact us with your comments.

For my part I would like to thank all those who have had sufficient confidence in the project to help get it off the ground and who then have offered the practical support necessary to bring things through to this stage. In particular I would like to thank my small editorial team and our printer and most of all my family who have had to bear with the consequences!!!

Sandy Marchant

Through the Church Door is grateful for the financial support received from: The Rural Development Commission, Hereford and Worcester Training and Enterprise Council, The Central Church Fund of the Church of England, The Edward Cadbury Trust, ACORA, Wychavon District Council, The Diocese of Hereford, the Diocese of Worcester and the Dean and Chapter of Worcester and Lichfield Cathedrals.

HOW TO USE THIS HANDBOOK

The book has been compiled to encourage you to explore some of the lesser known areas of the Heart of England. Please read this introduction before setting out.

Opening. Are the churches in this book open all the time?

The Country Churches While all churches included in this book welcome visitors no church can guarantee to be open all the time. The dates listed in the diary (correct at the time of going to press) are occasions when you can visit a church knowing that it will be open. You will find that many churches are open at times other than those listed. In many cases a telephone number has been included in the Gazetteer section - use it to plan or confirm your own arrangements. Each church entry includes suggestions of things to do and places to go locally and you are always welcome to join the local community for worship.

Please check at the beginning of each County Section in the Gazetteer; it lists churches which are regularly open and staffed.

The Town Churches This book deals principally with country churches but churches in local market towns have been included when they can indicate that they are open and staffed on a regular basis. These churches will be able to direct you to some of the country churches in their area.

Dates for Your Diary

The diary dates have been compiled from the individual entries and list the church activities known to be taking place on that day. For more information please consult the Gazetteer entries at the end of the book. **Although the telephone numbers are accurate you may find that they will have been affected by the 1995 renumbering procedures.**

The Gazetteer

Each church has been responsible for the compilation and presentation of its information. The Gazetteer lists all the churches participating in the project. They are arranged first on a county basis and then alphabetically by villages, Grid References are from the Landranger series of Ordnance Survey maps. Then follows the name of the church and the year it was dedicated, the diocese and an indication of the predominant architectural style. Where appropriate the listing of the church for architectural or historic merit has been added to complete this section.

Church Descriptions: Then follows a description of the church and its setting. This is not intended to replace the guide book. Each church and its setting is unique and churches have been asked to consider what is special about their own building. This is the basis on which the descriptions were compiled.

Finding and Parking: Local directions for motorists, have been included (and sometimes walkers and those travelling on public transport) Parking places have been chosen to cause minimum inconvenience to locals and visitors alike.

Looking Around: Many churches have information at hand to help you to appreciate the outside as well as the inside of their church buildings. Churchyards are places of considerable interest. Some are managed for the benefit of wildlife and contain species of animal and plant life rarely seen today. Others are winners of the best kept churchyard competition. Take time to appreciate the views from the churchyard, they can be spectacular.

Each church has indicated other places to visit both within its parish and beyond.

Comfort and Refreshment: Few churches can provide toilet facilities, where they can they have said so. Local picnic spots and places to eat and drink have been included, they can be very hospitable! Some parishes are working very closely with their neighbours to offer something special to visitors. Information printed in a box at the foot of an entry indicates where joint activity is taking place.

Christian Heritage

Each church is unique but linking each together is the common thread of the Christian faith. An understanding of the teachings of Christianity and the life of the Church can help in the interpretation of the things that can be seen in the walls, adornments and furnishings of each building. Each year a topic of Christian heritage will be put under the microscope. This year that topic is the 'Anglo-Saxon Church', next year it will consider 'Stories in Stone'. The first section of this book includes several short articles on the Anglo-Saxon church and its modern legacy. A map showing some of the surviving evidence of the period is included for you to use for your own exploration.

A DAY OUT IN THE COUNTRYSIDE

Visiting Country Churches
It is a good idea to wear good stout shoes if you intend to explore churchyards or walk the footpaths of the local area. Bring a pair of binoculars and use them to explore the glass and the bosses in the roof.

Visitors with Special Needs
All visitors are most welcome but occasionally the layout of the church or its position make it difficult for wheelchair access. Please consult the Gazetteer entry for each church to avoid disappointment.

Babies, Toddlers and Children
Babies, toddlers and children (of all ages) are all welcome. Look out for children's guides and activity sheets. Get on the detective trail!

Group Visits
Many churches welcome group visits (including school visits). They will make arrangements to meet special requests and will frequently provide teas or indicate places where they may be booked.

Special Interest Visits
It is hoped that the list of special interest activities will increase. This year your attention is drawn to three events:

1 In the Steps of St. Wulfstan: June 3rd. Churches throughout the area are piecing together the life of St. Wulfstan. A special map has been produced for the occasion and you are invited to 'Follow in the Steps of St. Wulfstan' around the Ancient Diocese of Worcester. (See list of churches.)

2 Embroideries and Tapestries Week July 5-9 Several churches are taking part in this week and will have their embroideries and tapestries on display. If your group would like to visit one or more churches during this week it can be arranged. Use the telephone numbers to organise for opening and special catering arrangements.

3 Church Detectives - August. August is holiday time and day trips can be fun. Why not use our church detective trail and discover some Anglo-Saxon evidence with your children and grandchildren, telephone 0905 841554 for details.

The Sponsored Cycle Ride 9th September You will see it described in many ways but it is the day when enthusiastic cyclists take to the road to visit as many churches as they can to raise funds for the church of their choice and their County Historic Churches Trust. Nearly all churches are open and ready to sign sponsorship forms on this occasion - If you like to take part consult your County Trust.

County Historic Churches Trusts

Herefordshire Historic Churches Trust. Mrs C.J.A. Galimore, Orchard House, Credenhill, Hereford HR4 7DA.

Gloucestershire Historic Churches Preservation Trust. J.K.Kerr Esq., A.I.C.S. Frocester Lodge, Nr. Stonehouse, Gloucestershire GL10 3TG

Oxfordshire Historic Churches Trust. R.H.Lethbridge Esq. Fawler Manor, Charlbury, Oxon OX7 3AH

Shropshire Historic Churches Trust. The Archdeacon of Salop, Tong Vicarage, Shifnal, Shropshire TF11 8PW

Warwickshire and Coventry Historic Churches Trust. Dr. C Brown,42 High Street, Warwick, CV34 4AS

Worcestershire and Dudley Historic Churches Trust. Michael Shaw Esq., The Pound, Chaddesley Corbett, Kidderminster, Worcs, DY10 4QL

Guided Walks and Talks

Several churches can provide guides to take you along footpaths between churches. Church Heritage rambles are interesting and a very good way of meeting local people. This information is in the Gazetteer.

If you would like someone to speak to your group about the country churches that appear in this book and many that do not, Tim Bridges or one of the county Historic Churches Trusts may be able to help. Contact Tim on 0905 722369.

Guide Books and Information

These will be available in the church and sometimes the village store. It is inappropriate to fill a small church with exhibition material but on some occasions churches are mounting special exhibitions on a short term basis. If you need to know something that is not immediately obvious do ask the welcomers. You will find them a mine of local and church information.

Entrance Charges

There are no charges but your donations are very welcome.

Security

Many churches now operate a ChurchWatch Scheme. No reference is made in this book to the treasures of individual churches. We feel sure that you will respect the items you see on display. They represent the gifts of local people throughout the ages, sometimes given in memory of individuals whose value to their community has been beyond price, as such they are irreplaceable. If you are asked to give your car number in return for the church key or sign the visitors' book please do so with good will. These simple measures can help keep our churches accessible.

1945 **1995**

WULFSTAN RETREAT (900th anniversary of St. Wulfstan of Worcester) 6th-8th October CANON DONALD ALLCHIN

50th ANNIVERSARY RETREAT 9th-12th October BISHOP DAVID JENKINS invited

RETREAT FESTIVAL 13th-15th October Bishop of Worcester Bishop of Stockport JABBOCK THEATRE

EMBROIDERY RETREAT 26th Aug - 1st Sept REVD. LEONARD CHILDS & TUTOR

RAKU CERAMIC RETREAT 17th-19th November SARA MAITLAND, SABINE BUTZLAFF

PAINTING & PRAYER RETREAT 18th-25th August REVD. JOHN SLYFIELD GLORIA OVERTON

POETRY & PRAYER RETREAT 20th-22nd January DIANE WALLS & GUY CORNWALL JONES

• CELEBRATIONS AT HOLLAND HOUSE •
MRS ELLIS HOLLAND
50 YEARS AS A RETREAT HOUSE

ELGAR RETREAT 12th-14th May FR. BILLY HEWITT SJ

ART HISTORY RETREAT 24th-26th February DOM SIMON McGURK OSB

MRS HOLLAND ORGANISED THE FIRST RETREAT IN OCTOBER 1945 & SUBSEQUENTLY GAVE HER HOUSE TO BE USED FOR RETREATS
HOLLAND HOUSE, RETREAT, CONFERENCE & LAITY CENTRE, CROPTHORNE, PERSHORE, WORCESTERSHIRE. TEL: (01386) 860330

OUR CHRISTIAN HERITAGE

THE ANGLO-SAXONS – WHEN THE NORMANS CAME:

The Anglo-Saxon Church

Christianity in Britain is very old. By the beginning of the fourth century there was an organised church. With the coming of the Anglo-Saxons in the fifth century it was largely destroyed. The British retreated before them to Wales and Cornwall. All had to begin all over again, the Anglo-Saxons who were pagans had to be converted. The work of conversion began with the Celtic monks (St Columba, Iona) from the north and the Roman mission sent by Gregory the Great which landed in 597. Gradually the work began.

Inevitably the church was a missionary church and Augustine and the Celtic monks reached out to the local rulers, the *bretwaldas*, of different regions of the country. If the ruler could be converted there was a good chance that his followers and people would do likewise. Broadly this is what happened. The missionaries were thorough in their work. They preached the Christian faith in the open air (later before 'preaching crosses'), they then instructed the people in the Christian faith and finally baptized them in rivers or lakes, confirmed them and admitted them to their first eucharist. In this the bishops played a leading part. Both for St Gregory and for the Celtic leaders a bishop was essentially a teaching bishop and he presided at the baptisms, and of course the confirmations, and celebrated the eucharist with the converts.

By the end of the seventh century the Roman and Celtic traditions had fused and thanks to the work of Theodore (from the Near East), Archbishop of Canterbury and the Roman abbot Adrian the church in England became organised. Theodore set up new dioceses (including Worcester). He divided others and thus broke down the previous "tribal" arrangements. His system was long lasting; parishes were much slower in coming. What was a very general pattern of pastoral activity was the establishment of minsters, staffed by a community of priests, assisted by young clerics, who evangelised the region surrounding them. The new Christians would go to the minsters for celebration of the liturgy, presided over by the bishop (if present) and the priests of the community, assisted by the young clerics who were being trained for pastoral work. The liturgy was anything but static. In the minsters it was sung to the primitive plainsong of the time. There would be a procession for the proclamation of the gospel and another when the people presented their gifts and went to receive holy communion.

The earliest churches seem to have been of the single-chamber kind (there were no screens) which seem to have developed rapidly into the two-chamber church, with nave and chancel. The windows were very narrow (and for long unglazed) and the interior rather dark. But the gloom was lightened by the candles burning around the altar. It is highly probable that the celebrant of the eucharist celebrated facing the people across the altar since celebration facing east came in generally on the continent in the ninth century. The whole rite then would have been clearly visible.

In such circumstances the Church's Year unfolded, marked by fast (Lent and vigil) and feasts — the great celebrations of Christmas, Holy Week: Palm Sunday, Maundy Thursday,(with the washing of the feet of the poor to whom food or alms were given), the singing of the Passion on Good Friday and the Creeping to the Cross, and on Holy Saturday the celebration of the Easter Vigil late in the day when the whole story of God's redeeming love from the Old Testament to the resurrection was enacted through word and sacrament. This was followed by the Fifty Days of Eastertide culminating in the Feast of Pentecost. (There was as yet no Trinity Sunday).

By the beginning of the eighth century the church in England could be said to be mature. Schools had been set up both in the north (Monkwearmouth and Jarrow, where St Bede, the Father of English History, taught) and in the south where under the influence of Theodore and Adrian not only Latin but also Greek could be learned. These and other schools were not merely academically important; they were training grounds for the clergy and what they learnt there they could communicate to their people. At the same time the language of the people, Anglo-Saxon, in which the clergy preached and taught (Bede translated the Gospel of St John into Anglo-Saxon) began to find expression in literature. Of this the Dream of the Rood by the oxherd Caedmon who saw Christ as a young warrior triumphing over death, is the best known.

But the most striking feature of the church's maturity was the missionary activity first of Willibrord to the Low Countries and the mission of Wynfrith of Crediton (later re-named, by the pope, Boniface) who evangelised much of west and south west Germany and who is acknowledged to this day there as the 'Apostle of Germany'. His body lies at Fulda where the bishops of the German-speaking countries meet for their annual conferences. It is noteworthy that women, nuns, assisted him in his work. Back in England women were playing an important part in the Christianisation of the country. There were abbesses, often of royal blood, presiding over double monasteries of monks and nuns. Their influence was pervasive and it is no accident that the famous Synod of Whitby (664) which marked the beginning of the fusion of the Celtic and Roman traditions took place in the monastery where St Hilda was abbess.

Unhappily the flourishing condition of the church as of the whole country was brutally interrupted by the invasion of the Norsemen towards the end of the ninth century and by the invasions of the Danes in the tenth century. They destroyed churches and monasteries, they looted their contents and slaughtered bishops (for example, St Alphege) and priests. They came to occupy much of England and it was only by the patience, courage and skill of King Alfred that they were pressed back to the eastern part of England called Danelaw. Alfred set about the restoration not only of the country but also the life of the church. No doubt there was much rebuilding of churches but Alfred had other things in mind. He gathered around him learned men (one from abroad), he began the restoration of the monastic schools and was much concerned that the clergy should be equipped or re-equipped for their pastoral work. Learning Latin late in life, he himself translated St Gregory's Pastoral Care, for like the saint he saw that bishops and priests must be preachers and teachers of the Christian faith. To give nourishment to the spiritual life he also translated the so-called Soliloquies of St Augustine. At his instance Werferth, Bishop of Worcester, translated the Dialogues of Pope Gregory the Great to provide more spiritual reading for the clergy, for religious, and even for the laity.

It could be said that Alfred laid the foundations of the revival of the church in the tenth century. The heart of this revival was monastic, brought about by three remarkable men: St Dunstan, Abbot of Glastonbury and later Archbishop of Canterbury, St Ethelwold, Bishop of Winchester, and St Oswald, Bishop of Worcester and York. These, with the help of kings like

Edgar, brought the full life of the Rule of St Benedict to the monasteries such as Worcester, the monastery where Wulfstan became a monk in the eleventh century. As before, the monastic revival was of concern to the whole church. There were the schools where boys and young men could be trained for the church, there they learned not only Latin and read the great Fathers of the Church but they also learned how to preach in the vernacular. They were greatly aided in this by the Homilies for the Church's Year and for certain saints' feasts, written by Aelfric, Abbot of Eynsham in Oxfordshire. There was indeed a great flowering of Anglo-Saxon culture at this time.

In the monasteries the liturgy became more elaborate and with the burial of a crucifix in the sepulchre on Good Friday and its 'resurrection' early on Easter morning, even dramatic. But once again, it needs to be said that this was important not only to monastic communities but to the church as a whole. The clerics and others (for monasteries at this time were not entirely enclosed communities) who took part in one way or another in the liturgy were set a standard they could live up to when and if they were ordained as priests.

In spite of wars and their unpleasant accompaniments - the early years of St Wulfstan were very disturbed - church life and the revival of the tenth century had effects in the eleventh. There were the beginnings of the parochial system and stone churches with stone altars were multiplied. The two-chamber church seems to have become common and over the chancel arch there was sometimes a great painted crucifixion with St Mary and St John on either side of Christ. Such pictures helped to instruct the people and had been called by St Gregory the Great the Biblia pauperum, the Bible of the Poor, for they learnt the Bible not only from sermons but through their eyes. The liturgy of the single priest in a church on the villa of a landowner was much simpler than that of the monasteries but it was sung (said Masses were known in the chapels of the monasteries but hardly elsewhere) and the whole local community attended every Sunday. Even as monk and priest Wulfstan preached assiduously to the people of Worcester and was criticised for it as some thought it was a bishop's job! As bishop he continued to do so, visiting his vast diocese that extended from Worcestershire to Bristol, confirming great numbers of children and celebrating the Mass for them.

In spite of the Norman invasion of 1066 the life of the Anglo-Saxon church continued. It was in good heart even if some of the grand foreign bishops and abbots looked down their noses at the church's 'old-fashioned' ways. Wulfstan himself seemed to sum up all that was best in devotion, pastoral zeal and biblical preaching in the Anglo-Saxon church.

Mgr J R Crichton

Discover the living legacy of the Anglo-Saxon church

follow in the STEPS OF ST WULFSTAN

around THE ANCIENT DIOCESE OF WORCESTER

on JUNE 3rd 1995

The Land that Wulfstan knew

The richness of our everyday speech gives us an immediate link with Wulfstan and his contemporaries. When we eat Apple, Plum or Pear, we taste fruits that they also knew by those names! It's the same with numerous birds, like Lark, Thrush and Nightingale, nowadays declining in numbers in our region. Familiar plants included Rose, Honeysuckle, Gorse and Cowslip, while Broom and Holly, Oak, Ash and Hawthorn grew here then, as they still do.

So you don't have to picture a countryside unimaginably different from today's. Anglo-Saxons, like us, distinguished between pasture and woodland, meadows and arable fields. Hedges were important, not only as boundaries, but to protect cultivated land from beasts grazing on common land and from woodland intruders like deer. A Midland peasant's regular duties included hedge maintenance. Our recent removal of miles of hedgerow, with resulting destruction of habitat, would have perplexed him.

Their landscape would have looked rougher than ours and smelled more raw and pungent. But fields and hedgerows were far more colourful, boasting a greater wealth of wild flowers, because they had not sprayed some to the verge of extinction.

Wulfstan in his travels would have seen a landscape busy with human movement, unlike the seemingly empty fields we know today, because farming was labour-intensive. Coppiced woodland was skillfully managed for building materials, fuel and utensils, as well as for pasture. Fertile resources were controlled far less wastefully than now, because it was more obvious to the Anglo-Saxons that survival and prosperity depended on their respectful relationship with the earth.

Some of their everyday wisdom would have put our ignorance to shame! Maybe you still teach your children to find Dock leaves to soothe Nettle stings, but general knowledge of the properties of other plants, for cooking or healing, is not widespread now.

Their night sky was truly dark, with only pinpricks of fire and candle-light showing where the settlements were. Because of that primary dependence on natural daylight and the changing seasons, our Anglo-Saxon ancestors had to live with the rhythms of nature, rather than despite them. Such harmony and co-operation are worth rediscovering in our present attempts to retrieve nature from man-made ruin.

Conflicts between exploitation and conservation in the region were known to Wulfstan's fellow countrymen. Indiscriminate felling of woodland had been punishable by fines for several centuries. There was unease at the growing demand for timber as fuel for Droitwich's expanding salt industry.

Here in Wulfstan's diocese, we retain some of the nation's most significant tracts of ancient woodland, such as Wyre Forest, notable in 1086 for its dearth of settlement place-names. A book of the period warned of the encroaching ploughman as "the gray enemy of the wood". His modern counterparts still exist.

Although they lost their political independence to the Normans, the Anglo-Saxons kept an identity alive in the landscape itself. As custodians of that same land, we can fall under a new Conquest and let economic forces rule us like Norman overlords. Or we can work to maintain and cherish a landscape which still bears traces that would be recognised by Wulfstan.

Rosemary Mann

Wulfstan and his Diocese

Wulfstan's diocese of Worcester was much larger than that of today although the population, of course, was much smaller. His see spread over the Shires of Worcester and Gloucester and a large part of Warwickshire. In the medieval bishoprics' league Wulfstan's church estates were the sixth wealthiest and included an enviable variety of land.

To the south lay the fertile valleys of the Severn and the Avon - land there was excellent for all arable farming, especially cereals. These were all important for life at the time. Bread was the staple of the eleventh century diet and the weak ale most people drank depended on barley as its main ingredient. Then further north, mainly north and west of Worcester and in Warwickshire, the land became more wooded with pasture interspersed. Today we might think of woodland as handy for timber and hunting, but centuries ago it had other surprising uses. Swine grazed amongst the trees and the villeins gathered honey from bees' nests in the tree trunks and branches. The Domesday book tells us that the bishop had the honey as well as the hunting in the forest of Malvern Chase - it was important enough for such a record to be made. Obviously as well, the woods provided fuel, valuable everywhere but essential in large quantities around Droitwich. Here furnaces burned constantly boiling the brine for salt production, a money spinner for the bishop as salting was the only known way of preserving food.

In Wulfstan's diocese by Domesday (1086) the bishop, besides being overlord of much land, held seventeen manors as his personal estates. These were mostly within thirty miles of Worcester and so could comfortably send in supplies for the bishop's Worcester household. They were also easily visited being about a day's ride from the centre. Nearest to the Cathedral lay the manors of Northwick, just north of the city and Wick over the river. A little further afield were Kempsey, Ripple, Fladbury, Bredon, Hartlebury, Hanbury and Alvechurch. Further away were Hampton and Stratford and Tredington in Warwickshire, Blockley, Cleeve, Withington and Bibury in Gloucestershire with Westbury near Bristol the most distant. A steward or bailiff would run the manor on the bishop's behalf and villeins and serfs did the work. The villeins (peasants) laboured for the lord, here the bishop, two, three or four days a week in exchange for a dwelling and land. The serfs, or more bluntly slaves, worked at the lord's will and were the poorest of medieval society. But they still had a home, however miserable, and the bishop's protection when needed.

Wulfstan also held as bishop some property in the small towns of the day. These gave him a foothold in urban society and, more importantly, the chance to make money in the town's trade and markets. Wulfstan possessed houses in Bristol, Gloucester, Warwick, Droitwich and Worcester, all centres of busy trade.

Enough is written about Wulfstan for us to imagine him moving about his diocese and lands. He would, of course, have had spiritual care of all the Worcester diocese although he was only landlord of parts of it. Every year with his Archdeacon Ailric preparing the way, Wulfstan made a visitation of an area. He would probably make a distant manor his headquarters and ride out daily to farms and villages, visiting priests and people. We are told he never passed a church without going in to pray and say a psalm, sometimes dismaying his entourage as the visitation fell further and further behind schedule. Often when he stopped, crowds of children would gather round, brought long distances to the saintly bishop who even when 'age was beginning to sprinkle his head with snow' would sign them with the cross in token of their confirmation. Where there was no church he asked for one to be built and he

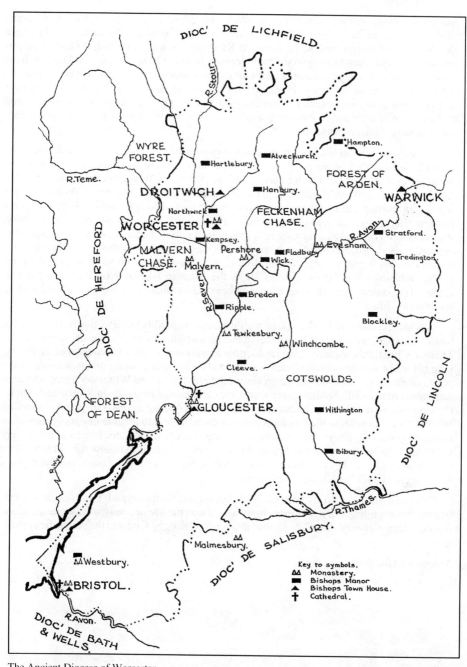

The Ancient Diocese of Worcester

made sure that on his own manors the churches were maintained in good repair. In accounts of his miracles too, we see Wulfstan in his diocese. At Cleeve in Gloucestershire he drove the Devil out of a tormented husbandman; at Kempsey the water in which Wulfstan had just washed his hands cured a man so sick with leprosy he was a living corpse. At Droitwich his written word healed Segild, a woman with limbs and joints so 'stiffened and knotted' that she could not rise from her bed. However, Wulfstan's miraculous power was not always compassionate. On one occasion at Longney-on-Severn where a nut tree overshadowed and darkened the church and its owner refused to cut it down Wulfstan cursed the tree, which subsequently withered and died.

On these journeys in his diocese Wulfstan would also have visited monastic houses. As a monk himself they were particularly dear to him. There were as many as fourteen monasteries in the diocese at Domesday. Evesham Abbey and Worcester Priory were perhaps the biggest, the monks at Worcester had increased from twelve to fifty during Wulfstan's rule as prior and bishop. But Gloucester was also important and there the abbot, Serlo, one of his greatest friends, would always welcome Wulfstan with warm hospitality. Tewkesbury, Westbury-on-Trim and Malvern, the religious houses established in his episcopate, would be especially cherished, and also Evesham where he was educated, but above all Worcester, his own priory. Wulfstan had entered it as a young man and there his parents had spent their last years. Whatever Wulfstan's feelings about the Norman take-over of 1066, once it was achieved the orderly Norman rule, even with heavy taxation, made good ground for building up monastic life.

As Wulfstan travelled his diocese he would accept hospitality but also give it. In his manor houses, and particularly in his Worcester home, he loved to care for his household and guests. This was Christian hospitality, given to all, poor as well as rich. As schoolmaster of the Priory, long before he was bishop, Wulfstan had insisted on his smart young pupils waiting on the poor as their guests. In 1062 when a group of cardinals had visited Worcester, three poor men were also entertained. Soldiers were sometimes attached to his home in Worcester; sent by the king they were to help the bishop guard the Severn crossing against rebels and marauding Welsh. Wulfstan entertained them as generously as he would anyone else, only their beer was to be curtailed! Ever since a savoury smelling goose had distracted him from his prayers the bishop had been a vegetarian, but he did not expect his guests to follow suit. Indeed when the cardinals arrived in Lent, Wulfstan was only eating leeks and cabbage, but the visitors were received with 'full honour and reverence'.

This is something of Wulfstan's life in his diocese and his household. His lifestyle was that of a medieval prelate, but it was more than that. It was the life of a holy and ascetic man, one truly of 'deep piety and dove-like simplicity, beloved alike by God and the people he entirely governed'.

Margaret Goodrich

Canonization: The Making of Saints

Since the beginning of the early Christian era, the idea of sainthood has fascinated people. This may be because so few people ever reach the status of being proclaimed a 'saint' by the authorities of the Roman Catholic Church. Canonization is an extraordinary event reserved for the select few.

How does the Church define a saint? - as one who because of his or her total faith and love for God and neighbour lived a life of heroic virtue in a constant manner and who imitated Christ's life and teaching.

Because so many saints have been gifted with unusual charisms and because the Church requires proof of miracles in order to canonize anyone, they are seen as signs of God's blessing upon the favoured person. Exceptionally good people with extraordinary love and faith are still hard to find. It is true that most people are basically good and kind: however, it takes a lot to become what Christ asked of us. All of us have the potential to become saints. The road is wide and the gate narrow. The faithful have never been promised an easy road to heaven. Those who stand out, 'saints', are important because they show us that it really can be done. They are reassuring figures to a world often searching for heroes. They are real-life-people, just like us, who have succeeded against all odds and we too can be inspired by their example.

In the early Christian era Martyrdom was the first recognised sign of sainthood. It is the death of a follower of Christ, brought about by the hatred of the faith. The victim, who must have died for the faith voluntarily joins in faith and action with that supreme sacrificial act of Christ who gave his life for many in order to set them free.

Authentic Martyrdom was important because in the first few centuries many pseudo-martyrs sprang up in the Church. Many heretics and schismatics died for their beliefs and so the Church had to be careful about who its true martyrs were. The Church was very serious about identifying and supporting only authentic martyrs and promoting proper veneration due to them. Canonization, as we know it, did not then exist. The granting of cult status came about through the spontaneous acclamation of the people (the faithful), who saw fit to venerate a particular martyr because of their direct witness to his or her dying for the faith.

An early sign of the ancient cult of martyrs was the presentation and veneration of their relics. After the local Bishop had approved a cult, the relics were often placed inside the altar as an act of respect. At times the remains of martyrs were buried under the altar or placed high above it. It was the celebration of the Mass each year in memory of the date of the martyr's death that gave rise to feast days for the saints. Saints' bodies were raised above the altar so that they could be easily venerated and it was eventually wrong to bury saints' bodies underground.

About the year 404 AD Vigilantes attacked the way that the church paid respect to relics of the saints. St. Jerome (342-420) defended the Church's stand. He claimed that the martyrs still prayed for the church militant after they reached their heavenly home, with more effect because they had overcome and triumphed. However St. Jerome was careful to point out the fundamental difference between worship of God and the veneration proper to the saints.

Around the 4th century Confessors became the object of devotion mainly because martyrdom was no longer possible in most places. How could Christians imitate Christ's life yet without dying as he had done?

The people soon focused upon those holy people who no longer died for the faith but were seen to lead outstanding lives.

The first British saint definitely authenticated was Edward the Confessor who was canonized in 1161 by Pope Alexander III. That same Pope declared that it was only with Papal authority that anyone could be declared a saint. By 1234 this rule was set.

Many regulations were established in order to ensure that the saints were properly honoured. In the 14th century we find the norms and procedures for canonization, such as the observance of appointed feast days, were well defined. A Papal commission of enquiry was set up in the form of a courtroom case; the servant of God was 'on Trial'.

After the 16th century the process was divided into two phases: one under the care of the local Bishop, the other initiated by the Pope. A revision of this process was itself abolished in 1983 and replaced with one called the Diocesan Inquiry. Pope John Paul II required that all historical documentation had to be gathered and studied in all cases. Only by using this method would the full truth about a saint come out.

From Belmont Abbey

St Wulfstan

St Wulfstan was Canonized by Pope Inocent in 1203. In 1218 his body was translated to a shrine in front of the High Altar in Worcester Cathedral.

THE ANGLO-SAXON LEGACY

Bishops and their Dioceses — Continuity and Change

1995 is the year of Wulfstan, recalling his death in 1095. It is well-known that he was according to his time, a social reformer. He held forth against the slave trade in Bristol, then within the Diocese of Worcester. He was a reforming bishop, travelling his diocese and calling on clergy and lay people to be totally committed in their Christian discipleship. If the clergy had wives they either had to renounce them or renounce their priesthood! The Cathedral and the monks who belonged to it were also to be brought into line. Because he was wise, Wulfstan was consulted by King Harold and retained in post by William the Conqueror.

Some two hundred years later Bishop Giffard is recorded as having left Westbury-on-Trim on January 6th with a retinue of one hundred and twenty mounted assistants. He arrived at Halesowen Abbey on January 25th and called at parish churches on the way. His sermon was from the Song of Solomon and the theme was, "You must pay your quota!" Which part of the Song of Songs was his text? It may have been the verse which speaks of the winter being over, the birds singing and the flowers appearing again, indicating the spring-time of the Church.

So in some ways bishops and their dioceses have not changed. A diocese is an area where the bishop has oversight. Like the Chief Shepherd, Jesus Christ, the bishop must care for all the people. He must have special responsibility for the clergy, enabling them to be spiritual leaders and pastors in their parishes. The bishop must stand for the faith in the nation. He must "constantly rebuke vice and patiently suffer for the truth's sake". He can never be solely concerned with the Church and in the past would sometimes take a leading role in the government of the country. When England became one nation in the ninth century, two bishops of Worcester held both the Archbishopric of York and the Bishopric of Worcester at one and the same time. This was to help keep the North and the Midlands together. The border bishops like Durham in the North and Hereford in the West were all-important for keeping out the Scots or Welsh. Indeed, sometimes the king billeted soldiers on the bishop to strengthen his hand! Certainly a hundred soldiers were at one time stationed at Hartlebury Castle, the historic home of the bishops of Worcester.

The structures of the Church have always tended to reflect the structures of the secular state and bishops are naturally characterised by their times. In the early days of Church history bishops were attached to the city states of the Mediterranean seaboard like Ephesus, Alexandria and Milan. In the so-called Dark Ages they tended to take refuge in monasteries and then in the Middle Ages they became feudal landlords to match their secular counterparts. In the eighteenth century they became grandees. Bishop Cornwall of Worcester declared that the Saloon, a large room by any standards, was too small to make a comfortable dining room!

What of the twentieth century? No doubt our critics would say that we have become bureaucrats, constantly in meetings, constantly going to conferences. The fact is that we must always refer back to our origins. And what are they? They are to be found in Jesus Christ, His mission and His ministry to the world. He sent His apostles into all the world to make disciples of all nations, to baptise, to teach the faith and to draw out its meaning for the world in each new generation. He promised to be with us to the end of time.

To preach, to convert, to build up the Church and to teach - those tasks belong to the office of a bishop in every age. As a twentieth century bishop I have a burning desire to make new disciples. Every church you visit has a font, probably the first thing you see. The font, or the fount, is the place of baptism, the source of the Church's new life. Then you see the lectern and pulpit, signs of the tradition of the Church in its Bible and the need to interpret it for modern people from the pulpit. The altar or holy table is the place where Christian faith is nurtured week by week.

There is also the responsibility to be involved in the life of the community and of the nation, involving bishops in journeys to Westminster, or consultations with local government or industry. Always, whether in the days of the horse with the retinue of a hundred knights, or in the days of a fax in the office and a Renault 25 on the road, the aim is to proclaim Christ and to bring His mind to bear on the issues of the day. In tenth century England as in twentieth century England, Christianity remains, "A Person to love and a life to live".

The message remains. Its content is unchanged but of course the context is utterly different. We now have universal education and literacy, great mobility and instant communication. Bishops no longer have social control - the Bishop of Winchester kept an awesome gaol - and they must make the Church's voice heard amongst the many others. We do not command the moral high ground. Instead we must work from within the situations in which we find ourselves. Wulfstan would have been the sole Christian leader in his area. Today we must work with many other Christian denominations and indeed with other ancient faiths.

The nub and kernel of our faith remains unchanged. "Jesus Christ is the same yesterday, today and forever". Times and circumstances change yet it is the faith of our fathers we proclaim and we must take our past into our future. This we are trying to do in 1995 and beyond.

+Philip Worcester

Monks and the Benedictine Heritage

There have been monasteries in Britain since Anglo-Saxon times. When Augustine and his missionary-monks arrived in Kent in 597 there were already monks observing the Celtic practices in such places as Glastonbury. Augustine introduced the Rule of St Benedict, which became the accepted norm.

It was in about the year 520 that St Benedict wrote his Rule of Life at Monte Cassino, in Italy. He based it on the Gospels together with the experiences of his monastic predecessors. His Rule has come to be considered one of the world's spiritual masterpieces. It describes the monastery as a completely self-contained and self-sufficient unit. It is the home of a spiritual family.

The way of life requires discipline and order, obedience and humility, a regular round of daily worship and personal prayer, work and study, love of the brethren, stability in a fixed monastic community and all under a Rule and an Abbot.

For St Benedict the celebration of the Divine Office and Liturgy is the work of God. This is the principal work of every monastery, centred on public prayer, recited or sung in the church at intervals throughout the day. For more than a thousand years the elaborate celebration, with chant and ceremony, of the Divine Office and other Liturgical functions, have been considered the chief duty to be accomplished by the monks of St Benedict.

Benedictine monasticism had extensive influence on the spiritual, intellectual, liturgical and apostolic life of the Western Church for several centuries.

In some places the non-monastic religious communities who served cathedrals adopted and adapted the Benedictine Rule to their own use.

Britain developed a distinctive tradition of monk-bishops, such as Dunstan, one of Wulfstan's predecessors. He had been Abbot of Glastonbury, became Bishop of Worcester in 957 and went on from there to become Archbishop of Canterbury.

A Synod was convened in Dunstan's time, to agree a common way of life, under royal patronage, for all English monastic communities. The resulting document was the "Regularis Concordia" which sets out the functions and duties of each day. Some of the English practices which it describes certainly differed from continental uses.

For example; a fire was allowed in a special room during winter. The pealing of bells was prolonged in the national fashion at Christmas and feasts. Processions were not only to be made in the monasteries but also in the streets nearby and the people were to take part and assist at the chief Mass. Daily Communion was also encouraged. English Monasticism was given an intimate connection with national life. The King and Queen being ex-officio patrons and guardians of the monastic institution had special prayers said for them and the Matin Mass was offered for them.

One more strange English rule in this code was concerned with the appointment of Bishops in the Monastic-serving Cathedrals. The Code lays down that the monastic community of the Cathedral should elect, if possible, one of their own members as Bishop who would conform to monastic life. This gave the English Episcopate a very strong monastic presence without parallel in the Western Church of that time.

Following Dunstan's time, an important and spontaneous revival took place in the Worcestershire area. Under Wulfstan the number of monks increased at the cathedral-monastery in Worcester and the estates were in good order. He was an exemplary monk-bishop and his standard of monastic life could not be improved upon even by the Norman Archbishop Lanfranc.

The Benedictine monasteries of this area continued to live by the Rule. They were affected by various movements over the centuries, such at the simpler Cistercian outlook, but the houses of Worcester, Gloucester, Evesham, Abingdon, Winchcombe, Tewkesbury, Deerhurst, Pershore, Great Malvern, Little Malvern, Leominster and St. Guthlac's Hereford prospered until the Dissolution.

Under Henry VIII, the English monasteries were dissolved. So from 1539 to the late eighteenth century, would-be English Benedictines had to be exiles on the continent, returning to their homeland in secret as missionary-monks. Their survival shows the readiness to adapt to hardships and danger while preserving the spiritual essentials.

A certain Dom Sigeburt Buckley, one of the monks of Westminster under the Worcester-shire-born Abbot Feckenham during Mary Tudor's brief monastic restoration (1556-59) was subsequently imprisoned in the Abbey's own gatehouse. Tradition has it that he passed on, secretly, all the privileges and customs of the old English Benedictines to two ex-patriate monks who visited him from Italy.

Meanwhile, Englishmen were founding Benedictine Houses on the continent and Cambray was founded for nuns. These houses were traditional in their observances. Their members were eager to re-convert the homeland. By the time of the French Revolution it was no longer possible for English monks to remain in France. So they returned to England. Gradually, in the nineteenth century, Abbeys were established and schools and parishes were attached to them. Some continental houses moved to England, including the nuns of Cambray who settled in Worcestershire, at Stanbrook.

Belmont Abbey, near Hereford came into being as the common house of studies for young monks from all the other houses. Under the Benedictine Bishop Thomas Joseph Brown (1796-1880) even the ancient cathedral - monastery connection was revived for a short time, Belmont serving as his Cathedral - Priory.

Today the Benedictines are still well represented in the Worcester, Hereford and Glouces-ter area. As well as the Abbeys of Stanbrook and Belmont, there are parishes run by other abbeys at Malvern and Cheltenham, and there is the Abbey of Prinknash close to Gloucester. This community of White-habited Benedictines is well known for its pottery industry and modern abbey buildings, on land which was once owned by the medieval abbey at Gloucester. Thus, in this region of England, the Rule of St Benedict is still being followed today.

From Belmont Abbey

The Life of Worcester Cathedral

A modern cathedral is a much more complex organisation than it was in St Wulfstan's time. We are now surrounded by the rules and regulations of planning authorities and conservation-ists. Monastic life was very disciplined. We, as a community are more diverse and our reliance on the goodwill of many volunteers creates a different ethos.

However, we can note continuity in the basic areas of the Benedictine life.

WORSHIP. Central to the Benedictine life was the Opus Dei - the work of God - the worship. The life of the community was focused on this. The seven offices were sung daily, along with the saying and singing of Masses. We still have the WORCESTER ANTIPHONER, dating from 1220. This contains all the music and liturgical instructions for a whole year in Worcester Cathedral. Much of the music at Worcester originated from the monastic life of Fleurie in France and was brought here by St Oswald before St Wulfstan's time. There was almost certainly a choir in his time.

We can trace a complete and unbroken tradition of worship. Daily Morning Prayer is said, the Eucharist is celebrated and Evening Prayer is sung or said. Around 2,000 acts of worship take place in Worcester Cathedral annually. In addition to the daily round, there are five services every Sunday and many services for special occasions.

All events have to be organised and every act of worship is planned in advance. The Cathedral clergy take it in turns to celebrate the Eucharist. Music plays a major role. We have two choirs at Worcester. The Cathedral choir consisting of boys and professional musicians and the Voluntary Choir who deputize for them and also sing at 6.30 pm every Sunday. We are fortunate having such a dedicated and skilled group of musicians providing more varied music than in any previous century.

The Cathedral as the Mother Church of the Diocese is the focus for special Diocesan events such as ordinations, the installation of canons and, occasionally, the enthronement of a Bishop. These services take a great deal of organisation and our regular worshippers help to give continuity to the worship. Our aim is to find excellence in worship, which is worthy of its task and helps to set a tone for worship throughout the Diocese.

HOSPITALITY. The Benedictines were famous for their hospitality. In the Middle Ages the Cathedral was a great centre of pilgrimage and from this source, income was derived for the Cathedral.

The word today is "Tourism". We have a major responsibility to our visitors. The "Ministry of Welcome" encourages many helpers to share in the process of welcoming the visitors. Large numbers of groups requiring guided tours visit the Cathedral and these all need organising. We repeatedly train new guides and welcomers and update our visitors' literature.

Inherited from the Benedictine tradition is caring for the socially deprived and we co-operate with other groups outside to provide help.

There are people who need counselling, and people with problems. Our Day Chaplains assist with this.

Whilst people find our tea bar friendly and welcoming, we are seeking to improve our catering facilities in order to expand our formal entertaining of visiting groups.

EDUCATION. Wulfstan's monastery was a great centre of learning with an ongoing process of education for young people and the monks. Today, our programme of education divides into six parts.

The Cathedral Library, housing a vast collection of books and manuscripts is a research centre for scholars worldwide; an essential provision which is demanding and costly.

Lectures, study days and other programmes are held for people wishing to study different aspects of the Christian faith.

We are committed to a programme for the Arts, music, the visual arts and drama.

Exhibitions are regularly held enabling our visitors to learn about the faith.

The King's School, part of our foundation, offers formal education to boys and girls aged 7 to 18 and provides education for the Cathedral choristers.

Work with children and school parties who come to learn about Cathedral life, the history and architecture.

All these are means of seeking to share an understanding of the Christian faith with those who come through our doors.

COMMUNITY. At the heart of Wulfstan's community lay the Monastic life. At the heart of Cathedral life today is the Cathedral College. This consists of the Dean and Chapter, the Vergers, Choristers, Lay Clerks, the masters and scholars of the King's School, the Cathedral Steward, the Architect and the Clerk of Works.

There are around 60 salaried staff and 500 voluntary workers. This requires good organisation and communication. The Cathedral was built for a Community and needs a community.

A large workforce maintains the building. We are in the middle of a massive £10 million restoration programme without which the life and work of the community could never be sustained.

As successors of the Benedictine tradition, the quality of our own community is important. It requires much love, care and sensitivity by all involved; attributes which Wulfstan himself demonstrated.

The role of the Cathedral, which holds the Bishop's seat, is not that of a Parish but is the servant of the Diocese of Worcester. We have a wider role to care for and respect the tradition into which we have entered. None of it would be possible without St Wulfstan who in many ways was our chief founder and benefactor.

Dean R. Jeffrey

The Norman Cathedral   *drawing by Peter Scholefield*

22

WORCESTER CATHEDRAL

1995

900TH ANNIVERSARY OF THE DEATH OF ST WULFSTAN

AN INVITATION

TO

PILGRIMAGE, WORSHIP, STUDY AND CELEBRATION

MAIN ACTS OF WORSHIP DURING THE YEAR
Sunday 22 January 3.30pm.   Service to launch the Wulfstan Year   *Preacher: The Dean*

6.30pm   Ecumenical Service at the Angel Centre to Launch the City Centre Church Covenant. *Preacher: The Bishop of Dudley*

Saturday 4 November   3.00pm   Thanksgiving Service for St. Wulfstan *Preacher: The Bishop of Worcester*

PREACHERS IN LENT
Special Course on The Future of the Church

5 March – The Bishop of Coventry   12 March – The Bishop of Bristol
19 March – The Bishop of Birmingham   26 March – The Bishop of Oxford
2 April – The Bishop of Gloucester

CONFERENCE ON ANGLO-SAXON SPIRITUALITY
6-8 October Holland House, Cropthorne

STUDY PROGRAMME: THE LIFE AND TIMES OF ST. WULFSTAN OF WORCESTER in conjunction
with Birmingham University Extra-Mural Department. Each from 10:00-16:30:

Saturday 28 January   St. Wulfstan's Life, Career and Cult

Saturday 25 February   St. Wulfstan's Cathedral: Architecture, Music and Worship

Saturday 29 April   St. Wulfstan's Bishopric and Monastery

Advance Booking essential. For details contact Mrs H Down, 52 Shrubbery Avenue, Worcester WR1 1QH

CONCERTS
Friday 20 January 19:00   Mahler's 9th Symphony with the BBC Symphony Orchestra conducted
by Libor Pesek

Saturday 25 March   J S Bach B Minor Mass with Worcester Festival Chorus and the
Bournemouth Sinfonietta

Thursday 20 April to
Sunday 23 April   Drie Koren Festival with the Choirs of Worcester, Breda and Haarlem Cathedrals

CHILDREN'S DAYS
Saturdays relating to St. Wulfstan - lots of activities relating to St. Wulfstan. Details from the Revd Sharon Swain, the Old Palace, Deansway, Worcester WR1 2JE

THE ST WULFSTAN PLAY
Specially written for the year by John Ward and directed by Richard Heyhow.

Performances in the Cathedral 19:00, 17-23 September plus Saturday matinee at 15:00 on September 23.

THE ST WULFSTAN EXHIBITION
21 January - 4 November in the Chapter House, will include details of his life, literature of the period and a model of his Norman Cathedral.

Further details from Mrs Jean Armstrong Tel: 0905 28854

COULD IT BE ANGLO-SAXON?

Looking for Anglo-Saxon Evidence - Through the Church Door.

Structure

Architectural work from the Anglo-Saxon period is not always easy to interpret. Many churches have continuous history back into the preconquest period, and several have masonry which may be of that date, but it is generally only the survival of recognisable features which allows us to be specific.

Remember that only a little survives of what once must have been. There are no Cathedrals of this date and the churches are often heavily altered and rebuilt. Apart from the great length of time from the period to the present, the lack of examples of Anglo-Saxon work is largely the result of a desire by the conquering Normans to eradicate Englishness. The best examples of Anglo-Saxon work to survive are in remoter parts of the country and away from places involved in the sweeping changes in politics after the conquest; they are, therefore, also not at the centres of Anglo-Saxon architectural innovation and development, such as Winchester or Canterbury.

Several churches contain the remains of Anglo-Saxon sculpture, particularly cross-shafts and cross-heads. That these were often recovered from Norman churches during nineteenth century rebuilding work, adds support to the idea of erasing the Anglo-Saxon style after the conquest. These crosses are important evidence for the nature of Anglo-Saxon worship before the Danish Raids of the ninth century. The country had a series of monastic 'minster' churches, such as at Wootton Wawen or Leominster, which sent out priests to preach within their large areas of jurisdiction. People would gather at meeting places marked by crosses. By the Conquest in 1066 there was an intricate series of church types from minsters to small country churches, and it is from the later period (the late ninth, tenth, and early eleventh centuries) that most examples of surviving church architecture can be seen today.

There are particular features which are recognisable in Anglo-Saxon buildings, though none are universal and many continued in use after the Conquest. This latter point applies to the West Midlands region, which was remote from the Norman centre of influence in London. Look out for tall narrow walls with squared stones or quoins at the corners. The walls are often divided by pilaster strips of dressed stone, which often project from rubble walls. This rubble was frequently plastered over, but much was laid in diagonal courses, giving a zigzag

A late Saxon or early Norman wall. Note the arrangement of the rubble stone work, the pilaster strips standing out from the wall and the long and short work on the corners

24

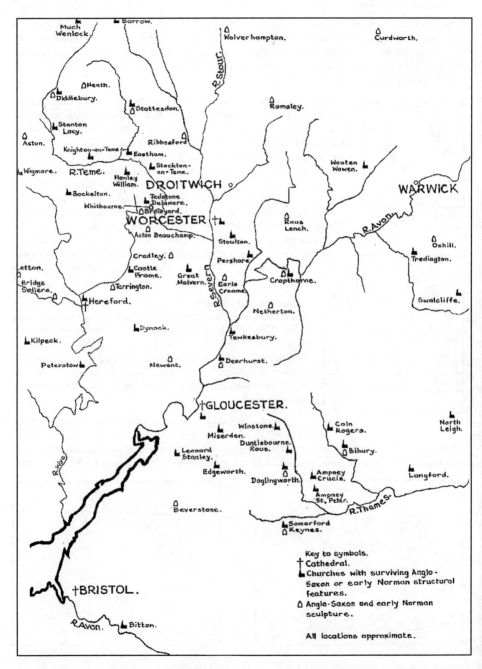

Looking for the Evidence: Some places to visit.

25

appearance known as herringbone masonry. This herringbone work is often highlighted as evidence for preconquest work in churches, but this should be treated with caution for the reasons given above. Of the quoins at the corners, the alternate long and short type are the most distinctive, and in the case of later buildings such as Odda's Chapel, Deerhurst, a tapering effect is used.

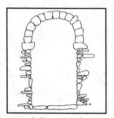

A simple Saxon window opening

Anglo-Saxon doors and windows are normally round headed, and thus similar to those of the Norman period. There are some triangular headed openings in later buildings, such as at the west end of Deerhurst church. Windows were only splayed to the inside in the early period, but by the tenth and eleventh centuries they were splayed both inside and out - often evidence for a later date when looking at a church. At this time, as towers were often added to churches, double openings were put in the belfries. Many doorways have hood-moulds to allow rainwater to run off, such as at Stanton Lacy. Where arches survive they are of similar construction to the doorways, round at the head, with massive shafts and capitals. Carving is rare, and painted decoration has disappeared, and so the arches stand elegant in their simplicity. There are good arches from the late Saxon period to be seen at Wootton Wawen and Deerhurst.

A triangular headed opening

Stone masonry held with good mortar has survived but it should be remembered that particularly in the forested areas of the West Midlands many church buildings may have been built of timber. This too would account for a lack of survivals, by contrast to areas of good building stone such as Gloucestershire or Northamptonshire. However, there is good evidence for timber roofs and internal features such as galleries, doors or ladders.

Church plans and analysis of features in surviving structures tell us much about Anglo-Saxon worship and lifestyle. Many were of a simple nave and chancel plan, to which were added 'particus' or side chambers. The simple nave and chancel can be seen at Odda's Chapel, Deerhurst, and

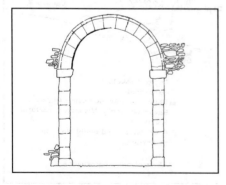

A simple Saxon or early Norman Chancel Arch

A more elaborate later Norman (mid 12th ccentury) Chancel Arch

examples of remains of particus at Deerhurst and Wootton Wawen. Other larger churches were of the basilica type, of which Brixworth in Northamptonshire is the most impressive survival. Doorways at upper levels indicate galleries and 'double decker churches', such as at Deerhurst, or in the case of Tredington a first floor entrance for greater security. Several larger churches have crypts housing relics of saints and burial chambers of wealthy patrons, of which Wulfstan's rebuilding of the crypt at Worcester Cathedral is a most remarkable example of the transition from Anglo-Saxon to Norman architecture.

As more detailed analysis of church buildings is undertaken, during the course of restoration or building works, so our knowledge of Anglo-Saxon church architecture becomes more extensive. Many churches of Anglo-Saxon origin may yet reveal features, such as blocked windows or fragments of carved stone, which are physical evidence for their important preconquest past.

Tim Bridges

Sculpture

Saxon and early (11th century) Norman sculptures are very unevenly distributed and too scattered to be easily compared.

A Saxon monster head

Typically Saxon carving is shallow, intricately patterned with leafy trails, and with strange birds and beasts which have a gentle quality, unlike the bold, deeply carved and menacing Norman "menagerie". There is an overlap between Saxon and Norman styles - Saxon masons were still working after the Norman conquest.

GLOUCESTERSHIRE

Look for a piece of Saxon stone set into an outside wall at BIBURY. Also some on the chancel arch. At DEERHURST, a huge battered monster head looms over the doorway, there are two heads with large teeth inside the doorway, and two more on the blocked chancel arch. What are these heads? It is anybody's guess! The font, carved with spirals and leafy trails, has come back to the church after being used as a washtub. Walk round the outside of the church and find the Deerhurst Angel.

DAGLINGWORTH has 4 sculptured panels - see St Peter holding the huge Key of Heaven.
At NEWENT, there is a piece of Cross-shaft - look carefully and you can find Adam and Eve.
SOMERFORD KEYNES has a large, broken sculpture, possibly the remains of two dolphins.
BEVERSTON has a large Saxon figure of Christ on the tower.

HEREFORDSHIRE

ACTON BEAUCHAMP has a fragment of a very fine cross-shaft, and CRADLEY has a single Saxon stone built into the tower. At LLANVEYNOE, there are two charming, childishly carved figures just inside the door.
ASTON, BRIDGE SOLLERS, BREDWARDINE, LETTON AND TARRINGTON have carvings which may date from the overlap period. The fonts at BROMYARD and WHITBOURNE may be pre-1066. See if you can find the Lamb of God on Whitbourne font.

SHROPSHIRE

Inside DIDDLEBURY church is a rather faint carving of little figures in a tree, probably the Tree of Life. At STOTTESDON over the inside of the tower doorway is a large carved stone with strange, savage, fighting creatures, certainly NOT gentle looking. WROXETER has a little procession of carved creatures on the outside, whilst UPPINGTON has a very curly, tendril-y Viking sort of dragon.

STAFFORDSHIRE

Apart from some very badly eroded cross-shafts at WOLVERHAMPTON, (formerly in Staffs.) there is nothing recognisably Saxon. ARMITAGE has an early font, with delightfully comic figures under arches, and ILAM font is also early. IPSTONES has two Viking-type dragons fighting, above the doorway.

WARWICKSHIRE

Little or no Saxon sculpture. The font at CURDWORTH is great fun - find the dragon's toothy grin - and OXHILL font, with Adam and Eve, is also early, possibly overlap.

WORCESTERSHIRE

CROPTHORNE has a splendid example of Saxon carving - a great cross-head worked with birds, beasts, and patterns. A fragment of another cross is at ROUS LENCH, where a man extends a bunch of grapes to a peacock.

On the ruined chapel at NETHERTON, near Elmley Castle, is a fire-breathing, flying dragon with a curly tail. This chapel is privately owned, so ask for permission to enter.

EARLS CROOME (Chancel Arch), and the doorways at RIBBESFORD and ROMSLEY all have carvings which may be of the overlap period.

Jean Lawes

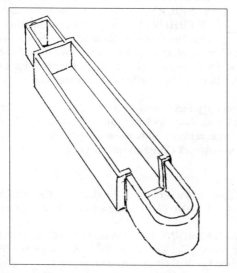

Early Anglo-Saxon churches were simple structures. Tall and narrow enough for a tree to span the width to carry the roof.

Later towers and side chambers were added, some had galleries at upper levels, others crypts to house the relics of saints.

BELMONT ABBEY, HEREFORD
A Benedictine Monastery

– Continuing the monastic tradition of hospitality –
The monks of Belmont welcome guests to:

Hedley Lodge Guesthouse
and
Centre for Retreats and Conferences

Conferences, meetings and Ecumenical gatherings
Retreats: pastoral, spiritual, artistic and cultural
Accommodation: member of the Heart of England Tourist Board

Visitors
Tours for groups and school parties
Abbey Shop and Tea Room
Extensive grounds and gardens

For details contact:
The Guestmaster, Belmont Abbey, Hereford HR2 9RZ   Tel: (0432) 277475

For our Retreat Calendar contact:
The Retreatmaster, Belmont Abbey, Hereford HR2 9RZ   Tel: (0432) 277388

THE GAZETTEER

with

DATES FOR YOUR DIARY

Special Through the Church Door Events

in 1995

Saturday June 3 :In the Steps of St Wulfstan

Embroideries and Tapestries Week: 3-8 July

The following churches will be exhibiting their embroideries and tapestries but it may be necessary to telephone for details.

Herefordshire
Stanford Bishop   St James the Greater

Shropshire
Hope Bagot   St John the Baptist

Warwickshire
Radford Semele   St Nicholas

Worcestershire
Bengeworth (Evesham) St Peter
Harvington   St James
Lower Broadheath   Christchurch
Malvern Link   Church of the Ascension
Malvern Link   Saint Matthias
Powick   St Peter
Stoulton   St Edmund King and Martyr

August :Be a Church Detective - for the young at heart!

Worcestershire
Malvern Link   Church of the Ascension
Malvern Link   Saint Matthias'
Telephone 01905 841554 for details of our special Anglo-Saxon Trail

Herefordshire
Stanford Bishop   St James the Greater

Shropshire
Hopesay   St Marys

Worcestershire
Malvern Link   Church of the Ascension
Salwarpe   St Michael

November 18/19: Plant a Tree Weekend

Don't forget the sponsored Cycle Ride: September 9

WATCH OUT FOR CYCLISTS!

The great majority of churches included in this first Gazetteer belong to the Church of England. They are to be found in three administrative counties - Hereford and Worcester and a part of both Shropshire and Warwickshire - for the purposes of church administration they fall into three other areas - the dioceses of Hereford, Worcester and a part of the diocese of Coventry. The Gazetteer is organised on a county basis. (Hereford and Worcester each comprising one section.) This is to make it easier to locate the individual churches. The churches are then listed alphabetically.

Each section begins with some general information relating to the county. Then follows a diary listing the dates when you can be sure that the churches will be open. Many are open at times other than those listed and you are welcome to use the contact numbers given to check the local situation.

The Diocese of Hereford

The Diocese consists of Herefordshire and the southern half of Shropshire. It is one of the most rural dioceses in the Church of England. There are 432 church buildings. Church buildings are focal points of the villages and link the past with the present worshipping community.

HEREFORDSHIRE

The River Wye and its tributaries, wooded valleys, views across rich farmland, 'black and white' houses, interesting churches and a majestic cathedral in Hereford contribute to Herefordshire's rural charm. This is the charm of a bygone age and a slower pace of life. Here among the machinery and buildings of modern agriculture is the home of the famous white faced Hereford cattle. The cathedral houses many fine treasures including the Chained Library and the world renowned Mappa Mundi. In the west Offa's Dyke reminds us of the division between England and Wales. A great number of motte and bailey castles, built to defend the area, survive as a testimony to the area's violent past. The villages and towns of the county support a wide range of sporting and cultural events and festivals. There are many footpaths to walk and the quiet lanes are ideal for scenic drives.

Brian Chave

Town Churches open daily
Hereford Cathedral
Leominster Priory
Ross on Wye   St Mary's Church
Belmont Abbey

Village churches. The county is a rich treasure house for those wanting to explore and there are many churches to find. Many are open at times other than those listed in this book. Spring time and harvest time are particularly good times to visit this area and you may wish to come for the Rogationtide and Harvestide festivals, including Big Apple in October. For further information and for details of where to stay contact:

Herefordshire Tourism. The Tourist Information Centre, Hereford.

The Countryside Service. Queenswood Country Park, Dinmore Hill, Leominster, Herefordshire HR6 0PY.

Village Festivals
June   Kington Festival
July   Madley Festival
October   Big Apple

Village churches - listed alphabetically with the names of nearby towns. Each Gazetteer entry gives a grid reference from the Landranger OS Map series. Most are on sheet nos. 148, 148 and 161

Acton Beauchamp	south-east of Bromyard
Almeley	south-east of Kington
Bredwardine	north-east of Hay on Wye
Brelston Green	south-west of Ross
Bullinghope	south of Hereford
Burghill	north-west of Hereford
Castle Frome	south of Bromyard
Clifford	north of Hay on Wye
Cusop	adjoining Hay on Wye
Dilwyn	south-west of Leominster
Dorstone	south-west of Hereford
Eardisley	south-west of Kington
Eaton Bishop	west of Hereford
Eye (Morton)	north of Leominster
Goodrich	south-west of Ross on Wye
Hardwicke	east of Hay of Wye
Kilpeck	south of Hereford
Kingstone	south-west of Hereford
Little Dewchurch	south of Hereford
Madley	west of Hereford
Moccas	west of Hereford
Peterchurch	west of Hereford
Putley	south-east of Hereford
Ross on Wye	west of Gloucester
Rowlstone	south-west of Hereford
Sellack	north-west of Ross on Wye
Sollers Hope	south-east of Hereford
St Weonards	west of Ross on Wye
Stanford Bishop	south-east of Bromyard
Sutton St Nicholas	north of Hereford
Turnastone	south-west of Hereford
Vowchurch	south-west of Hereford

Dates for Your Diary in Hereford

Many churches will be open at times other than those listed below. For up to date local information please use the contact numbers listed in each of the Gazetteer entries.

Diary dates are dates when you can be sure to find the church open. Where churches have made a regular arrangement to have their building open and staffed they are listed at the beginning of each of the monthly lists. For more details please consult the individual entries.

Special Through the Church Door activities are also listed at the beginning of each month as appropriate.

Joint Openings

The Golden Valley churches: Dorstone, Peterchurch, Turnastone and Vowchurch

The Border Link Churches: Bredwardine with Brobury, Cusop, Hardwicke and Moccas

January

15	Acton Beauchamp	11:30	

March

5	Little Dewchurch	15:00	

April

9	Little Dewchurch	15:00	
9	Sellack		
15	Castle Frome	10:00	17:00
26	Burghill		
27	Burghill		
28	Burghill		
29	Burghill		
30	Burghill		

May

6	Dorstone	9:00	17:00
6	Little Dewchurch		19:30
6	Peterchurch	10:00	17:00
6	Turnastone	10:00	18:00
6	Vowchurch	10:00	16:00
20	Bredwardine	10:00	18:00
20	Clifford	10:00	18:00
20	Cusop	10:00	18:00
20	Hardwicke	10:00	18:00
20	Moccas	10:00	18:00
21	Bredwardine	10:00	17:00
21	Clifford	10:00	17:00
21	Cusop	10:00	17:00
21	Hardwicke	10:00	17:00
21	Moccas	10:00	17:00

28	Almeley	10:00	17:00
29	Eye (Morton)		
29	Sutton St Nicholas	10:00	18:00

June

3 June In the Steps of St. Wulfstan

3	Acton Beauchamp		
3	Burghill		
3	Dorstone	9:00	17:00
3	Kilpeck		
3	Peterchurch	10:00	17:00
3	Putley		
3	Turnastone	10:00	18:00
3	Vowchurch	10:00	16:00
4	Little Dewchurch		15:00
7	Sollers Hope	10:00	18:00
9	Kington	10:00	18:00
10	Brelston Green, Marstow	10:00	17:00
10	Kington	10:00	18:00
11	Kington	10:00	18:00
17	Kington	10:00	18:00
18	Acton Beauchamp	15:15	
18	Kington	10:00	18:00
24	Bullinghope	10:30	
24	Kington	10:00	18:00
24	St Weonards		
25	Bullinghope	10:00	16:00
25	Peterchurch		
30	Eye (Morton)		

July

Embroideries and Tapestries Week 2-9 July

1	Dorstone	9:00	17:00
1	Eye (Morton)		
1	Peterchurch	10:00	17:00
1	Turnastone	10:00	18:00
1	Vowchurch	10:00	16:00
2	Eye (Morton)		
7	Kingstone	10:00	18:00
8	Kingstone	10:00	18:00
9	Ross on Wye		
9	Kingstone	10:30	
14	Sellack		
15	Little Dewchurch	11:00	16:00
22	Dilwyn	14:00	17:00
22	Eardisley		
23	Eardisley		
29	Dilwyn	14:00	17:00

August
Why not be a Church Detective this August?

5	Dilwyn	14:00	17:00
5	Dorstone	9:00	17:00
5	Little Dewchurch	13:00	18:00
5	Peterchurch	10:00	17:00
5	Turnastone	10:00	18:00
5	Vowchurch	10:00	16:00
12	Dilwyn	14:00	17:00
19	Dilwyn	14:00	17:00
26	Kilpeck		
27	Kilpeck		
28	Sutton St Nicholas	10:00	18:00
28	Kilpeck		

September
9 September:
The Sponsored Cycle Ride -
Watch out for Cyclists!

9	Bullinghope	10:00	16:00
9	Burghill		
9	Dorstone	9:00	17:00
9	Eye		
9	Goodrich		
9	Little Dewchurch		
9	Madley		
9	Peterchurch	10:00	17:00
9	Putley		
9	Sellack		
9	Sollers Hope	10:00	18:00
9	Stanford Bishop		
9	Turnastone	10:00	18:00
9	Vowchurch	10:00	18:00
15	Little Dewchurch	19:30	21:00
22	Goodrich	19:00	
23	Goodrich		
24	Goodrich	11:00	
24	Little Dewchurch	15:00	

October

1	Acton Beauchamp	11:30
5	Madley	

November
Plant a Tree Weekend 18 and 19 November

12	Castle Frome	11:20
18	Stanford Bishop	

December

10	Castle Frome	11:20
17	Acton Beauchamp	15:15

Ross on Wye

St Mary the Virgin

1316	*Hereford*
Attributed to Norman style.	*Grade 1*

Building of present church commenced in the last quarter of the 13th Century, but it conveys a 19th Century appearance. Made of local sandstone, roof boarded with pitch pine and retained by 8 sturdy sandstone pillars, pews also of pitch pine. Interior walls pointed. Stained glass windows a special feature. The several monuments attributed to local families are important. Set on the highest point of the town offers excellent views in all directions. Visitors always express delight on entry especially noticing the trees in an east window, were originally elm trees.

TRAVEL From the town centre proceed up Church St., Rectory on your left, to the South Gate. Car park at this point. From this point entry into the church is round to the North Porch. **PARK** Car park mentioned above, or in Church St. Coach Park off Homms Road.

OUTSIDE Plague Cross in the closed area of the churchyard. Council Park area to the South West of the church giving wonderful views of South Herefordshire. Beautiful autumn colours.

ACTIVITIES
Regular-**OPEN MON- SAT 9:30-17:30**
Strawberry Fayre 8th July biennial Patronal Festival Telephone for details. **SPECIAL** Bell Ringing teams are always welcome.

CONTACT Any arrangements can be made via the Rectory 0989 562175. Visitors very welcome

FOOD The Royal Hotel,Palace Pound.The King's Head, High St. The Prospect.The Lost Street Museum, Bowkend Street. Tourist Office in Brook End Street and Market House.

VISIT Wye Valley and Forest of Dean.

Acton Beauchamp 670 503

St Giles

Hereford
Georgian "Classical"

Probably founded in the 9th or 10th century but substantially rebuilt in the Georgian "Classical" style around 1800 this beautifully situated small church has a peaceful charm all of its own, and is well worth a visit especially during the spring when the churchyard snowdrops are followed by primroses and daffodils. The churchyard is managed with nature in mind, and there is a fine specimen of the rare Wild Service Tree as well as ancient yew trees - one possibly predating the church. Above the tower door is a lintel formed from the shaft of a finely carved Saxon Cross.

TRAVEL From Acton Green take the Bishops Frome road; then first turning right, and first right again. **PARK** By pond, church is then up hill across fenced off portion of field. Approached by narrow lane. Limited parking on road verges. Not suitable for coaches.

OUTSIDE Wild Service Tree. Part of Saxon Cross over tower door.

ACTIVITIES Sunday, 15th Jan, 11.30: Wassailing Service, followed by Wassailing of local orchards. 3 course lunch available by ticket £4.50 phone 0531 634 687.
Sunday, 18th June, 3.15 pm: Floral Songs of Praise. Many local gardens open from 1.30 pm - 6 pm. Home made teas available all afternoon.
Sunday 1st Oct, 11.30 am: Blessing of Animals Service. Well behaved animals welcome for a blessing at this happy Family Service.
Sunday 17th Dec, 3.15 pm: Victorian Candlelit Carol Service. Victorian style dress optional.

CONTACT Telephone number 0885 490708.

FOOD The Green Dragon and The Chase Inn Bishops Frome. The Majors Arms, Halmonds Frome. All provide home-cooked food. Hop Pocket Craft Centre and Tea Rooms, Bishops Frome.

VILLAGE Acton Beauchamp Roses - Specialist growers of Old Fashioned Roses.

VISIT Bromyard - historic half-timbered market town. Bromyard Downs - acres of open downs and common land. Lower Brockhampton Court - National Trust. Shortwood Open Farm, Pencombe. Castle Frome.

Almeley 332 516

St Mary

Hereford
Grade 1
Mainly Decorated

From the south porch of this beautiful church are fine views across the remains of a Norman motte and bailey castle towards the Welsh Border and the Black Mountains. An unusual feature of the interior is a painted ceiling over the eastern end of the nave with a pattern of Tudor roses. Notice also the fine geometrical east window of the chancel. Other interesting buildings in this small friendly village include Almeley Manor a fine timber framed private house part of which is 14th Century and a very early Quaker meeting house founded in 1672.

TRAVEL From A480 turn off at Woonton or Holme Marsh. From A4111 turn off at Eardisley. From A4112 turn off at Kinnersley. **PARK** Roadside parking is allowed in the village but there are not facilities for coaches.

OUTSIDE Look for the 13th century base of the west tower.

ACTIVITIES Saturday 27th and Sunday 28th May, 10 am - 5 pm. Refreshments will be available. There will be a sale of interesting garden plants and home made cakes. On the Sunday at 11 am there will be a Songs of Praise.
Sunday service 11 am (except some 5th Sundays in the month): all welcome.

FOOD The Bells public house is quite near the church and serves food.

VILLAGE There is a good village shop and the September Dairy farm shop sells ice-cream, dairy products, bacon and local cider.

Bredwardine (with Brobury)   148/335 445

St Andrew

Norman   *Hereford*

The church is predominantly Norman built of local white Tufa stone. The Chancel built in the late 12th century was probably built outside the earlier building. The font from the 17th century is an octagonal bowl each face has trefoiled arches, three of which enclose a rose, thistle and fleur de lys.

The Church at Brobury (St. Mary Magdalene), now a 'private home is also Norman. The two parishes united in 1851 when a priest looked after both churches.

TRAVEL Off the B4352, on the minor road between Bredwardine village and the Wye bridge. **PARK** on the approach path to the church.

OUTSIDE Revd Francis Kilvert's tomb on the north of the church. Bredwardine castle to the south.

ACTIVITIES Saturday 20th May, 10 am - 6 pm, Sunday 21st May, 10 am - 5 pm .21st May: Rogationtide. In the church you will find some information on our community and the local facilities available as well as information on the church itself.

SPECIAL Those wishing to join our celebration of Rogation are welcome.This involves visits to farms to bless the land (with a different itinerary for walkers and those who wish to use cars), followed by tea and a service at a farm. Please be at Hardwicke church at 2.30 pm.

CONTACT The Rector. The Rectory. Cusop. Hay-on-Wye. 0497 820634.

FOOD The Red Lion Hotel is situated in the village offering restaurant and bar facilities. Old Court offers a more peaceful Dinner (prior booking only).

VILLAGE Old Castle, Merbach Hill with its wonderful views.

If you are interested in staying for the weekend, a leaflet giving details of B&B and other accommodation is available by sending a stamped addressed envelope to Mark Robinson, The Haven, Hardwicke, via Hereford HR3 5TA

VISIT Arthur's Stone, Hay-on-Wye home of many books. The Border Link Group of Parishes-Bredwardine (with Brobury), Clifford, Cusop and Hardwicke and Moccas.

Rogationtide Weekend The Border Link parishes all look forward to meeting you and hope that you will have an enjoyable stay.

Brelston Green, Marstow   20/56

St Matthew

1857   *Hereford*
Victorian

A country church which in 1856 was moved from its original riverside site to a commanding position half a mile away. This small but welcoming church is on high ground looking over cottages, farms and streams towards Symonds Yat and Goodrich. The building is simple, but contains a marble carving of the Last Supper which is both lovely and unusual. Above this is a beautiful stained glass window - seen best in the morning. The churchyard cross/sundial was transferred from the original site and can be seen in the churchyard.

TRAVEL Coming from A49 (T) road, take the A4137 leading to Whitchurch. There is a sign for Marstow and Brelston on the left after about 5 miles. Follow this for 0.75 mile and St Matthew's stands on the right. Coming from A40(T) road, turn off at Goodrich Cross. Cross over the major road and follow signs to Marstow and Brelston for about 2 miles along a winding lane. The church can be seen from some way off. **PARK** Parking of cars is limited to 6-7 where lanes widen sufficiently to allow farm vehicles to pass.

OUTSIDE The churchyard cross/sundial.

ACTIVITIES Saturday 10th June, 10 am - 5 pm: St Matthew's will be open and visitors will be welcome.Come and see a display of summer flowers.

SPECIAL For those interested in seeing the site of the original ancient church, a walk or drive of about 0.5 mile towards Marstow Court can be arranged. Tea, coffee and soft drinks will be available.Sketch maps showing routes of circular walks (2-5 miles) within Marstow area will be available.

FOODThe Cross Keys, Goodrich Cross (2 miles). The Hostelry, Goodrich (3 miles). Little Chef, Whitchurch (2 miles). Picnic spots abound in the area, but the nearest facilities are at 2 miles.

VISIT Goodrich Castle with excellent parking and picnic site (3+ miles).Symonds Yat West. Outstanding riverside area with a variety of inns and restaurants; ferry boat over R. Wye; quiet walks and nature areas; less quiet Maze and Butterfly Farm (2 - 5 miles).Wye Valley Farm Symonds Yat East. Rare breeds of all sorts. Children welcomed. Picnic site. (4 miles).

Bullinghope   **510 370**

St. Peter

1878   *Hereford*
Early English   *Grade 2*

The church is built of local stone dressed with Bath Stone. Look at the Reredos in memory of Rev. E.W. Daniell who began plans for the new church. At the back of the church are memorials taken from the old churchyard. Also consider the unusual marble font consisting of an angel holding a large shell.

TRAVEL Off the A49, 1.5 miles south of Hereford. Follow signposts to Bullinghope. **PARK** Outside the church. Adequate for minibuses.

OUTSIDE From the well kept churchyard there are views to the Black Mountains to the west and Dinedor Hill to the east. The tower was erected to the memory of Capt. Robert De Winton after his death in 1904.

ACTIVITIES 24th & 25th June: Patronal weekend; the church will be open from 10.30 am onwards.

Sun 25th 6.30 pm Special Open Air Patronal Service in the old church ruins (in the grounds of the Cedars) NB in church if wet.
Sat 9th Sept: "The Great Bike Ride" 10 am - 4 pm.
Sunday Service at 11.15 am (excluding 5th Sundays).

CONTACT For additional opening times by request, Tel. 0432 - 268791.

FOOD Grafton Inn (A49 3 miles south of Hereford) Graftonbury Hotel (off A49 2 miles south of Hereford).

VISIT Dinedor Hill - Iron Age Hill Fort; 2 miles by footpath starting opposite the church. Ruins of old church (in Private Garden).

Burghill   **44N : 48E**

St Mary the Virgin

?1275   *Hereford*
Norman,extensively rebuilt 19th Century   *Grade 1*

Originally Burghill was an Anglo-Saxon hill fort (Burgh = hill of the fort) and the church stands on the site of an Anglo-Saxon settlement. Saxon remains have been found to the west of the building. Circa 1200, it was in the patronage of the Prior of the Priory of Llanthony 1334-1526. Sir Edward Elgar would cycle out to Burghill to sit in the churchyard to enjoy the peace. The stem of the font is late Norman, there is a fine screen and effigies of Sir John Milbourne and his wife in Alabaster c. 1440.

TRAVEL A4110 Canon Pyon road, turn left following sign post for Burghill at the bottom of the slope the road sweeps right and the church is on the right.

PARK Turn right before church to reach car park at the side of the church.

OUTSIDE Preaching Cross, Norman window in Chancel north wall. Hollow Yew Tree in churchyard.

ACTIVITIES Wednesday 26th - Sunday 30th April: Flower Festival.
Saturday 9th September: Cycle Ride.

SPECIAL Refreshments will be available at both events.

CONTACT Church Contact: 0432 760246.

FOOD The Royal Oak , on the A4110 just beyond the turning to Burghill, The Three Elms, at the fork of the A4110 and Tillington road, The Bell Inn on Tillington road beyond turning to Burghill.Picnic and barbecues at Queenswood,

VISIT Dinmore (A49 north). Walk up hill from church, fine view of Malvern Hills.

Dinmore Manor, Queens Wood Arboretum, Dinmore (A49 North).

Visit Stretton Sugwas church, with its fine example of a Norman Tympanum of the English School of Sculpture.

SPECIAL "I Spy" Sheet for Children in the church.

FOOD 5 pubs and Craft Centre Tea Room within 2.5 miles radius.

VILLAGE Hop Pocket Craft Centre,Footpath from churchyard.

VISIT Historic Market Town of Ledbury. Eastnor Castle; Newbridge Farm Park. Acton Beauchamp.

Font – St. Michael & All Angels – Castle Frome

Castle Frome   **668 459**

St Michael and All Angels

Norman   *Hereford*
                                  Grade 1

Originally a resting place for soldiers from the nearby Castle, the church is still a peaceful haven with wild flowers and animals hiding in its boundaries and buzzards soaring overhead. Inside there is lots to interest - the Unett tomb showing a cavalier, his wife and offspring (the plaque records 3 daughters, but 4 kneel round him!); opposite a crusader's head, his heart probably buried in the walls; the ancient sundial in the porch; and the much admired Romanesque font.

TRAVEL Signposted and visible, 150 yards off B4214. **PARK** Limited - no turning space for coaches.

OUTSIDE Beautiful views, ancient sundial in porch, very old yew tree.

ACTIVITIES 15th April, 10 am - 5 pm: Through the Church Door Day. At 5 pm Easter Tea with Easter Egg Hunt and light entertainment for children and adults. 8 pm, Lighting of the Easter Fire outside church and candlelit service of the Pascal Vigil. 12th November, 11.20 am: Remembrance Service - a special family service with children taking part. 10th December, 11.20 am: Christingle Service - A delightful service when we gather around the font with Christingles.

Clifford   **148/ 252 450**

St Mary

12th century   *Hereford*
Gothic

It is supposed that there must have been a church in pre-Norman times, but the present church is Early Norman, thought modified in the 16th and 19th Centuries, and was probably built as a church for the Cluniac priory established in the 12th Century further down the hill. The parish was once believed to be one of the four largest in the country, until losing to the new parish of Hardwicke in 1853, the part on the southern side of the Hay-Bredwardine road.

TRAVEL South side of the minor road which runs between the B4350 Hay-Whitney road and the B4352 Hay-Bredwardine road. **PARK** Parking available by churchyard wall.

OUTSIDE The churchyard is of particular interest in that it has been the focus of a Conservation Project since May 1989, and many varieties of plants and insects are found here. Excellent views of the Wye valley and the Black Mountains can be seen from the site.

ACTIVITIES Saturday 20th May, 10 am - 6 pm, Sunday 21st May, 10 am - 5 pm.

HEREFORDSHIRE

21st May: Rogationtide. In the church you will find some information on our community and the local facilities available as well as information on the church itself.

SPECIAL Those wishing to join our celebration of Rogation are welcome. This involves visits to farms to bless the land (with a different itinerary for walkers and those who wish to use cars), followed by tea and a service at a farm. Please be at Hardwicke church at 2.30 pm.

St. Mary's Church, Clifford.

CONTACT The Rector. The Rectory. Cusop. Hay-on Wye. 0497 820634.

VILLAGE The site of the castle by the Wye, built in the late 11th century can be visited by permission of the owners. If you are interested in staying for the weekend, a leaflet giving details of B&B and other accommodation is available by sending a stamped addressed envelope to Mark Robinson, The Haven, Hardwicke, via Hereford HR3 5TA.

VISIT Hay on Wye 2.5 miles to SW, is a market town best known for its large number of bookshops. The Border Link parishes of Bredwardine, Clifford, Cusop and Hardwicke.

> Rogationtide Weekend The Border Link parishes all look forward to meeting you and hope that you will have an enjoyable stay.

| Cusop | 148/ 240 415 |

St Mary

| Norman | *Hereford* |
| | *Grade 2* |

The present Norman church replaced an earlier, probably wooden, building dedicated to St Cewydd, a fifth century Celtic saint. Set on the hillside, amongst yews of great antiquity, it is a typical Border church; solid, unpretentious and very beautiful.

TRAVEL Off the Cusop - Dingle road, which itself leads off the B4348 Hay-Bredwardine road. **PARK** Parking available on the strip of grass between the churchyard gates.

OUTSIDE Our round churchyard and ancient yews, the largest of which is two thousand years old, indicate a pre-Christian site.

ACTIVITIES Saturday 20th May, 10 am - 6 pm, Sunday 21st May, 10 am - 5 pm.
21st May: Rogationtide. In the church you will find some information on our community and the local facilities available as well as information on the church itself.

SPECIAL For those interested in finding out more and exploring the churches of the **Border Link** parishes and the countryside in greater depth, there is an invitation to visitors to join our celebration of Rogationtide on Sunday 21st May 1995, in the afternoon. This involves visits to farms to bless the land (with a different itinerary for walkers and those who wish to use cars), followed by tea and a service at a farm. Please be at Hardwicke church (GR 271438) at 2.30 pm.

CONTACT The Rector. The Rectory. Cusop. Hay-on Wye. 0497 820634.

FOOD Hay, with its books, craft centre, interesting shops, pubs, cafes, river and picnic site is just half a mile away.

VILLAGE There are many lovely walks centred on the church, and details will be found there.

If you are interested in staying for the weekend, a leaflet giving details of B&B and other accommodation is available by sending a stamped addressed envelope to Mark Robinson, The Haven, Hardwicke, via Hereford HR3 5TA.

VISIT Hay-on-Wye. The other Border link churches-Bredwardine, Clifford, Moccas and Hardwicke.

> Rogationtide Weekend The Border Link parishes all look forward to meeting you and hope that you will have an enjoyable stay.

FOOD The Crown pub in the village serves food. There is a tea room half a mile East of the church down Common road. The village green is an ideal picnic site.

VILLAGE Village shop and post office.

VISIT Burton Court: large home between Dilwyn and Eardisland. Monkland, All Saints, 3 miles on the Leominster road. A 19th Century Vicar of this Norman church was Sir William Baker, the Hymn writer ("The King of Love my Shepherd is").

Dorstone   **315 418**

St Faith

1890 (restoration)   *Hereford*
Late Victorian Gothic   *Grade 2*

A church has stood on this site certainly since the 12th Century. Legend has it that Richard de Brito one of Thomas a Beckett's murderers built a chapel here as penance for his crime. The present church dates from 1890 replacing a previous one built in 1827. The arch of the tower is of local tufa which was the stone used in the old buildings. Note the 13th Century piscina in the south wall.

TRAVEL Dorstone is situated on the B4348 approx. 16 miles west of Hereford and 7 miles east of Hay-on-Wye. Bus service No.39 (Hereford-Brecon) runs on weekdays at 2 hourly intervals and stops by the village hall. **PARK** Cars may be parked alongside the church or on the playing fields opposite the churchyard, coaches may be parked by the village hall.

OUTSIDE In the churchyard look for the memorial cross and the sundial balls on the gate posts.

ACTIVITIES 6th May, 3rd June, 1st July and 5th August; 9 am - 5 pm; open with other Golden Valley churches.
9th September: Sponsored Cycle Ride.

SPECIAL A Mother's Union Safari encourages people to visit the Golden Valley churches. The visit ends with tea followed by a short service. Interested parties may ring for information.

CONTACT 0981 550 388.

Dilwyn   **415 547**

St Mary the Virgin

c. 1290   *Hereford*
Early English   *Grade 1*

St Mary's is on a rise in the centre of Dilwyn. The Norman tower is marked by the roof-line of an earlier building, pulled down when the present large church was built around 1290. Medieval features include chantry screens and piscinas, a recumbent knight, rood-loft stairs and some charming stained glass. Every century has seen some permanent change reflecting the continuity of worship in the village.

TRAVEL 6 miles South West of Leominster, just off the A4112 road to Hay and Brecon. **PARK** Parking for cars and coaches beside the road at the church gate.

OUTSIDE Roof line of earlier church on the side of the tower; signs of raising the nave roof, including 13th Century and 15th Century windows side by side; a fine 15th Century porch.

ACTIVITIES Regular: open every Saturday from 22nd July to 19th August, 2.00 pm to 5.00 pm.

CONTACT For details of services telephone the Team Office 0568 612124. Church members will be happpy to show visitors round on other days by arrangement. Please telephone 0544 318613.

FOOD The Pandy Inn (by village green). Picnics can be taken on the village green or on the playing field.

VILLAGE The Pandy Inn (oldest pub in Herefordshire), Village Hall (was village school which opened in early 17th Century), Castle Tump and Sundial on Village Green, interesting village houses.

VISIT Arthur's Stone (Neolithic burial mound 2000 or 3000 BC) Snodhill Castle (approx.1 mile from village). Merbach Hill - giving views of several counties. Footpaths shown on map by village hall. Peterchurch, Vowchurch and Turnastone.

Eardisley   313492

St Mary Magdalene

12th Century   *Hereford*
Norman/Early English   *Grade 1*

Standing among its ancient gravestones, with the fine Black and White Tithe Barns alongside, the church looks out on a more peaceful scene today than when it was founded some 900 years ago in the shadow of the castle of the Baskervilles. Inside is the remarkable 12th Century Font dramatically depicting an event in their family history. Near the pulpit is a Hereford Bishop's gravestone. Look on the organ to discover why his descendent, 200 years later, donated the instrument. Ponder the case of the Vicar who never was, and the Barnsley court battle which lasted 34 years - and gave Charles Dickens an idea. The Guide Sheet tells all nearby.

TRAVEL It stands on the west side of the A4111 at the Hereford end of the village. It is opposite the school. Yeomans (Tel.0432 356201) and Sargeants (Tel. 0544 230481) run buses from Hereford and Kington through the village on weekdays and Saturdays. **PARK** Use the lane off the A4111 between the churchyard and the Tithe Barns. Suitable for minibuses and small coaches. Large coaches down road opposite by school playing fields where they can be turned.

OUTSIDE The lych-gate, a fine Wellingtonia pine, the old preaching cross, the wrought iron gates to the church porch, the blacksmith's epitaph on a gravestone to the left of the porch.

ACTIVITIES Saturday 22nd and Sunday 23rd July (St Mary Magdalene Day): Exhibitions of village craft work and demonstrations. Village gardens open. Village Walks. **SPECIAL** Special Sunday Evening service Songs of Praise. Groups welcome. Catering is to order and guided tours can be arranged.

CONTACT Please telephone 0544 327256.

FOOD Tram Inn and The New Inn, both in Eardisley. The Great Oak.

Eaton Bishop   SO 443 391

St Michael and All Angels

Unknown   *Hereford*
Early English   *Grade 1*

The walls are of rubble and ashlar, dressings all of local sandstone. The roofs are predominantly tile covered with spire being covered in oak shingles. The West Tower is the oldest part of the church dating from the 11th Century and bears traces of Saxon influence. In the 13th Century the North and South arcades of the Nave were built and a clerestorey and aisles added. The Chancel was rebuilt in the 14th Century and bears contemporary painted glass of national importance. The church is set amidst a pleasant churchyard with some fine mature trees at the highest point of the village.

TRAVEL Take the A465 out of Hereford, branching left on to the B4349 follow the signs to Madley. Eaton Bishop lies to the north of the Clehonger/Madley road and the turning to the church is clearly marked with signs drawing attention to the unique 14th Century glass. **PARK** Roadside parking only.

OUTSIDE A fine churchyard cross and chest tombs together with some other interesting headstones.

CONTACT Church Contact: 0981 250 839.

FOOD The Ancient Camp Inn, Ruckhall. The Madley Arms, Madley.

Eye (Morton)   486 638

St Peter and St Paul

Hereford

Norman

Built in the late 12th Century, the oldest part is opposite the entrance via the 14th Century timber porch. Its special features include: Norman pillars, effigies in Lady chapel, curious vine carving on roof beam, carved font on 'modern' base and central aisle 'bent' at Chancel steps. Note the old monuments of an angel holding a shield and stone carving of St Peter and St Paul in the Choir. Also note the stone carved heads (corbels) on the principal arch which once held a wooden screen (rood loft). The church was restored in 1874 - the Bell Tower was rebuilt and the vestry added.

TRAVEL Drive south on A49 - turn right, past Ashton fruit farm at signpost to Morton/Eye and Luston or take B4361 (road to Ludlow from Leominster), and take the first right, past the Balance Inn at sign post to Morton/Eye and Berrington Hall. **PARK** Parking for cars, access not suitable for coaches.

ACTIVITIES Monday 29th May:Spring Bank Holiday 30th June, 1st, 2nd July: Flower Festival.
19th September: Cycle Ride Visitors very welcome 10 am - 7 pm.

SPECIAL Coffee/tea and soft drinks available. **Access for wheelchairs.**

FOOD Balance Inn - pub meals served.

VISIT Berrington Hall and Croft Castle (National Trust).Village Stores and Post Office in Luston.

Goodrich   572190

St Giles

Decorated

Hereford
Grade 2*

The graceful 14th Century spire is a familiar landmark, for the church, parts of which are at least 800 years old, stands on a promontory away from the present-day village and must be approached on foot by field paths. It is an impressive building consisting of two equal aisles, unusual in having no division between nave and chancel. There are a number of monuments to famous people outside and more inside, where the visitor can see fine woodwork and stained glass. The grandfather of Dean Swift, Thomas, was vicar here in the 17th Century and his tomb is under the altar.

TRAVEL Half a mile off the A40 Ross - Monmouth dual carriageway. No. 34 bus service from Ross to Monmouth passes within 200 yards of footpath to the church. Public footpath from Goodrich Village to Cross Keys Inn crosses the churchyard. **PARK** On unclassified public road at junction with private road and footpath or by the church notice board outside Old Vicarage. No suitable parking for coaches or minibuses.

OUTSIDE Cross, tombs of Sir Samuel Rush Meyrick K.B., Joshua Cristall (1st President of Society of Painters in Water Colour), Stone seat memorial 1719.

ACTIVITIES 9th September: Sponsored Bike Ride. 22nd-24th September: Harvest weekend.
Friday 22nd, 7 pm: Harvest evening service followed by supper in the Village Hall (phone 0600 890680). Sunday 24th, 11 am: Harvest Festival.

CONTACT The church may not always be open, but a notice is displayed in the porch indicating where the key may be obtained. **SPECIAL** Ancestor tracers will find helpful copy of burial register and plan of grave sites displayed in the porch. No close road access, **wheelchairs not advised.**

FOOD Cross Keys and Ye Hostelrie. Refreshments and picnic site at Goodrich Castle.

VILLAGE Goodrich Castle. General Stores and Post Office. Open Farm at Huntsham. Coppett Hill Common (good walking).

VISIT Ross-on-Wye, Symonds Yat, Forest of Dean, Walford Church and Marstow.

Hardwicke 148/ 271 438

Holy Trinity

1853   *Hereford*
Victorian

The church was built in 1851-3 to serve the new parish of Harwicke formed out of part of Clifford parish. Virtually unaltered since, the pleasing proportions and details make a harmonious whole. The stained glass windows provide valuable clues about the foundation of the church. Find the memorial plaque to the second vicar the Revd Thomas Webb, the eminent Astronomer. Look out for the plaques in honour of the dedicated service given by Hardwicke organists - only 3 in 140 years! **TRAVEL** On the B4348 between Hay and Dorstone. Half a mile from the junction with the B43352. Route 39 Hereford to Brecon bus passes the entrance. Footpaths link to the Wye Valley Walk which crosses the northern part of the parish. **PARK** Cars and minibuses can park off-road by the Lych gate.

OUTSIDE Look out for the Ha-ha which borders the front of a churchyard which is planted with yews, conifers and rhododendron trees.

ACTIVITIES Rogationtide Weekend - Saturday 20th May, 10 am - 6 pm, Sunday 21st May, 10 am - 5 pm 21st May: Rogationtide. In the church you will find some information on our community and the local facilities available as well as information on the church itself.
SPECIAL Those wishing to join our celebration of Rogation are welcome. This involves visits to farms to bless the land (with a different itinerary for walkers and those who wish to use cars), followed by tea and a service at a farm. Please be at Hardwicke church at 2.30 pm.

CONTACT The Rector. The Rectory. Cusop. Hay-on Wye. 0497 820634.

FOOD Royal Oak is close by and the Castlefields Inn is on the road to Bredwardine.

VILLAGE Walk up Merbach Hill and Little Mountain and enjoy the glorious views.

If you are interested in staying for the weekend, a leaflet giving details of B&B and other accommodation is available by sending a stamped addressed envelope to Mark Robinson, The Haven, Hardwicke, via Hereford HR3 5TA.

VISIT Hay-on-Wye with its bookshops and other facilities is three miles away. Churches at Bredwardine, Clifford, Cusop and Hardwicke.

> Rogationtide Weekend The Border Link parishes all look forward to meeting you and hope that you will have an enjoyable stay.

Kilpeck 445 305

St Mary and St David

1140   *Hereford*
Pure Norman   *Grade 1*

The Norman church is recognised worldwide for its remarkable Romanesque sculptures inside and out, the particular gem being the well preserved South Doorway, which is carved with all manner of Birds, Beasts and Serpents representing Creation, with the Tree of Life on the Tympanum. The jambs are intricately carved with figures as lively today as they were 900 years ago. The many figures on the Corbel Table range from grotesque "Beast eats Man" and "Dog and Rabbit" to "Sheila-na-Gig". The fine Chancel Arch has two moulded Orders carried on jambs depicting three Saints on either side.

TRAVEL 8 miles south of Hereford on the A465 towards Abergavenny turn left at the special sign on the Main Road. If coming from Ross on the A49 towards Hereford, follow the B4348 signposted Hay-on-Wye, through Much Dewchurch and take the first left, also specially signposted. **PARK** Parking available for 12+ cars.

OUTSIDE Scant remains of the 14th Century castle, site of the original medieval village and views of the Black Mountains.

ACTIVITIES 3rd June: In the steps of St Wulfstan.

Saturday 26th, Sunday 27th, Monday 28th August:Flower Festival entitled "Reflections of Village Life".

SPECIAL At the same time the local Art Club will hold their Exhibition in the Village Hall, where cold lunches, coffee and teas will be available.

CONTACT Please phone 01981 21315.

FOOD The Red Lion in the village - no food available. Black Swan at Much Dewchurch - food available. Three Horseshoes at Allensmore - food available.

VISIT A list of other interesting local churches is in the church. Information on church notice board.

Kingstone   424 357

St Michael and All Angels

Unknown   *Hereford*
Gothic   *Grade 2**

The church stands on a gently elevated site to the North of the medieval village mentioned in the Domesday Book as "Land of the King", King's Tun or King's Town. It is a well-kept welcoming building which has evolved since the early 12th Century with additions in the mid 14th Century and restoration in 1890. Some of the interesting features include a Norman arch at the South door, and a 13th Century "plum pudding" font. The vestry was refurbished in

1985 and a ringing platform installed. There is a fine new peal of eight bells.

TRAVEL From the west on B4348 turn left by Bull Ring Pub; from the east on B4348, turn right by Bull Ring. Church is on the right. Green Farm is on the right before the church. The Old School is on the right beyond the church. **PARK** A field will be open behind the church; its entrance is beside the Old School. Also some parking near the church and in Green Farm.

ACTIVITIES 7th, 8th and 9th July 10 am - 6 pm Flower Festival.
Friday 7th July, 7.30 pm: Amateur Operatic Society Concert.

SPECIAL Saturday 8th July, 2.00 pm: If desired a country walk can be arranged by public footpath, taking in one or two local churches (perhaps Madley and Eaton Bishop). The path passes close to BT Madley Satellite Earth Station. Strong shoes, walking clothes, seven or eight miles.

Sunday 9th July, 6.00 pm: Songs of Praise. Some gardens within the village will be open to visitors.

CONTACT Church Contact: 0981 250538.

FOOD The Bull Ring (very good pub food).

VISIT Madley and Eaton Bishop churches. Clehonger, Eaton Bishop, Allensmore and Thruxton.

Kington   292 568

St. Mary's

c. 1200   *Hereford*
Early English   *Grade 1*

During King John's reign the south tower of the stone church was built, the broach spire was rebuilt in 1794. The nave was rebuilt c.1300 and given aisles: with the Victorian addition of a further north aisle, the visitor's first impression is of a broad, open church. The next may be of "the noble chancel", (Pevsner) 13th century, with its group of Lancet windows. In the circular font, with the rope moulding, Kington babies have been baptised for 900 years. The Vaughan effigy is 15th Century. Entering the church's serene and prayerful atmosphere visitors will certainly see a lovingly tended church.

TRAVEL Off A44 on Hill on West side of Town. Regular buses from Hereford and Leominster. On Offa's Dyke path. The church stands on a hill, a pleasant walk from the centre of town. **PARK** North side of churchyard (cars only). Coaches can off-load on slip road to west of church. In town: Mill Street car park, the Square (coaches).

OUTSIDE The churchyard commands beautiful views down the Arrow valley, across meadows to Ridgebourne House and Hergest Ridge and looking up to the slopes of Bradnor Hill.

ACTIVITIES 9th, 10th, 11th, 17th, 18th, 24th June, 10 am - 6 pm: Church open as part of **Kington Festival**. 9th, 10th, 11th June: St Mary's Flower Festival. Teas available in nearby Parish House.
11th June, 6.30 pm: St Mary's Songs of Praise.
17th June: Kington Eisteddfod.
18th June, 7.30 pm: Kington Eisteddfod concert with M.U.Choir.
24th June: Kington Lion's Gala Day. **SPECIAL** Guided tours by arrangement on above dates - 0544 230 271. **Disabled facilities**: ramp. 1 wheelchair available. Toilet.

CONTACT 0544 230271

FOOD The Swan, the Royal Oak. Picnic Site: The Recreation Ground.

VISIT Hergest Croft Gardens (Teas, shops, toilets). Small Breeds Farm (refreshments, toilets). Hergest Ridge and Bradnor Hill: Walking areas.T.I.C. Mill Street.

Little Dewchurch 530 317

St David

rededicated 1870   *Hereford*
Victorian - Gothic   *Grade 2*

You will find this most interesting church set in a peaceful valley to the West of the village. The church, which dates from the 14th Century, was sympathetically restored in the 1870s, whilst the Norman Tower with its gargoyles was left intact. The near circular churchyard indicates this was probably a pre-Christian burial ground and holy place. The striking mosaic reredos behind the altar was designed by the well known West Country architect, Frederick Preedy. Unusually, he also designed and made the stained glass windows in which his "signature" of an open flower can be found etched into the blue sky. Look out for it on many other things around the church too.

TRAVEL Midway between Ross on Wye and Hereford (just under 7 miles from each). From Ross take A49 to Hereford taking the second right, go through Hoarwithy where one climbs the hill to Little Dewchurch. Turn left just after the Plough Pub. From Hereford take the back road (B4399) to Hoarwithy. At Little Dewchurch turn right by the Village Hall and School, the church is 0.25 mile up the lane. **PARK** There is ample parking to the South Side of the church where for special events it may be extended into a field.

OUTSIDE In the churchyard, where conservation is carefully balanced with other needs you will find an unrestored 14th Century Preaching Cross, and also the grave of a gentleman who in the late 1930s staked a claim to our Royal Throne - and even had his own banknotes printed!

ACTIVITIES Sun 5th March, 3 pm: Patronal Service. Sun 9th April, 3pm: Palm Sunday Procession with Donkey.
Sat 6th May, 7.30 - 9.00 pm: Musical Evening (1940s), in church.
Sun 4th June, 3 pm: (Pentecost) Teddy Bears' Picnic.
Sat 15th July 11 am - 4 pm: Crafts and Hobbies Display (in church).
Sat 5th August 1 pm - 6 pm: Broadway Lands Farm Country Walk and open garden (refreshments).
Sat 9th September, all day: The Cycle Ride and Event. Friday 15th September, 7.30 pm - 9.00 pm: Musical Evening "Fernleigh Singers" and "Just Brass" (in church).
Sun 24th September 3 pm: "Harvest of the Past". Encouraged to dress up - country style.

CONTACT 0432 840309 or 0432 840661.

FOOD The Plough Inn, Little Dewchurch. The Cottage of Content (pub meals), Carey.

VISIT St John the Baptist, Aconbury. The site of a 12th Century Nunnery where part of Derek Nimmo's "Hells Bells" was filmed. The church and area is frequently referred to in Dorothy Erskine's hitorical novel "The Lady of Hay".The Italian style church at Hoarwithy, overlooking the River Wye.

Madley   SO 420 388

Nativity of the Blessed Virgin Mary

prob. 6th century   *Hereford*
Norman and Early English   *Grade 1*

Come and follow the steps of the pilgrims as you explore this large and beautiful church building. In the 6th Century the important Celtic saint, Dyfrig or Dubricius, was born here and people came to visit his church. More pilgrims came in the 12th, 13th and 14th Centuries; there was then a special statue of Mary, hence the church's dedication. Madley church is ideal for the 'church detective', with a clear and fascinating building history. It has hardly been touched since the 14th Century; come and see the original wall paintings, stained glass and enormous Norman font.

TRAVEL On B4352 west of Hereford, (7 miles) regular buses (447, 448, 449) from Hereford. Good local footpaths. On B4352.

OUTSIDE Find the interesting tombstone inscriptions and ancient churchyard cross; enjoy the lovely setting of the church.

ACTIVITIES July: Week long Madley Festival : concerts by internationally renowned artists.
9th September: Cycle Ride day.
Thursday 5th October: Harvest Festival **SPECIAL** Children very welcome; also disabled people and wheelchairs. New 'church detective' style guide booklet.

CONTACT Rev. T Jones at Madley Vicarage 0981 250245 - for the following:Exploring the tower and crypt.Guided Tours Teas and lunches in church for pre-booked parties.

FOOD Red Lion, Madley.

VISIT Tyberton church 3 miles towards Hay, Moccas church and court, Dore Abbey.

Moccas   357 434

St Michael and All Angels

12th century   *Hereford*
Norman

A church (probably wooden) was established in the 5th century by St Dubricius, replaced in the 12th century by the present building, which is built from local tufa stone and, though restored in the 19th century, has not been altered significantly since it was built, making it an almost perfect example of a Norman village church. The area was manorial land from Norman times, and so the church eventually came to stand within a park.

TRAVEL Situated in the Moccas Court estate, the church is approached by a road through the park the entrance of which is just off the B4352 Bredwardine-Madley road. **PARK** At the foot of the mound on which the church stands: turn left before the cattle grid down a lane.

OUTSIDE The setting in Parkland studded with ancient oaks, is quite beautiful.

ACTIVITIES Saturday 20th May, 10 am - 6 pm, Sunday 21st May, 10 am - 5 pm.
21st May: Rogationtide. In the church you will find some information on our community and the local facilities available as well as information on the church itself. **SPECIAL** Those wishing to join our celebration of Rogation are welcome. This involves visits to farms to bless the land (with a different

itinerary for walkers and those who wish to use cars), followed by tea and a service at a farm. Please be at Hardwicke church at 2.30 pm.

CONTACT The Rector. The Rectory. Cusop. Hay-on Wye. 0497 820634.

FOOD The Red Lion Hotel in Bredwardine.

VILLAGE Visit Moccas Court which is open to the public on some afternoons in the summer.

If you are interested in staying for the weekend, a leaflet giving details of B&B and other accommodation is available by sending a stamped addressed envelope to Mark Robinson, The Haven, Hardwicke, via Hereford HR3 5TA.

VISIT The other Border Link churches Bredwardine, Clifford, Cusop and Hardwicke.

> Rogationtide Weekend The Border Link parishes all look forward to meeting you and hope that you will have an enjoyable stay.

Peterchurch   SO 345 385

St Peter

possibly 786 AD   *Hereford*
Norman   *Grade 1*

This quiet and imposing 12th Century Norman church is exceptional in having four sections with a double chancel. It has the original stone altar, Norman font and other interesting features. Although worship has continued uninterrupted since the church was built, from outside you can see the first floor level door on the north face of the tower which gave access to a refuge in times of trouble. The modern replacement spire was lowered onto the tower in 1972 and the church is a focal point for miles around, a symbol of God's presence in the heart of the beautiful Golden Valley.

TRAVEL Turn off B4348 in centre of Peterchurch between Boughton Arms and Stores and go down church road towards River Dore. Hereford - Brecon bus service passes through village. **PARK** At the church or in public car park opposite.

OUTSIDE Site of former Golden Valley Railway. Dog Acre, the old dog pound. Interesting tomb stones. Exceptionally old yew tree much coppiced for long bows.

ACTIVITIES 6th May, 3rd June, 1st July, 5th August, and 9th September, 10 am - 5 pm: Church open in conjuction with Vowchurch, Turnastone and Dorstone. Refreshments provided at one of the four churches.
9th September: Historic churches cycle ride.
25th June: Kilvert Society service.

Weekend following 29th June: Patronal festival.

SPECIAL Mini-guide for children, and of local places of interest and walks. Map of other churches of interest in this part of Herefordshire. **Easy access for the disabled.**

CONTACT Church Contact: 0981 550282.

FOOD Picnic site and playground opposite church. The Boughton Arms (50 yds). The Nag's Head (0.3 mile). The Old Bakery Tea Shop (0.5 mile).

VISIT Golden Valley Apiaries, Long Lane. Shepherd's Ice Cream, Cwm Farm. Snodhill Castle.

> Special Mothers Union Safari to the Golden Valley Churches - Peterchurch, Dorstone, Turnastone, Vowchurch

---

Putley   SO 646 376

Christchurch

1875   *Hereford*
Victorian Decorated   *Grade 2*

Putley Church stands on the outbuildings of a Roman villa. Rebuilt in 1875, reusing medieval materials (observe the rafters), it presents an amazing Anglo-Catholic interior - statuary, mosaics, alabaster altar, carved choirstalls and benchends, glass, metalwork, inlaid stonework, and a cheerful font with Noah's Ark. The pulpit and screen are made of the Jacobean squire's pew. Major statues represent all the New Testament writers; others show the Last Supper (notice the unhaloed Judas slinking out), the Emmaus Road, and Doubting Thomas. Mosaics depict Palm

46

Sunday, Nain, Abraham and Isaac, and the Via Dolorosa. Benchends have carvings of local plants and birds.

TRAVEL From Trumpet Inn, Ledbury - Hereford road, Junction A438/A417/A4172: go quarter of a mile towards Hereford; first left (sign Putley Common); one mile, left at postbox (sign Putley); quarter of a mile; first left (sign Lower Court, Putley Church). Buses: 476 (alight Poolend), 478, 479. **PARK** Ample parking and turning space.

OUTSIDE Roman and Norman remains in north door. Churchyard cross: Christ crucified; St Andrew; Mary and the Infant Jesus; a brainless archbishop (could be any of them, but probably Tuppence a Bucket).

ACTIVITIES April/May: Blossomtime.
3rd June: Open.
9th September: Cycle Ride
October: Big Apple   **Easy disabled access**.

CONTACT Opening at all reasonable hours, by appointment only (Tel: 0531 670264).

FOOD Butchers' Arms, Woolhope (N.G.R. SO 617358) Tel: 0432 860281. Picnics on Marcle Ridge above pub.

VILLAGE Putley Water Mill (Tel: 0531 670249).

VISIT Hellens House, Much Marcle (Tel: 0531 660347). Notable screens in Aylton and Pixley churches.

Rowlstone   SO 374 272
St Peter

Norman   *Hereford*

Visitors to Rowlstone will be rewarded by seeing a fine Norman arch with a pair of figures carved on either side. Could one figure represent St Peter to whom the church is dedicated? Look for the band of carved birds extending across the nave and find the pair of 15th Century rare iron candelabra in the chancel. Enjoy the peace of this friendly ancient church, make time to explore the area. Details of walks are in the church porch along with maps of the locality.

TRAVEL Signposted at Pontrilas on A465 Hereford-Abergavenny road. One and a half miles to church. Opposite telephone kiosk and before Walterstone turn. **PARK** Car park behind church.

OUTSIDE   Churchyard Cross, wildflowers, Tympanum of Christ in Majesty in the Porch, Green Man Carving.

CONTACT Church Contacts: 0981 240708; 0981 240322; 0981 240503.

FOOD Carpenters Arms, Walterstone. Temple Bar and Dog Inn, Ewyas Harold. Picnic in car park.

VILLAGE   Footpaths to Ewyas Harold and Llancillo. Walks round Rowlstone. Offa's Dyke walk. Good walking area.

VISIT Clodock, Kilpeck, Abbey Dore and Bacton churches.

Sellack   SO 566 277
St Tysilio

Hereford

In watermeadow setting by the Wye. Beautiful views. Well kept churchyard - look for grave with hand pointing upwards and the word 'gone'! 14th century porch leads into building certainly built in Norman days. A 7th century mention of site exists, (then Llandaff diocese). Continuous ministry recorded since 1291. Remains of Norman arches - a fine barrel roof - and a fine and rare stained glass east window (1630). Notes in the church record a civil war story about this window. The only English church dedicated to this Welsh saint. Built in red sandstone - a church of peace and beauty.

TRAVEL 1 mile west of Ross (A49) Sellack/ Hoarwithy turn right. 2.5 miles to war memorial cross roads, take Sellack/Strangford/Foy Road (right). Then after half a mile (approx.) turn left, signed Sellack church. By path from Kings Capel across Wye footbridge. **PARK** In lane and verges by church.

OUTSIDE 13th century Black and White cottage - oldest house in village.

ACTIVITIES 9th April, Palm Sunday: Rare Pax Cake ceremony.
14th July: 'Music on a Summer's Evening'.
9th September: Cycle Ride.
SPECIAL Guided tours and other activities including walks etc. organised during Summer.

CONTACT phone 01989 770759.

FOOD The Lough Pool Inn.

VISIT Kings Capel - village and church. Hoarwithy - village and Italianate church. Ross-on-Wye - market town.

believed to have been built by Robert Whittington, elder brother of Dick Whittington, three times Lord Mayor of London.

TRAVEL Turn off B4224 at bend on hill approx. 2 miles from Fownhope and 1.5 miles from How Caple. Lane signposted Sollers Hope 1, Much Marcle 4. Half a mile along twisting lane, then turn left at the signpost to Sollers Hope Church. **PARK** For approx. 8 cars near church gate. Minibus welcome. Access not possible for coaches.

OUTSIDE 15th Century Churchyard Cross, now the War Memorial. Carved 17th Century gravestones. Churchyard bordered by brook, cowslips in April.

ACTIVITIES Wednesday 7th June 10 am - 6 pm: Church open day.
Saturday 9th September 10 am - 6 pm: Church open day.

CONTACT Telephone: 098 986 226.

FOOD The Green Man, Fownhope; New Inn, Fownhope. Forge and Ferry, Fownhope. The Butchers' Arms, Woolhope. The Crown, Woolhope. The Slip Inn, Much Marcle. Lime Kilns.

VISIT How Caple Court Gardens. Brockhampton Church (thatched; Arts and Crafts). Westons' Cider Works, Much Marcle.

Sollers Hope SO613 332

St Michael's

c. 1390 *Hereford*
Decorated *Grade 2**

Small, mostly 14th Century stone church with timbered bell-turret, on the site of a Saxon church. Simple, with fine barrel roofs over a strikingly lofty interior. The Font is 900 years old. Fine woodwork on choir stalls early 20th Century. Some medieval glass. Four 13th Century stone coffin lids, one incised with a knight in chain-mail. Sollers Hope (-hope = enclosed valley, owned by de Solers family 11th and 12th Century) is now designated an Area of Outstanding Natural Beauty. It belonged to the Whittington family for 200 years (1300 - 1546). The church is

St Weonards 162 / 496244

St Weonard

Hereford
Grade 1

The tower of St Weonards church can be seen for miles from the surrounding countryside. The oldest part of the present building (south doorway, windows on either side of it and lower part of the south nave wall) dates from about 1300, but there was a church here many years earlier. The tower and north aisle were built in the 16th Century, also the top part of the south wall. St Weonard, an obscure Welsh saint, believed to have been a hermit woodcutter, is pictured with book and axe in the 19th Century glass of the east window of the north aisle.

TRAVEL The church of St Weonard stands to the east side of A466 (Hereford to Monmouth road), just over 10 miles from Hereford and 7 from Monmouth. There is a car park near the church: follow the road marked 'Mount Way'. **PARK** Car park on left. Coaches can turn with care at the entrance to Mount Way.

OUTSIDE Near the path, south of the church is the base of a 15th century cross, fitted for a sundial. In the porch notice the holy-water stoup, usually filled with flowers. Wonderful views from the churchyard.

ACTIVITIES 24th June: church open and manned. On the same day, Treago, a 15th century house in the valley on the opposite side of the main road is to be open. It is also hoped that a fete will be held at Treago on that day.

CONTACT Church Contact: 0981 580353

FOOD.The Garway Moon, Garway. The New Inn, at St Owen's Cross.

VILLAGE See the 'tump' (opposite the car park) which is a pre-historic mound, and Treago. Garway Hill, for magnificent views.

VISIT Garway Church of Knights Templars fame. Orcop church, also ancient, as is Welsh Newton Church where St John Kemble is buried. All the above are situated in an exceptional piece of countryside.

Stanford Bishop   682 515

St James the Greater

Late Norman (restored)

Hereford
Grade 2

A late Norman building standing amid fields on the highest point in the parish, commanding extensive views of the rolling Herefordshire countryside. The churchyard is circular indicating an ancient site of worship, the predominant feature being a yew of over 1,000 years old. On entering the church one is immediately struck by the peace and serenity of this simple building. Our greatest treasure is a chair said to have been used by St Augustine on his meeting with the Welsh bishops in 603. Also of interest to embroiderers is the modern altar frontal featuring hops and St James' symbol.

TRAVEL 4 miles south east of Bromyard. Signpost from B4220. **PARK** Adequate for cars and minibuses.

OUTSIDE Vast 1,200 years old yew tree set in circular churchyard with extensive views, including the Malvern Hills.

ACTIVITIES 3-8 July: Embroideries and Tapestries Week-modern embroidered altar frontal. 9th September: Sponsored Cycle Ride. 18th November: We hope to plant a tree to mark Tree Planting Sunday.

CONTACT the Churchwardens on 0886 884237 and 0886 884362.

FOOD Herefordshire House, half a mile on B4220. Several cafes in Bromyard and picnicing facilities on Bromyard Downs.

VISIT Linley Green mission church which is linked to Stanford Bishop. Built in 1883. Lower Brockhampton.

HEREFORDSHIRE

Sutton St Nicholas 149/ 534466

St Nicholas

12th,13th century

Hereford
Grade 1

The village overlooks the water meadows and is overlooked by the hill crowned with the Iron Age fort, Sutton Walls. The church lies at the south-eastern end of the village. The building dates mainly from the thirteenth and fourteenth centuries, its simple form distorted by the medieval chantry chapel forming a south transept. In the structure and furnishings we are provided with a visual history of the architectural setting of worship. Look for the medieval piscina, the Jacobean pulpit and screen. At the north-western end of the village is the church of St Michael where we experience a direct entry into the austerity of a plain Norman building. Look for the two fonts, one Norman, the other seventeenth century.

TRAVEL St Nicholas: turn left off A465 from Hereford for Sutton St Nicholas: turn right at village cross roads at the Golden Cross Inn, the church is on the right a short way down the road. **PARK** Limited: roadside only.

ACTIVITIES 29th May (Spring Bank Holiday) 28th August (Summer Bank Holiday).

VISIT The church of St Michael. For St Michael: turn left at village cross roads at Golden Cross Inn. The church is on the left in about 0.25 mile, at the very end of the village. Grid ref. 527462.

Turnastone 357 365

St Mary Magdalene

Hereford
Early English

Grade 2*

One of the smallest parishes (c.530 acres) in Hereford Diocese and with a population of 28, Turnastone still maintains its separate identity. The late 12th Century stone building, with a small wooden bell turret, is set in a churchyard which in spring boasts wild daffodils. The Nave and Chancel have a handsome ceiled wagon roof with some charming carving of country tools on the wooden bosses; there is an attractive

Jacobean pulpit. Look out for the hatted satyr on the memorial to Thomas ap Harry. We have four services a month, all from the Book of Common Prayer.

TRAVEL From the B4348 Allensmore to Hay road, take the turning marked Vowchurch and Michaelchurch Escley; leaving Vowchurch (which also welcomes visitors) on your left, cross the bridge over the River Dore and continue past Turnastone Court Farm on your right. Our church will then be in view. There is a limited bus service from Hereford (service 39 from Bus Station) four times a day matched by a return bus about an hour later. **PARK** There is limited parking next to the church but there are places nearby where it would be safe to park and from where a combined visit to us and Vowchurch would be possible. One coach.

OUTSIDE There are some interesting memorial stones in the churchyard, details given in the Guide. Several signed footpaths which offer attractive walks. See Peterchurch.

ACTIVITIES Activities arranged in conjunction with Peterchurch, Vowchurch and Dorstone. **SPECIAL** Guided tours are possible by arrangement.

CONTACT please ring 01981 550341 (churchwarden).

FOOD Licenced restaurant at Poston Mill (about 1 mile), two public houses in Peterchurch (2.5 miles).

VISIT Our sister churches of Vowchurch (0.25 mile by road), Peterchurch (along bridle path, 3 miles) and Dorstone. Also St Margaret's Church (screen), Bacton Church (Memorials) and Abbeydore (12th Century Abbey).Bridle path to Peterchurch 3 miles.

> **Special Mothers Union Safari to the Golden Valley Churches - Peterchurch, Dorstone, Turnastone, Vowchurch**

Vowchurch 362 365

St Bartholomew

1348 (re-dedicated)
Norman/Early English

Hereford
Grade 1

Our church, close to the River Dore, has an air of timelessness and tranquillity felt by many of our visitors. The church is Norman; part of the south and north walls are original, as is the window in the south wall. There was a major extension in the 14th Century and the church was re-dedicated at that time. Massive oak pillars support the roof trusses in a most unusual way. There is some interesting woodwork, particularly the altar rails, carved pew backs and chancel screen. The bell tower is supported on 4 large oak timbers and houses 3 bells. Approximately 100 kneelers depict some village features. The churchyard, sweeping down to the river, has an abundance of wild flowers, birds and small mammals.

TRAVEL The Vowchurch turning is 10 miles west of Hereford, 2 miles east of Peterchurch on the B4348. There is a limited bus service from Hereford and Brecon. **PARK** There is limited parking for cars and one coach.

OUTSIDE Look for the change in stonework on the north and south walls marking the extension in the 14th Century.

ACTIVITIES See Peterchurch entry. The church will be open and manned on Saturday: 6th May, 3rd June, 1st July and 5th August, 10 am - 4 pm. 9th September, 10 am - 6 pm: Sponsored Churches Cycle Ride. **SPECIAL** Near the porch entrance is the grave of Skeffington Dodgson, vicar of Vowchurch 1895-1910, brother of Lewis Carroll the author of 'Alice in Wonderland'. There is a permanent exhibition concerning Lewis Carroll's family. A mini-stall for plants, produce and second-hand books is occasionally extended to include hand-knits, toys etc. with light refreshments available.

FOOD Pub/restaurant in Peterchurch (2 miles). Picnic in the churchyard by the river.

VILLAGE On Saturday mornings in the Summer months there is a country market in the nearby village hall.

VISIT Our sister church at Turnastone is 0.25 mile up the road. A bridle path runs from Turnastone to St Peter's, Peterchurch (about 3 miles).

> **Special Mothers Union Safari to the Golden Valley Churches - Peterchurch, Dorstone, Turnastone, Vowchurch**

51

SOUTH SHROPSHIRE

"Clunton, Clunbury, Clungunford and Clun,

Are the quietest places under the sun".

A.E.Houseman

With its gently rolling hills, wild uplands and unpolluted rivers where otters hunt, South Shropshire is much as it was in Houseman's day. It is still possible to drive for a quarter of an hour without passing another car.

But the tranquillity of the scenery is deceptive. Nestled in a time-warp between England and Wales, this deeply rural backwater is nevertheless an active farming area, where the land is as productive and treasured as it has ever been.

And you have only to scratch the surface of the present calm to find history everywhere. From battles of national importance, to innumerable local feuds and border skirmishes, many of which have left their mark on the landscape in forts and castles of all ages. The region is rich in other links with our past: picturesque bridges, majestic abbeys and not least the many remote rural churches. These churches witnessed the events of the past, and often reflect them in their architecture and furnishings, just as they are witness to and part of the present day life of the communities around them.

Katherine Lack

St Wulfstan and Shropshire

Not long after the Norman Conquest Wulfstan was asked to administer the Diocese of Lichfield. Records show that when he travelled up the River Severn to Shrewsbury he prayed at a little wooden chapel near the junction of the River Severn and the River Meole. It was called St Peter's. When asked why he was attracted to St Peter's rather than St Mary's church in the centre of the town he replied;

"Believe me, this chapel, so little esteemed, will in time become the most glorious place in all Shrewsbury, and the joy of the entire region."

A monastery was founded there in 1083. Today we know the church as Shrewsbury Abbey.

Wulfstan must have stopped at the many churches along the banks of the River Severn. He was certainly present at the consecration of the church at Quatford.

Tourist Information
The Tourist Information Office
Castle Street, Ludlow, Shropshire.

Festivals in villages
Church Stretton Festival: last two weeks July
first two weeks of August
Lydbury North Festival 16-24 September

Town Churches

Shrewsbury	The Abbey Church
Ludlow	St Lawrence
Bridgnorth	St Mary Magdelene
Bishops Castle	St John the Baptist

Village Churches are listed alphabetically with the names of nearby towns. Each Gazetteer entry gives a grid reference from the Landranger OS Map series. Most are on sheet nos. 137 and 138.

Ashford Carbonell	south of Ludlow
Astley Abbotts	west of Wolverhampton
Bishop's Castle	north of Ludlow
Bridgnorth	south-west of Wolverhampton
Church Stretton	north of Ludlow
Claverley	west of Wolverhampton
Coalbrookdale	near Ironbridge, Telford
Cound	south-east of Shrewsbury
Dorrington	south of Shrewsbury
Farlow	north-east of Ludlow
Harley	north of Much Wenlock
Highley	south of Bridgnorth
Hope Bagot	north-east of Ludlow
Hopesay	north-west of Ludow
Leebotwood	west of Much Wenlock
Lydbury North	north-west of Ludlow
Quatford	south of Bridgnorth
Stapleton	south of Shrewsbury
Stokesay	north-west of Ludlow
Stottesdon ·	north-east of Ludlow

Dates for Your Diary in South Shropshire

Many churches will be open at times other than those listed below. For up to date local information please use the contact numbers listed in each of the Gazetteer entries.

Diary dates are dates when you can be sure to find the church open. Where churches have made a regular arrangement to have their building open and staffed they are listed at the beginning of each of the monthly lists. For more details please consult the individual entries.

Special Through the Church Door activities are also listed at the beginning of each month as appropriate.

January
Regular: Church Stretton: Wed-Sun

February
Regular: Church Stretton: Wed-Sun

March
Regular: Church Stretton   daily

April
Regular: Church Stretton   daily

6	Stottesdon	14:00	17:00
11	Leebotwood	10:00	15:00
20	Stottesdon	14:00	17:00

May
Regular: Church Stretton   daily

4	Stottesdon	14:00	17:00
13	Bishops Castle	10:00	18:00
18	Stottesdon	14:00	17:00
21	Ashford Carbonell	14:00	
21	Bridgnorth	12:00	18:00
22	Bridgnorth	10:00	18:00
26	Stapleton		
27	Stapleton		
28	Hopesay		
28	Stapleton		

June
3 June In the Steps Of St Wulfstan
Regular: check days and times above
         Church Stretton   daily

3	Cound		
3	Dorrington		
3	Highley		
3	Hopesay		
3	Quatford	10:00	17:00
3	Stokesay		
8	Stottesdon	14:00	17:00
10	Bishops Castle	10:00	18:00
22	Stottesdon	14:00	17:00
24	Bishops Castle		
24	Stokesay	9:00	18:00
25	Bishops Castle		
25	Farlow	14:00	18:00
25	Stokesay	9:00	18:00
26	Farlow	14:00	18:00
30	Dorrington		

July
Embroideries and Tapestries Week 3-9 July
Regular: Bridgnorth   daily
         Church Stretton   daily

1	Dorrington		
2	Dorrington		
2	Lydbury North	9:00	19:00
3	Dorrington		
6	Stottesdon	14:00	17:00
7	Hope Bagot	10:00	17:30
8	Bishops Castle	10:00	18:00
8	Hope Bagot	10:00	17:30
9	Hope Bagot	10:00	17:30
15	Claverley	10:00	21:00
15	Coalbrookdale	10:30	17:00
16	Claverley	10:00	21:00
16	Harley		
17	Claverley	10:00	21:00
18	Claverley	10:00	21:00
20	Stottesdon	14:00	17:00
22	Ashford Carbonell		
23	Quatford	14:00	17:00

August
Why not be a Church detective this August?
Regular: Church Stretton   daily
         Bridnorth   daily

3	Stottesdon	14:00	17:00
12	Bishop's Castle	10:00	16:00
17	Stottesdon	14:00	17:00
19	Coalbrookdale	10:30	17:00
26	Stokesay	10:00	18:00
27	Stokesay	10:00	18:00
28	Stokesay	10:00	18:00

September
9 September:
The Sponsored Cycle Ride - Watch out for Cyclists!
Regular: Church Stretton   daily
         Bridgnorth   daily

7	Stottesdon	14:00	17:00
9	Ashford Carbonell		
9	Bishop's Castle	10:00	16:00
9	Bridgnorth		
9	Harley		
9	Leebotwood	10:00	18:00
9	Quatford	10:00	18:00
9	Stokesay	10:00	18:00
9	Stottesdon	10:00	18:00
16	Lydbury North	9:00	19:00
17	Lydbury North	9:00	19:00
18	Lydbury North	9:00	19:00
19	Lydbury North	9:00	19:00
20	Lydbury North	9:00	19:00
21	Lydbury North	9:00	19:00
21	Stottesdon	14:00	17:00
22	Lydbury North	9:00	19:00
23	Lydbury North	9:00	19:00
24	Lydbury North	9:00	19:00

October
Regular: Church Stretton   daily

5	Stottesdon	14:00	17:00
16	Stottesdon	14:00	17:00

SHROPSHIRE

November
18 and 19 November: Plant a Tree Weekend
Regular: Church Stretton: Wed-Sun

December
Regular: Church Stretton: Wed-Sun
1   Bishop's Castle
2   Bishop's Castle
3   Bishop's Castle

c. 1300

1789

1808

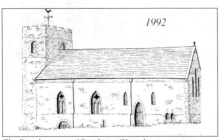

1992

The Development of Stapleton Church

Bishop's Castle   **SO 323884**

St John the Baptist

1860 (on rebuilding)   *Hereford*
Victoria Gothic

The church is attractively situated at the lower end of
Church Street. As you approach it is worth noting
the fine Lychgate and striking Norman tower, with
a red line marking an ancient form of ball game. The
churchyard offers pleasant surroundings for a stroll.
The interior of the church is a fine example of
Victorian 'Decorated' work giving an overall spacious
appearance.   A short history and description is
available. It is worth looking out for the original
Norman Font, fine 19th Century East window
dedicated to St John and carved wooden reredos.

TRAVEL Bishop's Castle is situated just off the
A488 23 miles South of Shrewsbury and 5 miles
North of Clun. It is on the Shropshire Way footpath.
PARK 2 Public Car Parks in Town; one suitable for
coaches.

ACTIVITIES Regularly Open and staffed on the
second Saturday of each month, May to September
inclusive (10 am - 4 pm).
24th, 25th June: The Midsummer Rejoicing and
Rushbearing.
1st, 2nd, 3rd December: Nativity Festival (exhibition
of Christmas Cribs).

CONTACT For special arrangements or further
details write to: 1 Lavender Bank, Bishop's Castle,
Shropshire, SY9 5BD enclosing S.A.E. or telephone
0588 650282.

FOOD The town has good catering facilities.

TOWN Has a wide variety of shops and tourist
information centre. **Toilets (including disabled)
available at Market car park**.

VISIT Bishop's Castle Railway Museum. 'House on
Crutches' Museum. Regular exhibitions by local
Artists.

Bridgnorth

St Mary Magdalene
1796   *Hereford*
Renaissance style   *Class B*

This Georgian church stands at the head of East Castle Street and is aligned in a north - south aspect. It was designed by THOMAS TELFORD, the famous engineer and built between 1792 -1794. The stone used was white sandstone, quarried locally, from Eardington. The outside is a regular Tuscan elevation and the North Tower with Cupola, contains the bells and a clock. The interior is arcaded with tall Ionic pillars

TRAVEL Main roads from Wolverhampton, Kidderminster, Stourbridge, Ludlow, Shrewsbury and Telford to the town centre. **PARK** No easy access or parking for coaches, there is little or no parking close to church, but it is within walking distance of the car parks.

OUTSIDE Look in the churchyard for a grave with a cast-iron gravestone, holding the remains of one of the Hazeldine family, the great ironfounders. Also, see if you can find the vertical gravestone of Charles de Preux, a Napoleonic General; this gravestone was moved when the church was enlarged in 1876.

ACTIVITIES Regular: Open daily from July to September.
19th - 22nd May: Flower Festival and Craft Displays.
9th September, 10am - 6pm: Cycle Ride.
Disabled access, all groups and parties welcome.

CONTACT Guided tours by prior appointment - please ring Parish office between 9 am - 12 noon weekdays, tel: 0746 767174. (No toilet on site).
FOOD Many places to eat - pubs, restaurants. Picnic in Castle grounds or on Severn Park.

VISIT Cliff Railway, Severn Valley Railway, Museum, Town Hall. There are guided tours of the Town, pm from the tourist information centre in Listley St. Motor Museum, at Stanmore, Stourbridge Rd.

Church Stretton   137/ SO 452 937

St Lawrence

Norman and early English   *Hereford*
                                      Grade 2

The Church of St Lawrence with its Norman structure and battlemented early English tower nestles amongst the Stretton hills. The beautiful 'Truss-rafter' roofs of the chancel and north transept are as early as any in the County. Behind the altar is a carved wood Jacobean Reredos.

TRAVEL By road: Church Stretton is off the A49 15 miles south of Shrewsbury. By train: daily services run between Shrewsbury, Church Stretton, Ludlow and beyond. The Church Tower can be seen from the Square in the High Street. Proceed up Church Way from the SW corner of the square. **PARK** Public car park for coaches and cars is off Easthope Road or High Street. Outside Sheila-na-gig above Norman North door; early English Lancet window on East wall; oak studded door to tower.

ACTIVITIES Regular: Open from November to February inclusive: Wednesdays - Sundays. From March - October: Staffed on Mondays and Tuesdays. Last two weeks in July and first two weeks in August: Church Stretton Festival and Festival Fringe. Saturday 9th September: Sponsored Cycle Ride. **SPECIAL** Parish Centre (opposite the church): Lunch is available on Mondays throughout the year from 12.00 - 1.00 pm. Tea and light refreshments are available on the last two Mondays in July and first two in August from 2.30 pm to 4.00 pm.

CONTACT Tel. 01694 724224.

FOOD Plenty of pubs, cafes and restaurants in Sandford Avenue and the High Street. Seasonal National Trust cafe and shop in Cardingmill Valley. Tourist Information Centre (01694 723133).

VILLAGE Walks in Rectory Woods; Antique Market and various gift shops. Market day: Thursday. Early closing: Wednesday.

VISIT Hill walking on the Long Mynd, accessible by car. Views. Stokesay Castle (nr. Craven Arms). Acton Scott Farm Museum (Marshbook). All Saints, Little Stretton (2 miles south). St Michael and All Angels at All Stretton a LEP Anglican/United Reform Church (1 mile north).

| Ashford Carbonell | SO 525 710 | Astley Abbotts | SO 709 962 |

St Mary Magdalene

Hereford

Norman

This small unpretentious Norman church stands on an elevated site above the River Teme and is surrounded by ancient yew trees. A walk around the outside enables one to appreciate the architecture and especially notice the blocked north doorway with its original dog-tooth mouldings and oak door, both c.1210. Inside the decoration is simple. However, the beautiful arrangement of windows at the east end is particularly noteworthy and includes a very unusual Vesica window. This architectural feature is said to have been common in the part in North West France from whence the Carbonel family came.

TRAVEL South of Ludlow leave the A49 as signposted and cross the two bridges (with care). Turn right into the village itself and the church lies behind the school which is the first building on the left. There is a wooden finger post. Go to the top of the hill where a small car park is available. **PARK** Small car park outside the church - cars only.

ACTIVITIES 21st May: Rogation Sunday, beating the bounds. Meet at church 2 pm, followed by barbecue.
22nd July: Patronal Festival, refreshments available and evening service.
9th September: Church Cycle Ride, light refreshments provided.

CONTACT Tel. 0584 74266.

FOOD Salwey Arms Hotel, Woofferton (Junction A49/A456). A very pleasant picnic site is to be found on the banks of the River Teme - pass through two wooden gates opposite the school and follow the cart track to the original ford crossing.

VISIT Treasures of Tenbury Ltd. - Burford gardens and nursery. Ludlow - Medieval market town.

St Calixtus

1138
Late Decorated Gothic

Hereford
Grade 2

Two miles from Bridgnorth situated in a quiet, rural village setting, the church is an original, which is little changed, with an exceptionally wide chancel with late decorated mullion windows of 1633. Look out for one of the few remaining Maiden's Garlands - said to be that of Hanah Phillips, drowned on the eve of her wedding in 1707. Notice also the plaque in memory of Francis Billingsley who fell during the siege of Bridgnorth in the Civil War.

TRAVEL Take B4373 Broseley road out of Bridgnorth. At crossroads (1.5 miles turn right into Astley Abbotts village. The church is on the left after another 0.5 mile. **PARK** Private cars have easy roadside access. Arrangements for coaches may be made with prior notification.

OUTSIDE Notice the grave on the north side of the churchyard, surrounded by iron railings, of John Phillips, F.R.C.S. said to have been killed by a lion from a travelling menagerie.

ACTIVITIES The church will be open to co-incide with the garden openings of nearby Stanley Hall, Astley Abbotts House and Dunval Hall. **SPECIAL** See National Gardens Scheme, Yellow Book.

CONTACT Church Contact: 0746 762813.

FOOD The Swan, Nordley. The Pheasant, Linley Brook.

VILLAGE The Lavender fields next to the church. The parish borders the River Severn. This is good walking country with an extensive network of scenic rights of way.

VISIT The Gardens at Stanley Hall, Astley Abbotts House and Dunval Hall are open during the year for various charities, including the National Gardens Scheme. See The Yellow Book.The Parish borders the River Severn and there is an extensive network of scenic rights of way. Additional walks in Stanley Park are available by prior arrangements. By prior appointment only, groups may be allowed to visit 17th century Stanley Hall.

Claverley	SO 7930 9342

All Saints

| *1094* | *Hereford* |
| *Norman, Perpendicular* | *Grade A* |

The fine medieval church of a large rural parish, on an ancient hill site. 15th Century Perpendicular work dominates the exterior - see especially the porch, nave upper windows and tower. The spacious interior reveals its long history: Saxon and Norman fonts, wall paintings (c.1200) of national importance, 14th Century chancel with a 1601 hammerbeam roof, 15th Century chapels, Jacobean oak pulpit, and many monuments. The hillside churchyard has rural views, a yew tree reputedly 1000 years old, and historic tombs. The church, 15th Century timber-framed Old Vicarage, medieval cross and lych-gate are the centre of an attractive historic village.

TRAVEL Claverley is signposted from the A454 Wolverhampton - Bridgnorth, A458 Stourbridge - Bridgnorth and B4176 Dudley - Telford roads. The village lies in rolling countryside, reached only by narrow lanes and a cutting through the rock. The churchyard is elevated above the street; the main entrance is through the lych-gate in the Bull Ring. Several public bus routes: details Shropshire Traveline Tel. 0345 056785. **PARK** Limited parking in the street; coaches can (just) turn round in the Bull Ring. All three pubs have large car parks for customers.

OUTSIDE The modern heads on the big east window - portraits of the churchwardens. An unusual memorial near the lych-gate to Richard Twentyman (died 1979) by the sculptor Tony Twentyman who lived and worked in Claverley; his monument (1994) is beside it.

ACTIVITIES During the very popular annual Flower Festival 15 - 18 July the church will be open and manned for visitors, with refreshments available, from 10.00 am - 9.00 pm. The bells are rung before the 9.30 am and 6.30 pm services on Sundays. **SPECIAL** Accompanied **wheelchair access** is possible to most parts of the church. Group parties, including schools are welcome; guided tours may be possible by prior arrangement.

CONTACT the Vicar, Prebendary R. Sharp Tel. 0746 710268.

FOOD The Kings Arms, The Crown and The Plough are close by; they all serve meals.

VILLAGE Post office and village shop. A network of public footpaths provides pleasant walks in the surrounding countryside.

VISIT Tuck Hill: Holy Innocents church (1865); woodland setting. Worfield: fine mediaeval church and historic village. Dudmaston (National Trust). Bridgnorth: historic hill town on the River Severn, with a cliff railway between High Town and Low Town; Severn Valley Railway: steam trains from Bridgnorth to Kidderminster.

Coalbrookdale

Holy Tinity

| *1854* | *Hereford* |
| *Victorian Gothic (Voysey of London)* | *Grade 2** |

The church stands on Church Hill, overlooking the village, the famous Coalbrookdale foundries ("the cradle of the industrial revolution"), and part of the Ironbridge Severn Gorge. It was built with money given by the Darby family, on land also given by the same family when they converted to Anglicanism from Quakerism.

TRAVEL From North or South. M54 junction 6 follow signs to Ironbridge Gorge and Much Wenlock, fourth roundabout downhill to Coalbrookdale. Turn sharp right down Darby road to Museum of Iron, or turn sharp left uphill after traffic lights. **PARK** None at church. Park in Museum of Iron at bottom of Church Hill.

OUTSIDE Tomb of Abraham Darby and wife. Can you find the memorial to Captain Webb (the first one to swim the Channel)?

57

SHROPSHIRE

ACTIVITIES 15th July and 19th August: Exhibition sale of local crafts, refreshments, guided tours, trips "up the tower", organ music (Harrison and Harrison organ), open 10.30 am to 5.00 pm.

CONTACT Open by arrangement: tel nos. 0952 433309, 432737, 433318.

FOOD Coalbrookdale Inn, the Grove Inn, numerous restaurants in Ironbridge, picnic site: river bank of Severn or Forge site in Coalbrookdale.

VISIT Museum of Iron, Rosehill House, Quaker Burial Ground, Pottery.The Ironbridge, Coalport China Works, Blists Hill Living Museum (at Madeley), ruins of Buildwas Abbey, Museum of the River.

CONTACT Telephone for details: 0743 761325 or 0743 761332.

FOOD Cound Lodge, on A458, 2 miles. Fox Inn, Cross Houses, on A458, 2 miles. The Bell, Cross Houses, on A458, 2 miles.

VISIT Severndale Nurseries: on A458 between Cross Houses and Cound. Attingham Park (N.T.). River Severn at Atcham, Cound Lodge and Cressage. Shrewsbury - (Brother Cadfael), Wenlock Edge (scenic), Much Wenlock (attractive little town). Ironbridge Shropshire Industrial Museum (12 miles) Acton Burnell Castle (English Heritage).

Cound   126/ 558 045

St Peter

c. early 12th C.   *Hereford*
mostly 13th C. medieval   *Grade 1*

In an attractive rural setting the church reflects the changing styles of country church architecture over the centuries. A Saxon church was reconstructed in stone early 12th Century, of which a notable survival is the Norman font. A south aisle was added in the mid 13th Century, later enlarged. The massive sandstone tower is late 14th Century. Part of a 15th Century restored 'doom' painting on the chancel arch and some carved 17th Century woodwork remain. A lofty chancel was added on the old foundations in Gothic style in 1862. Interesting memorials to past generations abound.

TRAVEL In Cound village, 7 miles south-east from Shrewsbury off A458. Turn right at signpost to village. Half mile to church, direction sign at memorial. **PARK** Limited. Space for 10 cars by adjacent Guild Hall or in road.

OUTSIDE Massive sandstone tower.

ACTIVITIES May: Church Fete.
3rd June: In the steps of St Wulfstan.
June: St Peter's Day.
October: Harvest Festival.
Christmas: Carol Service.

Dorrington   126/ 476 029

St Edward the Confessor

1845   *Hereford*
Victorian   *Grade 2*

St Edward's is a Victorian Anglo-Catholic church built in Shropshire stone dating from 1845 and extended early this century. The land, building and Vicarage were given by John Thomas Hope of Netley. A fine reredos and altar window, a balcony and fixed pews are internal features. Unusually the church was built on a North-South axis, with the altar at the South end. Two transepts originally provided private seating for the Netley Hall family (on the East) and the Vicarage family (on the West). There is still evidence of a fire-place in the old Vicarage pew (now the Baptistry).

TRAVEL By Road: Dorrington lies on A49 Shrewsbury-Hereford Road halfway between Shrewsbury and Church Stretton. The Church is located 100 yds west of the main road, opposite the school, on the lane signposted Picklescott. Bus: Shrewsbury to Ludlow service Mon-Sat, stops in village. **PARK** Limited on street. Special arrangements for events.

OUTSIDE Note fine stonework. Interesting family tombs South West corner of churchyard.

ACTIVITIES 3rd June: In the steps of St Wulfstan. 30th June - 3rd July: 150th Anniversary celebrations, Flower Festival, catering available.

Saturday 1st July 7.30 pm: Concert in church to be given by Shrewsbury Cantata Choir including music by Handel and Parry.

Sunday 2nd July 6.30 pm: Songs of Praise and Re-Dedication Service. Bishop of Hereford to attend. **SPECIAL Access for the disabled,** group parties and other visitors welcome by prior arrangment.

CONTACT Tel.: 01743 718574 or 01743 718768.

FOOD Horseshoes Inn, Dorrington. Country Friends Restaurant, Dorrington. Bridge Inn, Dorrington - camping available. Fox Inn, Ryton. Bottle and Glass, Picklescott.

VILLAGE List of local B&B accommodation available on church notice board. Village Stores and Post Office, Traditional Butcher, Simples Cane and Pine Furniture Store.

VISIT Shrewsbury, Church Stretton and South Shropshire Hills (Long Mynd).

Farlow   3640 3806

St Giles

1857   *Hereford*
Early English

Victorian church built in 1857 to replace a derelict chapel lower down the field. The new church incorporates the Norman doorway, the 'tub' font and bells from the previous church. There has been a chapel from at least as far back as 1386, and Farlow is mentioned in the Domesday Survey of 1086 when it was outlying land of Leominster Manor in Herefordshire. Farlow remained a detached part of Herefordshire and a chapelry of Stottesdon Parish until 1844 when it became a separate parish. Burial and marriage registers are held from 1858. The church is situated on the edge of an escarpment with an excellent view.

TRAVEL From the A4117 Ludlow to Cleobury Mortimer turn off at Hopton Bank petrol station between Doddington and Hopton Wafers, then second left after two miles. By bus the church is one mile from the thrice weekly bus service, see under

Stottesdon. **PARK** Parking in the lane outside the church. Coach turn around is possible but difficult.

OUTSIDE The churchyard is kept wild. Look for wild flowers.

ACTIVITIES 25th and 26th June, 2 pm - 6 pm: Flower Festival. **SPECIAL** Teas available in the school adjacent to the church 2 pm - 4 pm. Evensong at 6.30 pm.

CONTACT The church may be opened at other times by arrangement, Tel. 0746 718297.

FOOD "The Gate Hangs Well", booking advisable, Tel: 01584 890273. Coaches welcome by prior arrangement. Also "The Crown" at Hopton Wafers, Tel: 01299 270372. The Gobbett Nursery and Rare Breeds Centre, Tel: 0746 718276. Circuitous route needed for coaches to avoid steep twisting hill.

VISIT Silvington and Cleeton St Mary may also be visited by arrangement, Tel: 0746 718297.

Harley   SJ 596 015

St Mary

1846 (re-dedication)   *Hereford*
19th Century

The churchyard at Harley has probably been a site of religious importance for many hundreds of years, as evidenced by its circular shape, ancient yew tree and commanding position, with splendid views of Wenlock Edge to the south and across The Wrekin (NE). The 13th Century Tower is all that remains of the previous building but the 19th Century Nave and Chancel offer a simple, light and airy interior, embellished by comparatively rare box-pews, a notable

59

SHROPSHIRE

brass tablet to the Lacon family and two Harnage family hatchments. A warm welcome awaits visitors.

TRAVEL By car: 0.25 mile off A458, 2 miles North of Much Wenlock. Public transport (Shrewsbury/ Bridgnorth route) weekdays only. **PARK** Limited to roadside normally but extra space available (including minibuses etc.) on 16th July.

OUTSIDE Several interesting examples of different architectural styles within the village.

ACTIVITIES Sunday 16th July: Church open and staffed. There will also be a garden-party on that day from 3 pm at The Old Rectory (opposite the Church) followed by 'Songs of Praise' at 6.30 pm. **SPECIAL** A treasure-hunt will also be organised for children. 9th September: We look forward to welcoming cyclists, on the sponsored cycle ride. **SPECIAL** Brass-rubbing (Lacon tablet).

CONTACT Church open by arrangement (Tel: 0952 510321).

FOOD The Plume of Feathers (0.5 mile) offers meals and accommodation. Tel: 0952 727360.

VILLAGE Harley Nursery - for trees and shrubs.

VISIT Much Wenlock (Priory), Wenlock Edge (N.T.), Buildwas Abbey, Ironbridge, Wroxeter Roman city of Viroconium, Acton Burnell Castle, Attingham Park (N.T.).

Highley   **138/ 741832**

St Mary

Hereford

Norman

A Norman church, set in a gently sloping area on the South side of the village centre and within its own grounds. A fine tower, chancel and nave built of local pink and grey sandstone with a gabled, tiled roof. Stained glass East window depicting Christ the shepherd. Pipe organ with tracker action. Peal of 6 bells, two of which are medieval.

TRAVEL By road, on the B4555 off the B4363 between Bridgnorth and Bewdley. By bus, Whittle or Midland Red. By Severn Valley Railway from

Bridgnorth, Bewdley or Kidderminster. By horseback along the Jack Mytton long-distance bridleway. Footpaths from Alveley, and surrounding villages. **PARK** Easy free parking and turning in adjacent roads or the car park in the village centre.

OUTSIDE The churchyard contains an ancient Preaching Cross, a mixture of old and new memorials, seats for relaxation and a developing 'wild' area with meadow flowers and grasses.

ACTIVITIES 3rd June: In the steps of St Wulfstan.

CONTACT Please telephone the Vicarage (0746 861612) for help or information.

FOOD Oasis Centre cafe 300 yds into village. Bache Arms pub 400 yds into village. Picnic sites: Severn Valley Park, 0.5 mile down Station Road and adjacent to the railway line.

VILLAGE Toilets: in the village centre, at the Country Park and the station. Telephone in the village centre. Welfare recreation ground, with heated outdoor swimming pool.

VISIT The River Severn (0.75 mile), the Severn Valley Railway and Severn Valley Country Park. Ray's Farm and animal sanctuary (3 miles). Alveley Visitors Centre (1 mile across river footbridge). Golf driving range and par-3, 9-hole course in the village, open to visitors and a 9-hole course, for visiting Club members, adjacent to the river.

Hope Bagot 588 740

St John the Baptist

11th or 12th C	*Hereford*
Norman	*Grade A*

This attractive little Norman church, with its 13th Century tower, sits in a circular churchyard in secluded Hope Bagot, half way up Titterstone Clee. Inside, the finest feature is the Norman chancel arch. The pulpit is Carolean. Look out for the tale of the miller's drowning, in the Church Guide, and the lugubrious memorial in the choir. Outside is a yew tree believed to be at least 1,600 years old, and under its spread an ancient healing Holy Well, which must pre-date the church, and may explain its dedication to St John the Baptist. Perhaps the site was a place of worship before Christianity arrived.

TRAVEL From A49 (Ludlow by-pass) come up through Caynham or Henley to Knowbury; turn east in Knowbury along Hope Bagot Lane for 2 miles. From B4214 Tenbury-Clee Hill road, 4 miles out of Tenbury turn west along lane signed "Hope Bagot" for 2 miles. **PARK** Village Hall car park beside churchyard. Minibuses welcome; coaches by arrangement only.

OUTSIDE The wild flowers and grasses (of which there are well over 100 varieties). The well and yew tree. An early stone head built into the South Wall - can you find it?

ACTIVITIES 1st Sunday of month: Communion 8.30 am, 3rd Sunday of month: Evensong 6.30 pm. 7th - 9th July, 10 am - 5.30 pm: Exhibition of Embroideries and Tapestries.

SPECIAL On Saturday 8th July and Sunday 9th July refreshments and cream teas in village hall, and Detective Trail for children.

CONTACT either 0584 890608 or 0584 890270. Refreshments for parties; in village hall, by arrangement.

FOOD Bennets End Inn (tel. 0584 890220) and Penny Black Inn (tel. 0584 890589) in Hope Bagot Lane, Knowbury, half a mile away.

VILLAGE Rambles through the countryside - see leaflets on sale in church.

VISIT Ludlow town and castle - 7 miles. Titterstone Clee, for views - 4 miles. Treasures gardens and Garden Centre at Burford, near Tenbury Wells - 5 miles. Whitton Church - stained glass by William Morris - 1.25 miles.

Hopesay SO 389 834

St Mary's

c. 1192	*Hereford*
Early English - Rural	*Grade 1*

Country church, stone built, slate roof, small bell tower with striking clock and containing four bells. Said to have been started about 1192 AD it has a notably fine chestnut roof displaying quadrants supported by a rare system of wall plates and massive roof timbers. A Norman doorway is still in use. There is a chancel arch of stone said to be 14th Century.

TRAVEL From Craven Arms on the A49 trunk road, take B4368 westwards. Leave at Aston-on-Clun onto minor road going north which is signposted Hopesay. Turn left at Hopesay. **PARK** Poor facilities are available but the village road is generally quiet and empty.

OUTSIDE The Lych-Gate. Hopesay Wildlife Meadow to be found by walking through the churchyard. Hopesay Farm.

ACTIVITIES Last Sunday in May: ARBOR TREE DAY the last Tree Dressing Ceremony in England with Fete, tugs-of-war, dancing etc.
3rd June: In the steps of St Wulfstan.

SPECIAL Gardens can be opened on early request. Special arrangements can be made for school children to use the meadow for nature exploring, pond dipping etc.

FOOD Picnic site in Hopesay, Wildlife Meadow itself. Refreshments at Kangaroo Inn, Aston-in-Clun or the Engine and Tender at Broome.

VILLAGE Two Iron Age Forts: Burrow Hill and Wart Hill. Good walking paths and bridleway. Hopesay Common is owned by the National Trust. Accommodation at Hesterworth 0.25 mile away.

VISIT Clun, Clunton and Clunbury - of A E Houseman fame. Lydbury North, Hopesay and Edgton.

SHROPSHIRE
Leebotwood   **SO 470 986**

St Mary's

Hereford
Norman Rectangle   *Grade 2*

St Mary's Church, 800 years old, is set in peaceful churchyard. A simple stone (Norman) rectangle with tower. Interior wall painting "Adoration of the Kings" c. 1200. Stained glass East Window "Faith, Hope, Charity". Wall memorials, box pews, original roof timbers with two carved dragons, original teaching pews sited in Gallery.

TRAVEL Quarter mile from A49 on Woolstaston Road via Station Road. Midland Red Shrewsbury/ Ludlow, two hourly service. Footpaths from Lower Wood and Walk Mills. **PARK** Grass verge outside church (beware T-junction) and low railway bridge.

OUTSIDE Churchyard entrance leads to seats overlooking excellent views of South Shropshire Hills, Lawley, Caradoc, Long Mynd. Note superb beech, oak, yew trees, wild birds: nuthatch, woodpecker, owl; various wild flowers. Find unusual tombstones including one Coalbrookdale Cast iron. Note War Memorial.

ACTIVITIES Church beautifully decorated at Christmas, Easter and Harvest.
18th April, 10 am - 3 pm: Decorated Church.
9th September, 10 am - 6 pm: Sponsored Cycle Ride when the church is manned 10.00 am - 6.00 pm.

CONTACT Church opened by arrangement: Tel. 0694 751208. **SPECIAL** Guided Tours also by arrangement: Tel. 0694 751208. **Access for wheel chairs.**

FOOD Thatched Pound Inn, Leebotwood. Little Chef half mile south A49.

VILLAGE Brook House Farm Shop, Home made jams, fruit and veg.

VISIT Church Stretton market town 3 miles S. A49 Shrewsbury county town 10 miles N. A49. Country walks to S. Shropshire Hills.

Lydbury North   **3586**

St Michael and All Angels

Hereford
Norman   *Grade 1*

Note the centuries of buttressing on the huge clock tower (built 1728, and still going well). A unique roughly carved bell frame (1660) supports a ring of six bells. The nave (1150) contains a fine set of Jacobean pews, mainly pre 1617, and above the Tudor Rood Screen, the Creed, Commandments and Lord's Prayer were inscribed in 1615. From the Plowdon Roman Catholic Chapel leads an interesting rood loft staircase and above the Southern Walcot Chapel is the church school room, used from 1663 to 1847.

TRAVEL Travelling south-east from Bishop's Castle on the B4385 for approximately 3 miles, St Michael and All Angels is situated in the middle of a well maintained churchyard. **PARK** There is ample parking space on the B4385 opposite the church.

OUTSIDE The Oak Door at the south porch, allegedly scarred by bullets dating from the Civil War.

ACTIVITIES 2nd July, 9 am - 7 pm: Lydbury North Open Gardens Day. 16th - 24th September, 9 am - 7 pm: Village Festival. **The re-surfaced path provides easy access to the church by wheelchair.**

FOOD The local Powis Arms provides meals and a picnic area.

VILLAGE The village contains a well stocked General Store and Post Office. The famous Bury

Ditches Iron Age Fort. Many beautiful walks.

VISIT Walcot Hall - open to the public on certain days. Long Mynd, famous for its breathtaking views. Hopesay and church.

Quatford   739 907

St Mary Magdalene

1086	Hereford
Gothic	Grade 2

The church is sited on a hill overlooking an ancient fortified mound (Camp Hill), and the River Severn. It consists of Chancel, Nave, West Tower, South Aisle and South Porch, and is built of local red sandstone and Tufa. The Chancel is Norman with a splendid arch, the Nave was rebuilt in 1714 using re-used materials, the windows being 14th century. There are medieval floor tiles, a Piscina of the decorated period, two ancient altar tomb lids and the Font is Norman with 14th century decoration. The South Aisle and Porch are early Victorian with some interesting stained glass.

TRAVEL Situated just off, but visible from, the A442 Bridgnorth to Kidderminster Road, about 2.5 miles from Bridgnorth. Midland Red Bus route Bridgnorth - Kidderminster. **PARK** Adjacent to the church, suitable for coaches.

OUTSIDE The churchyard is maintained to encourage many species of wild flowers and is specially noted for its Snowdrops and Cowslips, but there are flowers for most of the year. There are some interesting monuments, look out for the Cast Iron ones.

ACTIVITIES 3rd June, 10 am - 5 pm: In the steps of St Wulfstan (Wulfstan was one of our consecrating bishops in the 11th century). 23rd July, 2 pm - 5 pm: Patronal Sunday. 9th September, 10 am - 6 pm: Sponsored Cycle Ride. **Access at present is difficult for the disabled. SPECIAL** We welcome group visits and will give a talk and guided tour.

CONTACT We will open by arrangement, contact 0746 766126.

FOOD The Danery Inn is almost next to the church. Meals are available.

VISIT The River Severn. Midland Motor Museum - 1 mile; Dudmaston Hall (N.T.) - 1.5 miles Severn Valley Railway - 2 miles.

Stapleton   SJ 471046

St John the Baptist

1291	Hereford
Medieval	Grade 2*

Stapleton Church is highly unusual in that it was constructed on two levels in the 13th Century. The undercroft, entered by a wide round-headed door in the south wall and lit only by a few slits, was used for tithes or animals. Entrance to the upper floor was by two pointed-arch doors on the south wall (lost) and north wall (existing). See also change in wall thickness, and piscina (recess) high on the chancel south wall. Apart from addition of tower and vestry and other changes in the 18-19th Century, the church is substantially unaltered since the two floors were thrown into one in the later Middle Ages.

TRAVEL Turn off A49 half mile north of Dorrington for quarter of a mile. **PARK** On the road outside.

OUTSIDE See illustrations on page 54

ACTIVITIES 26th-28th May, 9 am-5 pm: Stapleton Flower Festival.

FOOD Dorrington - Country Friends (Good Food Guide Entry).

VILLAGE Castle mound by church.

VISIT Hill walking on the hills around Church Stretton, 5 miles from Acton Burnell Castle, 3.5 miles from Shrewsbury.

Stokesay   SO 436 818

St John the Baptist

pre-1165	Hereford
Commonwealth	Grade 2*

There are Norman pillars to the south doorway but most of the church was destroyed in the Civil War. As a result it is one of the few churches built/rebuilt in Commonwealth/Restoration times. The nave was rebuilt in 1654 but the chancel not until 1664. The wall paintings were done in 1683. The box and

SHROPSHIRE

canopied pews were made in those times but there are a few primitive pews from the previous building. The church is in a rural setting detached from the town and adjacent to Stokesay castle. There are no steps so that access is easy.

TRAVEL On the A49 from Craven Arms go southwards a short distance towards Ludlow, then follow signposts to Stokesay Castle. From the station go south on the footpath alongside the A49. **PARK** Large field by Stokesay Castle.

OUTSIDE Stokesay Castle - a fortified manor house in the care of English Heritage - a grade 1 listed building.

ACTIVITIES 3rd June: In the steps of St Wulfstan. 24th, 25th June, 9 am - 6 pm: Friends of Stokesay and Patronal Weekend. 26th - 28th August, 10 am - 6 pm, Bank Holiday Festival. 9th September, 10 am - 6 pm: Cycle Ride. **SPECIAL** Printed guides for adults and children are available as well as postcards, etc.

CONTACT Guided tours by arrangement: ring 01588 672797 or 676129.

FOOD Craven Arms Hotel (A49/B4368 junction), Stokesay Castle Hotel (signs on A49), Stables Inn (Dale Street), or picnic in the car park. Refreshments can be obtained also in Stokesay Castle, at the Pump Pottery (adjacent to the Castle car park) and at the Station cafe (Shrewsbury Road).

VILLAGE Stokesay Castle. 'Walks around Stokesay' published by Shropshire Books (75p). History of Craven Arms (£1.50) from the newsagents, etc.

VISIT Newton (south east Craven Arms) is a conservation area. There is a public footpath on the eastern side of the River Onny from Stokesay bridge to Newton and hence to Craven Arms. Norton Camp, an Iron Age hillfort.

Stottesdon   3673 2829

St Mary the Blessed Virgin

before 1086	*Hereford*
Norman/Early English	*Grade 1*

Imposing church with fine Norman tower. In Norman times it was a mission church reaching out to the surrounding district. It contains an exceptionally fine carved Norman font from about 1170, also the old west doorway with pre-conquest carvings, now behind the organ. Wood carvings on pulpit, lectern and communion table. 4 bells re-cast by A Rudhall of Gloucester in 1752, now unringable and only open to bona fide bell ringers by special request. Norman arches in north aisle. 18th Century roof beams on south aisle. Organ by various unknown builders built up from early 18th Century instrument. The carvings make the church suitable for visits by blind people.

TRAVEL From B4363 Bridgnorth-Cleobury Mortimer turn off at Kinlet or Billingsley. From B4364 Bridgnorth-Ludlow turn off at Wheathill or Cleobury North. Church is up a short drive from the signpost in the centre of the village. Very limited bus service Wed, Thur, Sat mornings from Cleobury Mortimer, Talbot Hotel. Connecting bus services from Ludlow and Bewdley/Kidderminster. **PARK** 2 cars only in churchyard, other vehicles use village car park beside school.

OUTSIDE Some interesting gravestones have survived, including a few early iron ones. The Hall farmhouse next to the church is the 16th century Hall and is the oldest house in the village.

ACTIVITIES Regular: Church open April to October, every 1st and 3rd Thursday in the month, 2 pm -5 pm Sat 9th September, 10 am - 6 pm: Sponsored cycle ride.

SPECIAL Details of local walks can be obtained in the church.

CONTACT Open other times by arrangement. Tel. 0746 718297.

FOOD "Fighting Cocks" in the village, closed Mondays except Bank Holidays, lunches on demand or by prior arrangement, Tel. 0746 718270. Rays Farm Country Matters (3 miles) open all year, teas available. Tel. Kinlet 455.

VISIT Severn Valley Railway (7 miles); enquiries Tel. 01299 403816. Farlow, Silvington and Cleeton St Mary all may be visited by arrangement Tel: 0174 632297.

WARWICKSHIRE

Warwickshire churches have at their heart the famous new Cathedral at Coventry, with its many international connections. The south of the county has one focus in Stratford upon Avon, with others in Warwick/Leamington Spa and Rugby. With easy access both to London and Birmingham the county has many small manufacturing and distribution bases, yet most of the land is attractive rural countryside, so is popular with serious walkers as well as those wanting to take gentle strolls amongst its gentle hills and pleasant small valleys, or go along the Heart of England Way. The South West of the County stretches along the edge of the Cotswolds, while throughout the county there are interesting small villages hidden away along traditional country lanes. As well as its churches, the earliest of which are on Saxon or even possibly Roman sites, there are also many other places of historic interest for the visitor to see, with also places to spend a short stay. Many areas to the West of the County, near Alcester, have Roman connections, while many of the Churches are Medieval, associated with some of the great families of England, or are linked to the Oxford or Evangelical movements of the last century.

Francis Ballinger

St. Wulfstan and Warwickshire

The ancient diocese of Worcester included much of south-west Warwickshire. St Wulfstan was born in Long Itchington and spent his early years in the county. From the age of five he attended the monastery school at Evesham Abbey and so would have travelled through many of the villages we know today on his way to and from school. At seven he was sent to the Monastic School at Peterborough but records show that he came home from time to time and took part in village games and festivities.

Tourist Information contact:
The Tourist Information Office,
Stratford upon Avon, Warwickshire.

Town Churches
Stratford upon Avon	Holy Trinity
Warwick	St Mary
Coventry Cathedral	

Village churches are listed alphabetically with the names of nearby towns. Each Gazetteer entry gives a grid reference from the Landranger OS Map series. Most are on sheet no. 151.

Bidford-on-Avon	south of Stratford
Brailes	south-east of Shipston on Stour
Claverdon	north of Stratford
Coughton (C of E)	east of Redditch
Coughton (RC)	east of Redditch
Ettington	south-east of Stratford
Long Itchington	east of Warwick
Norton Lindsey	south-west of Warwick
Pillerton Hersey	south-east of Stratford
Preston Bagot	north-west of Warwick
Priors Marston	south-east of Warwick
Radford Semele	south-east of Warwick
Ratley	north-east of Shipston
Salford Priors	north of Evesham
Tysoe	north-east of Shipston
Walton	south-east of Stratford
Wellesbourne	south-east of Stratford
Whatcote	north-east of Shipston
Wootton Wawen	south-west of Warwick

Dates for your Diary in Warwickshire

Many churches will be open at times other than those listed below. For up to date local information please use the contact numbers listed in each of the Gazetteer entries.

Diary dates are dates when you can be sure to find the church open. Where churches have made a regular arrangement to have their building open and staffed they are listed at the beginning of each of the monthly lists. For more details please consult the individual entries.

Special Through the Church Door activities are also listed at the beginning of each month as appropriate.

WARWICKSHIRE
Dates for your Diary
in Warwickshire

February

5	Brailes	15:30	

April

Regular	Bidford-on-Avon		
	Mon, Wed, Fri,	14:00	16:00
	Coughton	Sat	Sun
2	Tysoe	14:30	17:00
17	Bidford-on-Avon	14:00	16:00
23	Brailes	18:30	
24	Bidford-on-Avon	14:00	16:00

May

Regular	Bidford-on-Avon		
	Mon, Wed, Fri,	14:00	16:00
	Coughton	daily	
1	Wellesbourne	11:00	15:00
4	Norton Lindsey		
6	Brailes	10:00	16:00
7	Tysoe	14:30	17:00
7	Wootton Wawen	15:00	
11	Norton Lindsey		
18	Norton Lindsey		
20	Wootton Wawen	10:00	
25	Norton Lindsey		
27	Bidford-on-Avon		
27	Wellesbourne	11:00	15:00
28	Wellesbourne	11:00	15:00
29	Wellesbourne	11:00	15:00

June
3 June In the Steps of St. Wulfstan

Regular	Bidford-on-Avon		
	Mon, Wed, Fri,	14:00	16:00
	Coughton	daily	
1	Norton Lindsey		
3	Coughton		
3	Long Itchington	10:00	18:30
3	Norton Lindsey		
3	Ratley		
3	Salford Priors		
3	Tysoe		
3	Whatcote	11:00	18:00
4	Tysoe	14:30	17:00
4	Wootton Wawen	15:00	
8	Norton Lindsey		
10	Long Itchington	10:00	18:30
10	Priors Marston	14:00	18:00
11	Claverdon	12:30	17:00
22	Norton Lindsey		
29	Norton Lindsey		

July
Embroideries and Tapestries 3-9 July

Regular	Bidford-on-Avon		
	Mon, Wed, Fri,	14:00	16:00
	Coughton	daily	
2	Tysoe	14:30	17:00
2	Whatcote		
2	Wootton Wawen	15:00	
6	Norton Lindsey		
8	Wellesbourne	11:00	15:00
13	Norton Lindsey		

20	Norton Lindsey		
27	Norton Lindsey		
30	Ettington	14:00	18:00
30	Pillerton Hersey	14:00	18:00
30	Wellesbourne	11:00	15:00

August
Why not be a Church Detective this August?

Regular	Bidford-on-Avon		
	Mon, Wed, Fri,	14:00	16:00
	Coughton	daily	
3	Norton Lindsey		
5	Walton		
5	Wellesbourne	11:00	15:00
6	Ettington	14:00	18:00
6	Pillerton Hersey	14:00	18:00
6	Tysoe	14:30	17:00
6	Wellesbourne	11:00	15:00
6	Wellesbourne	11:00	15:00
6	Wootton Wawen	15:00	
10	Norton Lindsey		
12	Brailes	10:00	16:00
12	Claverdon	12:30	17:00
13	Ettington	14:00	18:00
13	Pillerton Hersey	14:00	18:00
13	Walton	14:00	18:00
13	Wellesbourne	11:00	15:00
17	Norton Lindsey		
20	Ettington	14:00	18:00
20	Pillerton Hersey	14:00	18:00
20	Wellesbourne	11:00	15:00
24	Norton Lindsey		
27	Ettington	14:00	18:00
27	Pillerton Hersey	14:00	18:00
27	Walton	14:00	18:00
27	Wellesbourne	11:00	15:00
28	Bidford-on-Avon		
28	Wellesbourne	11:00	15:00
28	Whatcote		
29	Ratley		
30	Ratley		
31	Norton Lindsey		

September
9 September - Sponsored Cycle Ride

Regular	Bidford-on-Avon		
	Mon, Wed, Fri,	14:00	16:00
	Coughton	daily	
3	Wootton Wawen	15:00	
3	Tysoe	14:30	17:00
7	Norton Lindsey		
9	Claverdon	11:00	17:00
9	Long Itchington	10:00	17:00
9	Priors Marston	10:00	18:00
9	Ratley		
9	Salford Priors		
11	Bidford-on-Avon	14:00	16:00
14	Norton Lindsey		
21	Norton Lindsey		
24	Preston Bagot	10:00	16:00
28	Norton Lindsey		

October

Regular	Coughton	Sat	Sun
1	Brailes	10:30	18:30
1	Tysoe	14:30	17:00
1	Walton	17:30	

66

Bidford-on-Avon SP 101518

St Laurence

c.1215   *Coventry*
Victorian "renovated" Early English   *Grade 2*

A comparatively large but simple country parish church, with tower and chancel largely as built ca. 1215. The nave was enlarged in 1845 and the old roof line can be seen on the interior tower wall. The interior was redecorated in 1991 and has a light feel to it. The monument to Dorothy Skipwith on the south side of the chancel is a feature. Set in the heart of the village on a small rise on the north bank of the River Avon, the church affords views of the Cotswolds and Bredon Hill. The river life is varied and fascinating.

TRAVEL From B439, follow signs to the village centre at roundabout, and turn left at the traffic lights. From B4085, turn right at traffic lights immediately beyond the bridge. The church is about 150 yards on the right from the lights. **PARK** Free parking in the village car park by the roundabout on the B439 about 200 yards from the church. Short term parking may be possible in the village square by the church.

OUTSIDE The lych gate dedicated to Queen Victoria's Diamond Jubilee. A monument on the East end (north of the window). Views over the river.

ACTIVITIES Regular: The church is open from Easter to end September from 2 pm - 4 pm, Mondays, Wednesdays and Fridays. Also open Wednesday mornings 10 am - 12 noon. (Coffee in Church Hall opposite 10.30 am - 11.30 am).
Saturday morning 27th May: Spring Market.
28th August (August bank holiday): Bidford Carnival.

CONTACT The Vicarage (0789 772217) or (0789 772401) for other times.

FOOD The Bull's Head (sandwiches only), The Anglo-Saxon, The Bridge Inn, and The Frog and Bulrush are all in the High Street. Picnic in the "Big Meadow" on the south bank of the river.

VILLAGE The High Street, Big Meadow, river side walk to Marcliff.

VISIT The Cotswolds, Stratford-upon-Avon, Evesham, Ragley Hall (Alcester) are all close at hand. Salford Priors, Temple Grafton, Binton, Exhall and Wixford.

Brailes 151 315394

St George's

               Coventry
Decorated   *Grade 1*

One of the largest and most beautiful churches in Warwickshire. Known as "The Cathedral of the Feldon", the countryside or field-land south of the River Avon. The size of the church reflects the medieval prosperity of the village, once the third largest town in the county. The church was founded in Saxon times, but most of the present building dates from the 14th Century. The tower is 120 feet high and contains the second heaviest peal of six bells in the world. Inside, note the pattern-book font, fine tracery and carved stone faces on the corbels, plus the well-known matchstick model and tapestry panels. The church is situated in the centre of Lower Brailes.

TRAVEL 4 miles due east of Shipston-on-Stour, on the B4035 between Shipston and Banbury. **PARK** Parking for cars, minibuses, or one coach in front of church.

OUTSIDE (1) The fine openwork parapet of the south aisle. (2) The carvings on the string-course below the nave parapet on the south side. (3) The 16th and 17th Century tombstones ranged along the south porch and nave.

ACTIVITIES 5th February, 3.30 pm: Christingle Service.
23rd April, 6.30 pm: St George's Day Songs of Praise.
6th May, 10 am - 4 pm: May Market. Church will be manned.

12th August Village Show Church manned 10 am - 4 pm. 1st October, 10.30 am and 6.30 pm: Harvest Festival. **SPECIAL** Guided tours can be provided for groups. The church hall is available by arrangement and teas can be booked. **There is easy access to church for wheelchairs (one low step).**

CONTACT Please telephone Vicarage initially on 0608 685230.

FOOD The George Hotel is situated opposite the church. Also, The Gate Inn situated in Upper Brailes. Picnic area available on request.

VILLAGE Shops and post office. Castle Hill. Roman Catholic Church of St Peter and St Paul.

VISIT Shipston-on-Stour (4 miles), Whichford Pottery (4 miles), Hook Norton Brewery (5 miles), Broughton Castle (7 miles). There are footpaths to neighbouring parish churches such as Sutton-under-Brailes, Tysoe, Whatcote and Winterton.

Claverdon **SP 198 645**

St Michael and All Angels

Unknown   *Coventry*
Decorated with perpendicular tower   *Grade B*

A priest for "Claverdone" was mentioned in Domesday, so it probable there was an Anglo-Saxon church. A list of vicars dates from the 13th Century. The earliest part of the present building is the 14th Century chancel, on the north side of which stands the early 17th Century alabaster tomb of Thomas Spencer, second son of Sir John Spencer of Althorpe. Victorian alterations and extensions were carried

out and the most recent restoration has been to the 15th Century tower. Memorial and charity tablets record the past, and the artistic talent of present parishioners features in beautifully worked kneelers, altar frontal etc.

TRAVEL Claverdon is on the A4189 (formerly B4095) between Warwick and Henley in Arden. Approaching from Warwick, the church can be seen on the hill. In the village, turn into Church Road by the former forge with horseshoe entrance, and the church is a few hundred yards on the right. **PARK** Parking in Church Centre car park, on the right just before Vicarage and church. Minibuses welcome, but regret no coaches.

OUTSIDE Pleasant southerly views. Interesting old graves, all recorded in churchyard survey, include the burial place of Thomas Spencer's steward Christopher Flecknoe, marked by a recess and slab in chancel's south wall.

ACTIVITIES Sunday, 11th June, 12.30 pm - 5 pm: to coincide with gardens open at Holywell, a hamlet about 2 miles from church. Refreshments available at Holywell.
Saturday 12th August, 12.30 pm - 5 pm: to coincide with Claverdon Flower Show, on village recreation field, where refreshments will be available.
Saturday 9th September, 11 am - 5 pm: Sponsored Cycle Ride.

FOOD Red Lion and Crown Inn, both in village (meals served). Pleasant picnic places on Yarningale Common, about 1.5 miles from church.

VISIT Yarningale Common, with Stratford Canal. Henley in Arden, Hatton Craft Centre.

Coughton **150/ SP 084 605**

St Peter

c. 1450   *Coventry*
Tudor   *Grade 1*

The present church appears to be on the site of an earlier building and lies in a parkland setting next to Coughton Court (N.T.). It is a Grade 1 listed building, mainly in the Tudor style, light and airy, the peace of which many visitors find inspiring. Features include a fine porch, an early font, a clock (c.1690), Throckmorton family tombs, a noted brass, a selection of early glass and modern needlework. Guide books may be purchased in church.

TRAVEL Coughton village is mid-way between Studley and Alcester on A435. St Peter's church to East of main road across parkland and next to Coughton Court. **PARK** Use N.T. car park when Coughton Court open to public, otherwise church approach.

OUTSIDE On south side in churchyard sundial with four faces.

ACTIVITIES 3rd June: In the steps of St Wulfstan. **SPECIAL Wheelchair ramps in porch**.

CONTACT Parties please phone 0527 892372 or 0789 762487.

FOOD Coughton Court. Throckmorton Arms at Coughton (on A435 to N), Green Dragon, Sambourne (1.5 miles).

VISIT Coughton Court and gardens. *R.C. church close by. Alcester (2 miles) ancient market town (good parking) Stratford-on-Avon (9 miles). Footpaths along River Arrow to Studley and Alcester.

> **Site shared with Coughton RC Church**

St Peter, St Paul & St Elizabeth, (RC).

1856   *Birmingham*
Gothic   *Grade 2*

Built by the Throckmorton family in the grounds of Coughton Court. Designed by well known ecclesiastical architect, Charles Hansom. Tall, circular bell spire, steep roof. Open interior with tall, pitched roof. Tribune adjoins sanctuary for family worship. Adjoining presbytery built at the same time. In the grounds at Coughton Court.

TRAVEL Take Coughton Fields Lane off A435, 2 miles north of Alcester. **PARK** As for visiting Coughton Court.

OUTSIDE Coughton Court and Church of England Parish Church.

ACTIVITIES Regular: April - Saturdays and Sundays, 12 noon - 5 pm. Easter Monday to Wednesday, 12 noon - 5 pm.
May to September - Daily (except Thurs and Fri) 12 noon - 5 pm. October - Saturday and Sunday, 12 noon - 5 pm.

FOOD Coughton Court restaurant on days house is open. Throckmorton Arms pub on A435.

VISIT Coughton Court. Coughton Parish Church (C of E). Ragley Hall.

> **Site shared with Coughton C.of E. church**

WARWICKSHIRE

Ettington   SP 267 490

Holy Trinity and St Thomas of Canterbury

1903   *Coventry*
"modern" structure, 14th Century style

Set on rising ground at the western end of the village, this is the third church to be built in the parish on three different sites. A completely Edwardian church dedicated in 1903, with tower dedicated in 1909, it is based on much earlier design ideas. The "Good Shepherd" East window is very characteristic of Christopher Whall, the leading stained glass designer/maker in Edwardian times. Memorials (mostly from the earlier buildings) include a 1603 husband and wife brass and a 1868 memorial to the Vicar's brother killed in a Maori rising.

TRAVEL From the A422/A429 roundabout drive down into the village to the first crossroads; turn right, the church is on the right. From the Fosse/A422 crossroads drive along the village street, at the end of the village turn left into Halford Road. **PARK** On Halford Road outside church. No problem for coaches.

ACTIVITIES Regular: All Sundays in August: 2 pm - 6 pm.
Sunday 30th July : 2 pm - 6 pm.
SPECIAL An excellent recent guide to church history and features is on sale. Advice on short walks will be available. **No access problem for disabled before (single) chancel step.**

Ettington open same days as
Pillerton, Wellesbourne and Walton.

FOOD The White Horse and the Chequers both on the main (Banbury) road at the other (east) end of the village. Houndshill 1 mile towards Stratford-upon-Avon on the A422.

VILLAGE Shops opening times will be posted in church. Friends Meeting House (1680s) also in Halford Road. Good viewpoint in Rookery Lane of local hills (as far as Bredon).

VISIT Pillerton Hersey (church/teas), Walton (church/watermill), Wellesbourne (church).

Long Itchington

Holy Trinity

                                 Coventry
Norman   *Grade 1*

St Wulfstan was born in Long Itchington. The church contains a chapel dedicated to St Wulfstan with a window containing a coloured glass roundel depicting his legend.

TRAVEL Long Itchington is on the A423, two miles north of Southam. **PARK** Parking in the village square adjacent to the church, which has room for coaches.

OUTSIDE The church once had a spire whcich was struck by lightening in 1762. The base is still visible.

ACTIVITIES Open 3rd June 10 am - 6.30 pm.
10th June, 10 am - 6.30 pm: Parish Festival.
9th September, 10 am - 5 pm: Cycle Ride.
SPECIAL Village nature trail - details in church.

CONTACT   Open   by appointment, tel. 0926 813409.

VILLAGE The village has several pubs which offer meals. The canal runs through the village, and there is easy access from the tow-path for those who take their holidays on canal barges.

Norton Lindsey   229 631

The Holy Trinity

Gothic

Coventry
*Grade 2**

The Saxon font is all that remains of the original building. Around 1330 a chancel, bellcote and porch were added to the early 13th century nave. The Victorian restoration of 1874 consisted of a new roof, bell-turret and porch, addition of the North aisle and recasting of one of the 1330 bells. The vestry dates from 1880. Superb Victorian stained glass windows, including "The Transfiguration" by Hardman, characterise this small village church that occupies an idyllic setting. A magnificent yew tree and secluded Garden of Rest are features of the churchyard, which commands extensive views to the East and South East.

TRAVEL The church is at the end of Church Road, 130 yards round the corner from the New Inn close to the centre of Norton Lindsey, which is 0.5 mile south of the A4189 Warwick/Henley-in-Arden road, 2 miles North of the A46 Stratford Northern bypass and 3.5 miles from junction 15 of the M40 motorway. **PARK** On street parking is available.

ACTIVITIES Regular: Open every Thursday from 1st May to 30th September.

SPECIAL Guided tours by appointment, of the church and village lasting about 1 hr 30mins. The morning tour begins with coffee and biscuits in the Church Room at 10.30 am. The second tour starts at the Church Room at 2.30 pm and ends with afternoon tea and scones. Both tours include an exhibition of local history. 3rd June, 10 am - 5.30 pm: (Wake Festival Weekend) Floral and other displays in celebration of the community. 3rd June, 7.30pm: Musical entertainment by the youth of the village.

CONTACT Telephone 0789 731292 or 0926 842661 to make arrangements for your visit. Groups of up to 20 persons can be accommodated. **The Church Room has a toilet equipped for the disabled and there is wheelchair access throughout.**

FOOD The New Inn serves a choice of home-made food and light snacks at lunch-time and in the evening. If you wish to start or finish your visit with a meal, please book with the tour or phone the New Inn independently 0926 842303.

VISIT Warwick Castle is 4 miles to the East. Hatton Country World is 2.5 miles to the North. Good cross country footpaths link the United Benefice of Wolverton with Norton Lindsey and Langley.

Pillerton Hersey   SP 298 488

St Mary the Virgin

Some 13th Century, much 15th Century

Coventry
*Grade 2**

Set in a Conservation Area which includes a large former Vicarage in brick and stone-built, village-centre farm houses and associated barns (all now residential), the earliest parts of the present church are 13th Century (the chancel). There are many 15th Century features (note especially the fine nave roof) and alterations and extensions were made up to early Victorian times. Much early green-tinted glass remains, giving an "exceptionally light" church. Find the George III coat of arms - incorporating the Elector of Hanover's arms - and a converted barrel organ.

TRAVEL Signposted along the Walton Lane from the War Memorial Green in the centre of the village. **PARK** In the cul-de-sac alongside the Church Wall, Minibuses no problem but larger coaches not able to park near church at busy times. Find the memorial to "our venerable wheelwright".

ACTIVITIES Regular: All Sundays in August: 2 pm - 6 pm.
Open Sunday 30th July: 2 pm - 6 pm.

SPECIAL The Friends of the church are providing teas on Open Days: 3.30 to 5.30 pm **Disabled - shallow steps at gate but all the same level thereafter.** An excellent leaflet, pinpointing important features, is on sale.

WARWICKSHIRE

FOOD The Chequers and The White Horse in Ettington

VILLAGE Find the cartwash on the edge of the Village Green (on the road to Butlers Marston). Walton (church/watermill), Ettington(church), Wellesbourne (church).

Ettington, Pillerton Hersey, Walton and Wellesbourne

Preston Bagot   **151/175 661**

All Saints

Norman   *Coventry*
                                                     Grade B

The church stands in a field on top of a hill overlooking Preston Bagot and the countryside towards the villages of Claverdon and Wootton Wawen. Originally a small Norman chapel it has been extended, modified and restored but still retains much of its original simplicity. Its principal charm lies in that simplicity, its setting and its fine stained glass windows.

TRAVEL From Henley in Arden take the A4189 towards Warwick. After one and a half miles just past the Crab Mill Inn turn left, then fork right and the church is at the top of the hill on the left. **PARK** Small car park, cars and minibuses only.

ACTIVITIES Easter Monday and last Sunday in September (Harvest Festival) Open from 10 am to 4 pm Sunday Service - all welcome - 9.30 am less 5th Sunday.

CONTACT Open on request: telephone 0926 - 84 2307/2339/2317/2440.

FOOD Crab Mill Inn, Haven Tea Rooms, Farningale Common Picnic site.

VISIT Hatton Craft Centre. Claverdon Church.

Priors Marston   **151/ 490576**

St Leonard

13th - 19th century   *Coventry*
                                                     Grade 2

The church stands in a peaceful setting in this conservation village in a naturally beautiful part of the county. Dating from the 13th century the church has seen a number of changes. The original north wall and aisle remain. The tower is mainly 17th century. The remainder was largely rebuilt in the 1860s including the addition of a new Vestry. Much of the stained glass also dates from this time - look out for particularly good quality in the South Porch. Two new windows, rich in style and colour, were installed in 1993. Look out also for the 14th century cross head in the window sill to the north of the Altar - recently found in a garden nearby.

TRAVEL Take the Shuckburgh (& Napton) road leading north from the village green. The church is signposted off to the right via either School Lane or Vicarage Lane. Look out for temporary signs. **PARK** School Lane or Vicarage Lane. Not easy for coaches.

OUTSIDE There are two remarkable cedar trees, about 180 years old, in the churchyard.

ACTIVITIES Saturday 10th June, 2pm - 6 pm: church open; village fete in the school grounds. Teas at fete.
Saturday 9th September, 10 am - 6 pm: Diocesan cycle ride day, church open and manned. Teas in church.
SPECIAL Leaflets will be available describing the church, local footpaths, with detailed historical notes etc. Also displays showing a survey of the churchyard and a plan of the village.

FOOD The Holly Bush, Holly Bush Lane. The Falcon, Holly Bush Lane. Both provide food.

VILLAGE Marston Hill - views to the Malverns and beyond.

VISIT Canons Ashby. Elizabethan Manor House. N.T.Walks at Boddington Reservoir, Fawsley Park and the canal towpath at Marston Doles.

Radford Semele

St Nicholas

| 1100 | Coventry |
| Medieval to Victorian | Grade 2 |

Radford Semele is mentioned in the Domesday Book. The church is set back behind fields from the main road in well kept open churchyard. Delightful lych-gate in listed churchyard wall. The fabric dates from the 12th Century with extensive restoration in 1889 including the north Aisle, Vestry, Chancel including the Chancel Arch. There is a dedication window in the Norman Arch,on the South Wall. Handsome reredos motifs are reflected in the rich embroidery and tapestry work. The Chancel has an encaustic tile dado. There is a Foster and Andrews organ with a Willis trumpet. The tower has a ring of 4 bells, in the key of G natural which are rung weekly. There is a George III hatchment and charity board. The clock was added to the tower in 1991.

TRAVEL Off A425 Leamington Spa to Southam Road. Left hand turn into Church Lane. Bus from Leamington Spa. **PARK** Parking available for cars, minibuses and a single coach.

OUTSIDE Lych-gate and attractive church tower.

ACTIVITIES 8th July: Embroideries and Tapestries
9th September: Sponsored Bicycle Ride
1st October: Harvest Festival.
SPECIAL Special visits for children, history groups, ancestor tracers, M.U. and W.I. groups. **The church welcomes disabled visitors.** Guided tours can be arranged.

CONTACT The keys are available at the Vicarage parish office. For parties on other dates tel: 0926 420066.

FOOD The White Lion, an old thatched and timbered pub, serves family meals. Play area for children.

VILLAGE The Grand Union Canal - Radford Bottomlock (half a mile), Diocesan Retreat House, Offchurch (one mile).

VISIT Ufton Fields Nature Reserve (four miles), Chesterton Windmill, Warwick Castle, Leamington Spa.

Ratley   SP 383 473

St Peter ad Vincula

| 1190 | Coventry |
| Medieval: Middle Period | Grade 2* |

The church is built of local Hornton stone (ironstone), set in a peaceful churchyard. The village of Ratley is tucked in on the eastern side of the Edgehill Escarpment, on the edge of the Cotswolds area of outstanding beauty. The church dates from the 12th Century, with building continuing until the early 14th Century, when the tower was completed. Notice that the pillars of the arches have no capitals, a style not often seen. How many arches meet on the pillar at the south-east end of the nave? The church is used weekly for worship, and is at the heart of the village community.

TRAVEL From the A422 follow the signs to Edgehill and Ratley at Upton House. On the B4100 follow the signs to Edgehill (B4086) at the top of Warmington Hill. Along Edgehill, follow the sign into Ratley, and continue to the bottom of the village. The church is situated next to the Rose and Crown. **PARK** Limited parking on the road by the church and pub. Extra parking suitable for coaches is available at the Village Hall at the top of the village.

OUTSIDE There is a medieval preaching cross in the churchyard. Notice also the salting trough, used for salting pork by the main gate. See if you can find the natural spring (the Gogs) to the west of the churchyard.

ACTIVITIES 3rd June: In the steps of St Wulfstan

WARWICKSHIRE

Saturday 29th and Sunday 30th July: the church will be open for a Patronal Festival celebration.

9th September: the church will be open for the annual Historic Churches Sponsored Cycle Ride. There will be a Summer Concert in July: date to be arranged.

In December there will be a performance of the Messiah.

On Good Friday there is annually a ten mile pilgrimage of witness linking the four parishes of the benefice, starting at Shotteswell Church at 11am and ending at Ratley Church at 3pm.

SPECIAL The church can be opened by arrangement. Also teas and light lunches can be arranged if pre-booked.

CONTACT Please phone 0295 - 670453 or 0295 - 670554. **There are steps down into the church from the main door, but entrance by the South door is on the level.**

FOOD Rose and Crown next to Church. The Castle Inn, Edgehill. Picnic site: Edgehill Country Park on B4086.

VISIT Upton House: National Trust House and Garden. Farnborough Hall: National Trust House and Garden and Edgehill Battle Museum (looking for a new location).

Salford Priors   **SP 077510**

St Matthew

Coventry

Norman onwards

The church is situated on the eastern edge of the village, overlooking the flood plain of the Rivers Arrow and Avon. On the site of a former Saxon Church, it has Norman origins and has been altered or added to extensively throughout the subsequent 900 years; the last major change occurring as late as 1991! Indeed every century from the 11th is represented in its architecture. It contains a wealth of monumental memorials and other artifacts of great interest.

TRAVEL On the B439 Stratford to Evesham road, 1.5 miles south of Bidford on Avon. **PARK** Adjacent car park, suitable for minibuses and coaches (in small numbers).

OUTSIDE Look out for the splendid Norman Doorway, also the unusual, embattled, Beacon Tower on the south side of the building.

ACTIVITIES 3rd June: In the steps of St Wulfstan. 9th September: Sponsored cycle ride. Visitors welcome at all times.

CONTACT If locked, key is available from Churchwardens (Address and telephone numbers in church porch).

FOOD The Bell (B439). The Queen's Head (A435), Iron Cross. The Blossom Valley Inn (B439) & Salford Hall, Abbots Salford. Picnic: Twyford Country Centre, Evesham (B439).

VISIT Dunnington Forge (01789 490125). Limebridge Plant Centre (A435). Golls Nurseries and Aquatics (A435). Ragley Hall (Arrow - A435). Twyford Country Centre and Falconry Centre (Evesham - B439). Middle Littleton Tithe Barn (National Trust). Domestic Fowl Trust (Honeybourne).

Tysoe   **151/ 341 444**

The Assumption of the Blessed Virgin Mary

Pre-conquest   *Coventry*
Norman and Perpendicular   *Grade 1*

Tysoe, made up of Upper, Middle and Lower, nestles at the foot of the Edge Hill escarpment on the Warwickshire /Oxfordshire border. St Mary's is a large parish church built in local Hornton stone dating from Norman times. Considerably altered over the centuries culminating in a scraped interior by the Victorians to reveal the myriad of masonry

74

changes. Nave, north and south aisles, large choir, rood screen loft stairs, fine tower with 6 bells.

TRAVEL On the edge of Middle Tysoe, next to the church school. **PARK** Road parking near to lych-gate.

OUTSIDE Set in 1.5 acre churchyard which is dotted with Primroses in Spring. Restored pinnacles and parapets. Some Norman evidence in tower. "Saxon" preaching cross located next to ancient Yew tree. Many medieval tombstones.

ACTIVITIES Regular: Open 1st Sunday of each month April - October, 2.30 pm - 5 pm (except June when open 3/6/95): Church open. Come and enjoy "Teas in the Tower Tea Room".
3rd June: In the steps of St Wulfstan.
SPECIAL Sunday 2nd July: Open day: 3 lectures; "Bats in the Belfry" by Jilly Sargent, "Saxon and Norman Churches in South Warwickshire" by Tim Bridges (of Birmingham University), "Churches in the Landscape" by Richard Morris (of the Council for British Archaeology). Also visits to nearby Upton House and the private church of Compton Wynates.

CONTACT Access for bellringers etc. please contact churchwardens on either 0295 680274 or 0295 680369.

FOOD Peacock Inn, Tysoe. Lovely picnic spots along the escarpment footpaths.

VILLAGE Warwickshire Centenary Way footpath runs through Tysoe. Meg's Cakes, Compton Windmill, Thatched Police House.

VISIT Upton House, Edge Hill, Burton Dassett Hills, Gliding/Karting centre at Shenington, Charlecote Park, Warwick Castle, Stratford-upon-Avon. Whatcote and Oxhill.

Walton   **SP 285 524**

St James

	Coventry
Georgian	*Grade B*

St James' Church, Walton d'Eivile, is an attractive neo-classical building which stands in a beautiful setting of lawns and lake close to Walton Hall, the Victorian mansion designed by Sir Gilbert Scott.

Particularly impressive are the plaster-work ceiling installed in 1843 and the east window by Clayton and Bell of London, a magnificent representation of the Crucifixion which was put up in memory of Sir Charles Mordaunt at the beginning of this century. Walton Hall is now a hotel and timeshare complex, 'timesharers' from all over the world joining parishioners at weekly services, making the church a truly international centre.

TRAVEL Follow the Walton Hall signs off the Wellesbourne by-pass (A429). **PARK** Easy.

OUTSIDE In the churchyard tombstones of the Mordaunt family, as well as people who lived and worked on the estate and in the big house, including Henry Bird the butler 'Loyal and faithful servant to three generations of the Mordaunt family'.

ACTIVITIES 5th August: Annual fete, craft fair and exemption dog show. This popular event is held on the lawns in front of the church.
Church will be open Sunday 13th August, 2 pm - 6 pm
Sunday 27th August, 2 pm - 6 pm
Sunday 1st October, 5.30 pm: Harvest Festival.
SPECIAL A history of the church is available.
Several steps make access difficult for the disabled.

FOOD The Conservatory Restaurant and bar are open all day at Walton Hall. The Wellesbourne Watermill (on B4086). There is a picnic area, and light lunches and teas are served in the barn where there is good access for the disabled.

VILLAGE The Wellesbourne Watermill (on B4086) open Thursday - Sunday, 10.30 am - 4.30 pm, demonstrates milling and rural crafts.

VISIT Wellesbourne church, Pillerton Hersey and Ettington.

Ettington, Pillerton Hersey, Walton and Wellesbourne

WARWICKSHIRE

Wellesbourne

151/ SP 278557

St Peter

12th Century   *Coventry*
From Norman to Victorian   *Grade B*

St Peter's lies on the northern edge of Wellesbourne Hastings, behind the King's Head Hotel. The footpath past the church leads over the Dene brook to the old twin village of Wellesbourne Mountford, making together modern Wellesbourne. Your first impression of St Peter's may be of a substantial Victorian church with an older south front and perhaps an older Tower. And you are right, the church was almost wholly rebuilt and enlarged in 1847-48. Once inside however then you are challenged to find where the new and the old are grafted together. You will soon find the old Norman chancel arch, and guides will help you to see the other features.

TRAVEL Turn from the new by-pass, A429, to the village centre on the B4086 and turn right at the King's Head Hotel. The tower can be seen from the by-pass through the trees. **PARK** Cars may normally park in the Church Centre car park. Coaches should park in Church Street, by the church gate.

OUTSIDE Look for a reset late 13th Century quatrefoil bull's eye window of weather beaten Edgehill stone below the east window of the south aisle that a restorer or mason must have felt worthy of keeping, why?

ACTIVITIES Regular: All Sundays in August.
Mon 1st May: open Sat 27th - Mon 29th May: Wellesbourne Arts Festival weekend, Art display in church.
Sat. June 3rd.
Sat 8th July: Wellesbourne Festival.
Sun 30th July.
Sat 5th (links to Walton fete).
Mon 28th August: open.
August openings-teas at Pillerton Hersey Opening times: 11.00 am - 3.00 pm. **No access problems for the disabled**.

CONTACT Visiting parties by special arrangement - Tel. 01789-841573.

FOOD The King's Head Hotel is next to the church. The Wellesbourne Hotel is on the Kineton Road, and The Stag is to be found in Chestnut Square. All provide meals. Wellesbourne Water Mill - see entry for Walton.

VILLAGE A very pleasant walk through the old village begins at the church. Follow the path beyond the churchyard, cross the footbridge over the Dene, turn left along the river, and keep turning left to return to Church Street, 15-30 minutes.

VISIT Charlecote House, National Trust Property. Wellesbourne Airfield Museum - Sundays and Bank Holidays, 10 am - 4 pm. Teas available.

Whatcote

St Peter

c. 1150   *Coventry*
Saxon/Norman   *Grade 2**

This ancient village church, nestling in the folds of the South Warwickshire countryside, lies only a few miles from Stratford-on-Avon and the North Cotswolds. Within five miles of its walls lie some of the area's loveliest churches. The present building of Saxon/Norman origin contains some interesting memorials and a Saxon font. The simple serenity of the interior is reflected in the view from the doorway, bringing to mind "this blessed land". The Centenary Way footpath crosses the churchyard, with its medieval preaching cross, making St Peter's the ideal place for both bodily and spiritual refreshment.

TRAVEL Whatcote is signed from A422 Banbury to Stratford road and the A3400 Oxford to Stratford road. The church will be signed on open days.
PARK On roads near the church. Car parking will be arranged on special open days. Coaches by appointment only. Please ring (0295) 680628.

OUTSIDE Look out for the four windows in the tower - all of differing architectural styles. In the churchyard is the grave of Dr William Lovelock, musician.

ACTIVITIES "Whatcote, past and present" display in church during the summer months.
3rd June, 11 am - 6 pm: St Wulfstan's Day celebrations, refreshments and village produce available.
Sunday 2nd July: St Peter's Day annual open air service.
Monday 28th August: Church open, cream teas will be served on the village green from 2.00 pm (Coffee from 11.00 am).

CONTACT It is possible for St Peter's to be open to welcome visitors (including groups) at any reasonable time when light refreshments would be available. Please ring 0295 680628.

FOOD Royal Oak in village, 12th Century hostelry with Civil War connections will provide bar meals.

VILLAGE Maps for local walks will be available in church along with details of other places of interest.

VISIT Shipston-on-Stour - picturesque market town with plenty of choice of accommodation and places to eat. Upton House (N.T.) Edgehill. St Peter's church is part of the united benefice with St Lawrence's, Oxhill and St Mary the Virgin, Tysoe, both lovely old churches.

Wootton Wawen   SP 15 633

St Peter

730 AD   *Coventry*
Anglo Saxon, Norman, Early English,
Decorated, Perpendicular   *Grade 1*

St Peter's is an ancient minster church. An unusual shape with 4 parts built around the crossing tower which sharing several building periods produces a very varied exterior. Look for the base of the Saxon Tower, the oldest part of the church, now used as the Sanctuary with the High Altar. Notice the old chests and the Chain Library. Find out who were the old families living in Wootton Wawen. The original nave is now used for regular worship. Identify the figures in the West Window - the story of the "Te Deum". Notice the restoration work of 1994 - plastering the roof of the Lady Chapel, re-plastering the south and west walls of the Saxon Tower, re-leading of the nave roof, replacing finials on the roof with stone from Grinshill in Shropshire.

TRAVEL A3400, 2 miles South of Henley in Arden and 6 miles North of Stratford upon Avon. A good bus service and trains from Birmingham to Stratford upon Avon. **PARK** Space for 12-15 cars. Coaches at Wootton Hall (by arrangement).

OUTSIDE Double leaf-strip round east window. Iron herses originally for protecting grave mounds. Gravestone of Henry Houghton who was injured at Waterloo. Grave monuments to Fieldham, Capewell-Hughes and Williams. Grave of huntsman of William Somerville (Poet).

ACTIVITIES Regular: Guided tours first Sunday each month at 3.00 pm, May to end of September. Saturday May 10am: The Anglo-Saxon Church, a study morning. Phone for details.

CONTACT Please contact the Vicarage 0564 792659 for parties over 20.

FOOD Bulls Head Inn, Navigation Inn. Evenings: Country Club, back of Wootton Hall.

VILLAGE Local farms provide bed and breakfast. Canal basin and aqueduct by Navigation Inn. Farm shop and Craft Centre on the A3400. Wootton Hall and the weir by the bridge. Wootton Wawen is a good place for walking near to the Heart of England Way. Choice of footpaths, Heart of England Way.Henley-in-Arden, Alcester.

> ### An Anglo-Saxon Minster Church

WORCESTERSHIRE

The Diocese of Worcester has as much natural beauty as any other diocese in England, with outstanding stretches of countryside as you follow its two main rivers of the Severn and the Teme.

From West to East the diocese stretches from the delights of the Teme Valley to the edge of the Cotswolds with Broadway and the Vale of Evesham.

In the North there is Dudley and the Black Country with the Clent Hills and the edge of the Lickey Hills, while to the South there are the sheltering Malvern Hills.

In fact, wherever you are in the diocese you are always within easy striking distance of attractive countryside with meadows, woods, lush green hills, rough common land and orchards of apples and cherries.

Added to all this, there are beautiful old buildings and rural churches which are waiting to welcome visitors and to share their treasures and history with them.
John Willis

Tourist Information in Worcestershire
Worcester Tourist Information Office. The Guildhall, High Street, Worcester. Tel: 0905 726311.

Countryside Information
Hereford and Worcester Countryside Service County Hall, Spetchley Road, Worcester. Tel: 0905 763763.

Town Churches
Worcester Cathedral
Pershore   Abbey Church of Holy Cross
Kidderminster   St Mary and All Saints
Evesham   All Saints, and St Lawrence

Village Churches are listed alphabetically with the names of nearby towns. Each Gazetteer entry gives a grid reference from the Landranger OS Maps series. Most are on sheet no. 150.

Alfrick	south-west of Worcester
Bayton	south-west of Bewdley
Bengeworth	west of Evesham
Besford	south-west of Pershore
Birlingham	south of Pershore
Blakedown	south of Stourbridge
Bretforton	west of Evesham
Bricklehampton	west of Evesham
Broadway	south-west of Evesham
Callow End	east of Powick
Chaddesley Corbett	north-west of Bromsgrove
Church Lench	north of Evesham
Churchill in Halfshire	south of Stourbridge
Cookhill	south of Redditch
Cowleigh	Malvern
Croome D'Abitot	south-west of Pershore
Cropthorne	north-west of Evesham
Crowle	east of Worcester
Defford	south of Pershore
Dodford	north of Bromsgrove
Doverdale	north-west of Droitwich
Drakes Broughton	north-west of Pershore
Eastham	east of Tenbury Wells
Eckington	south of Pershore
Elmley Castle	south-west of Evesham
Far Forest	west of Bewdley
Fladbury	north-west of Pershore
Great Comberton	south of Pershore
Grimley	north of Worcester
Hanbury	south of Bromsgrove
Hanley William	east of Tenbury Wells
Hartlebury	south of Kidderminster
Harvington	north-west of Evesham
Heightington	west of Stourport
Himbleton	south-east of Droitwich
Hindlip	north-east of Worcester
Holt Heath	north of Worcester
Inkberrow	south of Redditch
Kempsey	south-east of Worcester

Knightwick	west of Worcester
Kyre Wyard	south-east of Tenbury Wells
Leigh	south-west of Worcester
Little Comberton	south of Pershore
Lower Broadheath	west of Worcester
Malvern Link	north Malvern
Malvern Link	north Malvern
Mamble	south-west of Bewdley
North Piddle	north of Pershore
Norton	south-east of Worcester
Norton (Evesham)	north of Evesham
Oddingley	south of Droitwich
Offenham	north-east of Evesham
Ombersley	west of Droitwich
Pirton	west of Pershore
Powick	south of Worcester
Rochford	east of Tenbury Wells
Rock	south-west of Bewdley
Romsley	south of Halesowen
Rous Lench	north of Evesham
Salwarpe	south of Droitwich
Sedgeberrow	south of Evesham
Severn Stoke	south-east of Malvern
Stoke Bliss	south-east of Tenbury Wells
Stone	south of Kidderminster
Stoulton	south-east of Worcester
Tenbury Wells	south-east of Ludlow
Tibberton	north-east of Worcester
Trimpley	north-west of Kidderminster
Upton Snodsbury	north of Pershore
Upton upon Severn	east of Malvern
Warndon Villages	east Worcester
Wick	east of Pershore
Wribbenhall	south-west of Kidderminster
Wyre Piddle	north-east of Pershore

HOLLAND HOUSE

Cropthorne, Pershore
Worcestershire WR10 3NB
Telephone: 01386 860330

HOLLAND HOUSE

is a retreat, conference and laity centre.

In October of this year it will be
celebrating the 50th anniversary of the
first retreat.

**For a programme of Retreats,
Quiet Days, Day and Evening
Courses and Special Events
contact**

HOLLAND HOUSE

*The Gardens are open for the
Cropthorne Walkabout on*

May 7th, 2-6pm – May 8th, 11am-6pm
and for the National Gardens Scheme
on Sundays
19th March and 9th July, 2.30-5pm

1945 – 1995

Dates for your Diary
in Worcestershire

Many churches will be open at times other than those listed below. For up-to-date local information please use the contact numbers listed in each of the gazetteer entries.

Diary dates are dates when you can be sure to find the church open. Where churches have made a regular arrangement to have their building open and staffed they are listed at the beginning of each of the monthly lists. For more details please consult the individual entries.

Special Through the Church Door activities are also listed at the beginning of each month as appropriate.

Joint Activities

Bayton, Far Forest Heightington, Mamble and Rock Eastham, Hanley William, Kyre Wyard, Stoke Bliss, and Rochford.

January

Regular:	Dodford	Tue	11:00	12:00
	Holt Heath	Weekends		
	Malvern Link	Sun	8:00	12:00
	(St. Matthias)	Thurs	10:00	12:00
	Pershore	daily		
7	Eckington		9:00	12:30
15	Lower Broadheath		18:30	
21	Malvern Link (St Matthias)		19:30	
28	Evesham		19:30	21:30
29	Rochford		12:00	15:00

February

Regular:	Dodford	Tues	11:00	12:00
	Holt Heath	Weekends		
	Malvern Link	Sun	8:00	12:00
	(St. Matthias)	Thurs	10:00	12:00
	Pershore	daily		
4	Eckington		9:00	12:30

March

Regular:	Dodford	Tues	11:00	12:00
	Holt Heath	Weekends		
	Malvern Link	Sun	8:00	12:00
	(St. Matthias)	Thurs	10:00	12:00

	Pershore	daily		
4	Eckington		9:00	12:30
19	Eastham		11:00	16:00
19	Hanley William		11:00	16:00

April

Regular:	Dodford	Tues	11:00	12:00
	Evesham	Weekends from 16 April		
	Holt Heath	Weekends		
	Malvern Link	Sun	8:00	12:00
	(St. Matthias)	Thurs	10:00	12:00
	Pershore	daily		
1	Eckington		9:00	12:30
1	Romsley		14:00	17:00
8	Romsley		14:00	17:00
15	Cookhill		10:00	16:00
15	Romsley		14:00	17:00
15	Wribbenhall		10:00	16:00
16	Cookhill		9:30	20:45
16	Lower Broadheath		14:30	18:30
16	Powick		10:00	16:00
17	Evesham			
17	Kyre Wyard		11:00	16:00
17	Rochford		11:00	17:00
19	Dodford		11:00	18:00
22	Hartlebury		14:00	17:00
22	Romsley		14:00	17:00
23	Hartlebury		14:00	17:00
29	Romsley		14:00	17:00

May

Regular:	Dodford	Tue	11:00	12:00
	Evesham	Weekends		
	Holt Heath	Weekends		
	Malvern Link	Sun	8:00	12:00
	(St. Matthias)	Thurs	10:00	12:00
	Pershore	daily		
6	Broadway		10:00	18:00
6	Eckington		9:00	18:00
6	Romsley		14:00	17:00
7	Eckington		9:00	18:00
7	Cropthorne			
8	Eckington		9:00	12:30
13	Romsley		14:00	17:00
14	Knightwick (with Doddenham)		14:00	17:00

80

14	Upton Snodsbury		
20	Malvern Link (St Matthias)	19:30	
20	Romsley	14:00	17:00
21	Bayton		
21	Evesham		
21	Far Forest		
21	Heightington		
21	Kyre Wyard	11:00	17:00
21	Mamble		
21	Norton (Evesham)		
21	Rock		
21	Stoke Bliss	11:00	17:00
27	Bretforton	10:00	
27	Knightwick (with Doddenham)	11:00	17:00
27	Romsley	14:00	17:00
28	Bretforton	10:00	
28	Knightwick (with Doddenham)	14:00	17:00
29	Bretforton	10:00	
29	Knightwick (with Doddenham)	11:00	17:00

June

3 June: In the Steps of St Wulfstan

Regular:	Dodford	Tues	11:00	12:00
	Evesham	Weekends		
	Holt Heath	Weekends		
	Kidderminster	Daily		
	Malvern Link	Sun	8:00	12:00
	(St. Matthias)	Thurs	10:00	12:00
	Pershore	Daily		

3	Alfrick		
3	Bengeworth (Evesham)	9:30	18:00
3	Birlingham		
3	Blakedown	14:00	17:00
3	Broadway		
3	Church Lench		
3	Churchill in Halfshire	14:00	17:00
3	Cowleigh (Malvern)		
3	Cropthorne		
3	Crowle	11:00	16:00
3	Defford		
3	Drakes Broughton		
3	Eckington	9:00	12:30
3	Evesham		
3	Grimley		
3	Hanbury		
3	Hartlebury	10:00	17:00

3	Harvington		
3	Himbleton		
3	Hindlip	10:00	16:00
3	Inkberrow		
3	Kidderminster		
3	Leigh	10:00	18:00
3	Lower Broadheath	10:00	18:00
3	Malvern Link (C of A)		
3	Malvern Link (St Matthias)	10:00	18:00
3	Norton	10:00	17:00
3	Oddingley		
3	Pershore	9:00	18:00
3	Pirton		
3	Powick	10:00	18:00
3	Romsley	14:00	17:00
3	Rous Lench		
3	Salwarpe	10:00	16:00
3	Sedgeberrow	14:00	17:00
3	Stoulton	10:00	18:00
3	Tenbury Wells		
3	Warndon Villages	11:00	16:00
3	Wribbenhall	14:00	17:30
4	Bretforton	19:00	
4	Hanley William		
4	Powick	10:00	18:00
4	Sedgeberrow	14:00	17:00
5	Dodford	11:00	18:00
10	Bayton		
10	Crowle	14:00	17:00
10	Offenham		
10	Pershore		
10	Romsley	14:00	17:00
10	Tenbury Wells		
10	Trimpley	10:00	17:00
11	Knightwick (with Doddenham)	14:00	17:00
11	Norton (Evesham)		
16	Severn Stoke		
17	Bretforton		
17	Evesham	19:30	
17	Great Comberton	14:00	18:00
17	Malvern Link (St Matthias)		
17	Romsley	14:00	17:00
17	Tenbury Wells		
18	Bretforton		
18	Broadway	14:00	17:00
18	Great Comberton	14:00	18:00
18	Malvern Link (St Matthias)		

WORCESTERSHIRE

23	Blakedown	9:30	17:30
23	Lower Broadheath	12:00	20:00
24	Blakedown	9:30	17:30
24	Crowle	11:00	17:00
24	Doverdale	10:00	17:00
24	Eckington	13:30	16:00
24	Elmley Castle	14:00	18:00
24	Himbleton	10:00	18:00
24	Holt Heath		
24	Lower Broadheath	10:00	18:00
24	Mamble		
24	Oddingley		
24	Romsley	14:00	17:00
24	Rous Lench	14:30	
24	Sedgeberrow	10:00	17:00
24	Tenbury Wells		
24	Tibberton	10:00	16:00
25	Doverdale	10:00	17:00
25	Eastham	11:00	17:00
25	Elmley Castle	14:00	18:00
25	Himbleton		
25	Holt Heath		
25	Lower Broadheath	10:00	18:00
25	Rous Lench	12:00	18:30
25	Sedgeberrow	12:00	17:00
25	Severn Stoke		
29	Powick	10:00	18:00

July

Embroideries and Tapestries Week 3-9 July

Regular Dates

	Dodford	Tue	11:00	12:00
	Evesham	Weekends		
	Holt Heath	Weekends		
	Kidderminster	Daily		
	Malvern Link	Sun	8:00	12:00
	(St. Matthias)	Thurs	10:00	12:00
	Pershore	Daily		

1	Blakedown	9:30	17:30
1	Churchill in Halfshire	13:00	19:00
1	Eckington	9:00	12:30
1	Heightington		
1	Kempsey		
1	Rock		
1	Romsley	14:00	17:00
1	Tenbury Wells		

1	Warndon Villages	11:00	16:00
2	Blakedown	9:30	17:30
2	Churchill in Halfshire	13:00	19:00
2	Norton (Evesham)		
2	Warndon Villages	11:00	16:00
3	Norton	10:00	17:00
5	Powick	10:00	18:00
8	Bengeworth (Evesham)	10:00	20:00
8	Broadway	11:00	18:00
8	Church Lench		
8	Far Forest		
8	Harvington		
8	Lower Broadheath	10:00	18:00
8	Malvern Link (St Matthias)	10:00	14:00
8	Malvern Link (C of A)		
8	Romsley	14:00	17:00
8	Salwarpe	14:00	17:00
8	Tenbury Wells		
8	Upton upon Severn	10:00	18:00
8	Warndon Villages	11:00	16:00
9	Broadway	11:00	18:00
9	Church Lench		
9	Harvington		
9	Knightwick (with Doddenham)	14:00	17:00
9	Lower Broadheath	10:00	18:00
9	Malvern Link (St Matthias)	8:00	17:00
9	Malvern Link (C of A)		
9	Upton upon Severn	14:00	18:00
9	Warndon Villages	11:00	16:00
14	Hartlebury	10:30	17:00
15	Bayton		
15	Hartlebury	10:30	17:00
15	Romsley	14:00	17:00
15	Tenbury Wells		
15	Upton Snodsbury		
15	Warndon Villages	11:00	16:00
16	Bayton		
16	Croome D'Abitot		
16	Romsley		
16	Warndon Villages	11:00	16:00
22	Romsley	14:00	17:00
22	Tenbury Wells		
22	Warndon Villages	11:00	16:00
23	Evesham	15:00	17:00
23	Warndon Villages	11:00	16:00
25	Callow End	10:00	18:00
25	Harvington		

29	Hanley William	10:00	16:00
29	Romsley	14:00	17:00
29	Stoke Bliss	12:00	17:00
29	Tenbury Wells		
29	Warndon Villages	11:00	16:00
30	Evesham	15:00	17:00
30	Warndon Villages	11:00	16:00

August
Why not be a Church detective this August?

Regular:	Dodford	Tue	11:00	12:00
	Evesham	Weekends		
	Holt Heath	Weekends		
	Kidderminster	Daily		
	Malvern Link	Sun	8:00	12:00
	(St. Matthias)	Thurs	10:00	12:00
	Pershore	daily		

5	Eckington	9:00	12:30
5	Kempsey	14:00	16:00
5	Romsley	14:00	17:00
5	Warndon Villages	11:00	16:00
6	Evesham	15:00	17:00
6	Malvern Link(St Matthias)		
6	Warndon Villages	11:00	16:00
12	Broadway	14:00	17:00
12	Kempsey	14:00	16:00
12	Romsley	14:00	17:00
12	Warndon Villages	11:00	16:00
13	Evesham	15:00	17:00
13	Knightwick (with Doddenham)	14:00	17:00
13	Warndon Villages	11:00	16:00
16	Hartlebury	10:30	17:00
19	Kempsey	14:00	16:00
19	Kyre Wyard	11:00	17:00
19	Romsley	14:00	17:00
19	Salwarpe	14:00	17:00
19	Stoke Bliss	11:00	17:00
19	Warndon Villages	11:00	16:00
20	Evesham	15:00	17:00
20	Malvern Link(St Matthias)	14:00	18:00
20	Warndon Villages	11:00	16:00
26	Great Comberton	14:00	17:00
26	Kempsey	14:00	16:00
26	Romsley	14:00	17:00
26	Warndon Villages	11:00	16:00
27	Evesham	15:00	17:00

27	Warndon Villages	11:00	16:00

September
9 September: Sponsored Cycle Ride.

Regular:	Dodford	Tue	11:00	12:00
	Evesham	Weekends to 24 September		
	Holt Heath	Weekends		
	Kidderminster	Daily		
	Malvern Link	Sun	8:00	12:00
	(St. Matthias)	Thurs	10:00	12:00
	Pershore	daily		

1	Harvington		
2	Eckington	9:00	12:30
2	Fladbury		
2	Harvington		
2	Romsley	14:00	17:00
2	Wick	14:30	17:00
3	Fladbury	12:00	18:00
3	Harvington		
9	Alfrick	**watch out for**	
9	Bengeworth (Evesham)	**cyclists !!!!!**	
9	Besford		
9	Bricklehampton	10:00	18:00
9	Cookhill	10:00	16:00
9	Cowleigh (Malvern)		
9	Croome D'Abitot	10:00	18:00
9	Cropthorne		
9	Crowle	11:00	17:00
9	Defford		
9	Drakes Broughton		
9	Eckington	10:00	18:00
9	Elmley Castle	10:00	18:00
9	Evesham		
9	Great Comberton	10:00	18:00
9	Hanbury	10:00	18:00
9	Hartlebury	10:00	16:00
9	Harvington		
9	Himbleton		
9	Hindlip		
9	Holt Heath		
9	Knightwick		
9	Leigh		
9	Lower Broadheath	10:00	
9	Malvern Link (St Matthias)		
9	Malvern Link (C of A)		

WORCESTERSHIRE

9	Norton	10:00	17:00
9	Norton (Evesham)	10:00	16:00
9	Oddingley		
9	Pirton		
9	Powick	10:00	18:00
9	Romsley		17:00
9	Salwarpe	11:00	17:00
9	Severn Stoke		
9	Stoulton	10:00	18:00
9	Tibberton	10:00	16:00
9	Trimpley	10:00	17:00
9	Upton Snodsbury		
9	Upton upon Severn	10:00	18:00
16	Cookhill	10:00	16:00
16	Ombersley	12:00	16:00
16	Romsley	14:00	17:00
16	Wribbenhall	10:00	16:00
17	Cookhill	9:30	20:45
17	Wribbenhall	11:30	16:30
22	Evesham		
23	Blakedown		
23	Evesham		
23	Rochford	11:00	17:00
23	Romsley	14:00	17:00
23	Sedgeberrow	14:00	17:00
24	Blakedown		
24	Evesham		
24	Malvern Link (C of A)	16:00	
24	Sedgeberrow	14:00	17:00
25	Evesham		
30	Broadway	19:30	20:00
30	Romsley	14:00	17:00

October

Regular:	Dodford	Tue	11:00	12:00
	Holt Heath	Weekends		
	Malvern Link	Sun	8:00	12:00
	(St. Matthias)	Thurs	10:00	12:00
	Pershore	daily		

1	Bayton		
1	Bricklehampton	10:00	17:00
1	Broadway		
1	Callow End	10:00	16:00
1	Dodford	11:00	18:00
1	Far Forest		
1	Hartlebury	14:00	16:30
1	Heightington		

1	Lower Broadheath	14:00	18:30
1	Mamble		
1	Offenham		
1	Rock		
7	Eckington	9:00	12:30
8	Hanbury	11:00	
8	Powick	10:00	16:00
22	Eastham	11:00	17:00

November

18/19 November Plant a Tree Weekend

Regular:	Dodford	Tue	11:00	12:00
	Holt Heath	Weekends		
	Malvern Link	Sun	8:00	12:00
	(St. Matthias)	Thurs	10:00	12:00
	Pershore	Daily		

4	Eckington	9:00	12:30
18	Malvern Link (C of A)		
19	Salwarpe	12:00	15:00

December

Regular:	Dodford	Tues	11:00	12:00
	Holt Heath	Weekends		
	Malvern Link	Sun	8:00	12:00
	(St. Matthias)	Thurs	10:00	12:00
	Pershore	Daily		

2	Eckington	9:00	12:30
2	Mamble		

Kidderminster   **835769**

St Mary and All Saints

1315   *Worcester*
Perpendicular   *Grade 1*

This church is large (total exterior length 215 feet) and full of historical and architectural interest. Visitors should be aware of the connection with Church Street, over the Ringway. Inside, the Baxter Pillar is the second from the east in the north side of the nave. The church has been recently re-ordered most beautifully. The attractive stained glass is Victorian. The exquisite Whittall Chapel, added in 1922 and designed by Sir Giles Gilbert Scott, has stained glass depicting St Mary, Joan of Arc and Florence Nightingale.

TRAVEL The main approach to the church is by means of a sub-way for pedestrians from Church Street and through the Horsefair and Churchfields by car. **PARK** There are ample facilities provided by Wyre Forest District Council near the church, and some on the road in Clensmore Street. Coaches are welcome.

OUTSIDE The church gardens behind the church are well kept. The Richard Baxter statue is near the church and the canal.

ACTIVITIES Regular: Open June to September: Monday to Saturday 10.30 am - 12.30 pm and 2.30 pm - 4.30 pm, except Monday mornings and Saturday afternoons.
3rd June: In the steps of St Wulfstan. **SPECIAL The church is suitable for disabled visitors.** Arrangements can be made for group parties, history and interest groups.

CONTACT Telephone: 0526 755454 for further information.

FOOD Several restaurants in Mill Street. Picnic sites - the church ground or St George's Park, Radford Avenue.

TOWN The River Stour and the Staffordshire-Worcestershire Canal are next to the church. Not too far from Wyre Forest Glades Leisure Centre, Bromsgrove Street and the Severn Valley Railway, Comberton Hill. Nearby are the Trinity Methodist Church and Baxter Church.

The Parish of Droitwich Spa

Birthplace on 18th October 1595

of

EDWARD WINSLOW

Old Vigornian — Pilgrim Father

Governor on three occasions of Plymouth Colony

Commissioner for Cromwell on an Expedition to the West Indies

The 400th anniversary of his birth and baptism will be celebrated in October 1995.

For more information contact: **The Droitwich Parish Centre**
Telephone: 0905 794925

Evesham

CP 037 437

All Saints

Late 12th Century *Worcester*
Perpendicular

The setting is unusual. The church lies in one churchyard together with the redundant Church of St Lawrence and the detached early 16th Century Bell Tower, the latter having a ring of 14 bells. These buildings are within the original Abbey wall, the Benedictine Abbey itself having completely disappeared, except for one cloister arch. The church is built in a mixture of styles, displaying examples of all architectural periods; from Norman (West Wall of Nave) to Tudor (West Porch and beautiful Lichfield Chapel), but not pure Gothic of the early English period. The Chancel is Victorian as is most of the stained glass.

TRAVEL Easily accessible from market square via the 12th Century Abbot Reginald Gateway, Abbey Park via Bell Tower, and gate on Vine Street. **PARK** Abbeygates Shopping Arcade (access, lower Bridge St.), and Merstow Green and old Brewery Car parks (Takes coaches).

OUTSIDE 12th Century Abbot Reginald's Gateway and Church House. Redundant Church of St Lawrence. Bell Tower. Old Abbey Wall on South Side of churchyard. Imagine the enormous Benedictine Abbey beyond the wall, at one time the 3rd greatest in the country. Remains of Cloister Arch in Abbey Park.

ACTIVITIES 28th January, 7.30 pm - 9.00 pm: "The Cowl and the Crown" Monastic life in words and music.
17th April: Organ recitals, 11.30 am, 2.00 pm, 4.00 pm.
21st May: Rogation Sunday - Beating the Bounds.

SPECIAL A walk followed by tea in Church House - all welcome. Friends of Church and Bell Tower. 3rd June: 'In the steps of St Wulfstan'. Church open day - display in church on "Monasticism in Evesham". 17th June, 7.30 pm: Concert by 'Musica in Ecclesia'. English music before 1600. Organised by Evesham and District Music Club.
9th September: Church open for Sponsored Cycle Ride "Historic Churches Preservation Trust". 22nd - 24th September: Flower Festival. Organised by Evesham Floral Society and All Saints. Sunday Organ recitals during the Summer: 23rd, 30th July. 6th, 13th, 20th, 27th August at 3.00 pm & 4.00 pm. Cups of tea available. 16th April - 24th September: Church open and manned at weekends.

CONTACT Church could be opened by special arrangement. Tel. Church Office: 0386 442213. **Disabled facilities.**

FOOD Many eating places within reach in the Town.

TOWN Almonry Museum - an outstanding local museum (also the Tourist Information Centre). Abbey Park and River area. Walk to Hampton Ferry.

VISIT Many interesting surrounding villages. Cotswolds and Bredon Hill within easy reach.

Pershore

Abbey Church of Holy Cross

Norman and Early English

Worcester
Grade 1

Former Abbey church in attractive Georgian riverside town of Pershore. Impressive Norman crossing (rebuilt 1102), Early English Choir (13th century) with unusual combined triforium/clerestory and magnificent vaulted roof set with intricately carved bosses. 14th century Lantern Tower with famous suspended ringing platform. (Pershore's bellringers have to have a head for heights!) Only part of the original Abbey church remains to serve as the parish church. The rest of the church, along with the monastic buildings, was pulled down at the time of the Dissolution of the Monasteries. The former nave may have been similar to that at Tewkesbury, stretching from the present west doors to the iron gates beyond. Pershore Abbey is still a fine place to wander quietly, or to sit and imagine the events of its long history, enjoying its inspirational atmosphere.

TRAVEL A44 to Pershore from M5, Evesham or Worcester. Also by Midland Red bus, or train (Pershore station is approx. 1 mile from the town, some connecting buses.) Boats moor on the River Avon. The Abbey, visible for miles around, is set in Abbey Park, close to the High Street. **PARK** Parking spaces in Broad Street and Church Row, as well as in Abbey Park. Also main town car park off the High Street.

OUTSIDE The line of trees marking the position of the pillars of the former nave; the cloister arch; roof lines of earlier roofs; the blocked doorway on the south wall of the South Transept which once led from the monks' sleeping quarters to the Abbey church; carvings, sedilia, etc. from a former chapel.

ACTIVITIES: OPEN DAILY

SPECIAL Saturday 3rd June, 9 am - 6 pm: In the steps of St Wulfstan, visitors are welcome all day. Manchester Boys' Choir will be giving a concert in Pershore Abbey at 7.30 pm. Throughout day: Musica in Ecclesia.
June 10th: A complete Monastic Day with all the Offices being sung. Visitors are welcome during all parts of the day. Visitors' Centre serving teas in St Andrew's Centre beside the Abbey, Sat & Sun afternoons in summer.

CONTACT Guided tours by appointment: Please ring Verger 0386 561520. Teas and refreshments for visiting groups by arrangement. Further information on visiting and many other concerts and activities from Pershore (0386) 561520 and 552071.

FOOD Plenty of places for tea, coffee and refreshments in Pershore, also pubs. Picnic site by Pershore Bridge (A44 towards Evesham), parking and information but no toilets by bridge.

TOWN Public convenience in Church Row close to Abbey. Also town car park. Pershore College of Horticulture, RHS Centre & Plant Centre. Pershore's many interesting shops & boutiques.

VISIT St Mary's, Wick. St Nicholas, Pinvin. St James', Birlingham. Visit Tewkesbury Abbey and look for similarities in style.

WORCESTERSHIRE
Alfrick   SO 748 529

St Mary Magdalene

Worcester

Late Norman/Early English

Situated on a hillock just south of the green with its war memorial, this beautiful little 13th Century sandstone church is a place of peace and tranquility. It lies midway between the Nature Reserves of Ravenshill and the Knapp, in an area of outstanding natural beauty. The ancient timbered porch leads into the Norman Nave with a barrel vault of old timbers. The Chancel was added in the 14th Century and the North Transept built in 1885. Now known as the Lulsey Chapel it houses the ancient font and a 12th century figure transferred from the St Giles, Church Lulsley now closed.

TRAVEL Take the A4103 from Worcester. In approx. 4 miles turn right at traffic island at Bransford. Bear right for Leigh and Alfrick. In about 4 miles at Alfrick turn left at crossroads (village shop, green with war memorial). The church is 150 yards on the right. **PARK** Limited parking outside gate in lane. Car park open by special arrangement with churchwarden 0886 - 884249. Other parking at village hall.

OUTSIDE A unique bellcote of wooden shingles bears a sundial which reads "on this moment hangs eternity". 12th Century buttress on north wall, 14th Century buttress at east end. Three Norman windows at western end. Tomb of Allies family. Jabez, son of Wiliam, born 1787 at Lulsley, wrote on 'The Antiquites and Folklore of Worcestershire.'

ACTIVITIES 3rd June: St Wulfstan celebrations. 9th September: Sponsored cycle ride.

FOOD Ploughman's Lunch at The Swan Inn, Alfrick. Extensive menu at the Fox and Hounds, Lulsley. Picnic site at Ravenshill Nature Reserve.

VISIT Ravenshill Nature Reserve, Knapp Papermill Reserve. On the Suckley hills is "Worcestershire Way" (passing into woodland of S.S.I). Lower Brockhampton - (National Trust) a moated manor house, near Bromyard on A44. Leigh Tithe Barn (English Heritage).

Bayton   3691 2732

St Bartholomew

Worcester

Norman with heavy Victorian restoration.

First stand beside the 19th Century Tower and enjoy the superb view of the Clee Hills and beyond. Then enter through the round-arched, dog-toothed Norman doorway and look left to examine the fine Norman font, and a 19th Century hatchment comprising the heraldic emblems of the Meyseys of neighbouring Shakenhurst, whose family also presented the beautiful east window depicting light from the risen Christ, descending upon the church below. Gaze up at the impressive roof tie-beams, and choir stalls. Sadly most other medieval features disappeared in the heavy 1905 restoration.

TRAVEL From Clows Top take the B4202 towards Cleobury Mortimer. In 0.5 mile bear left towards Bayton village. In village bear left and then take the next right opposite the Wheatsheaf Inn. Proceed 300 yards, turn left down lane to church. **PARK** At the end of the lane adjacent to the church.

OUTSIDE Memorial stone against south wall.

ACTIVITIES 21st May: Rogation Sunday Walk
10th June: Summer Concert
15th July: Bayton Church Fete, set in lovely gardens and grounds.
16th July: Songs of Praise Service.
SPECIAL 1st October: Wyre Forest Autumn Colours.

CONTACT For any further information or openings by arrangement, ring: 0299 832249.

FOOD Wheatsheaf Inn - meals each evening and lunches Friday and weekends.

VILLAGE Folk Festival - Wheatsheaf Inn on May Bank Holiday.

VISIT Towns of Ludlow, Bridgnorth and Cleobury Mortimer. Mamble, Rock, Heightington and Far Forest.

Bayton, Far Forest, Heightington, Mamble, Rock

Bengeworth (Evesham)   **SP 04 43**

St Peter's

1872   *Worcester*
Victorian

St Peter's Church serves the rapidly expanding Parish of Bengeworth and is an oasis of peace on the outskirts of Evesham. The spire, with its two clock faces, is a popular landmark. The original medieval church fell into disrepair and regrettably was demolished leaving only the remains of the porch. Built on a new site St Peter's houses some of the interesting relics linking past and present. Stained glass enthusiasts will enjoy the varied scenes depicted in the windows.

Do not miss the old church stained glass incorporated in the new extension door. Churchyard seats offer a welcome rest for passers-by!

TRAVEL Junction B4035 and A44 (Oxford Rd.). Top of Port Street. Evesham is served by local buses, National Express Coaches, Main Line Rail. **PARK** Limited parking for cars or minibus in church grounds. Paid parking within walking distance also free parking in adjacent roads.

OUTSIDE The Garden of Remembrance for Cremations. A Victorian Font.

ACTIVITIES 3rd June, 9.30 am - 6 pm: "In the steps of St Wulfstan". A small display relating to the life of St Wulfstan. Light refreshments will be available.
8th July, 10 am - 8 pm: Bengeworth Traders Annual Street Market held in Port St. **SPECIAL** In co-operation with the traders, St Peter's will be marking the day with a Festival of Flowers to depict the many shops and businesses to be found in Port St. Lunches and teas will be available in church. Please note that part of Port St. will be closed to traffic. As part of "Embroideries and Tapestries Week" a group will be working on Church kneelers.
9th September: Cycle Ride.

CONTACT Hospitality with light refreshments offered to groups with prior arrangements. Tel: 0386 446164. **Ramp and cloakroom facilities for the disabled.**

FOOD Numerous, of all varieties within minutes of the church. A grass area near the west doors of the church is suitable for picnics.

VISIT Riverside and Parks - 5 mins. For those researching ancestors, the Bengeworth cemetery is approx. 200 yards from the church. An excellent Museum situated in the Almonry in the centre of Evesham also houses the Tourist Information Centre.

Besford   **150/ SO 911 448**

St Peter

early 14th Century   *Worcester*
Medieval timber construction   *Grade 2*

Situated in the beautiful Worcestershire countryside Besford church features a rare timber-framed nave

WORCESTERSHIRE

of the 14th Century. Look out for the original wooden west window and the blocked north doorway. On entry you will find a beautiful nave dominated by a massive wooden vault and lined with panels from the old box pews. Note the original rood screen. The Victorian chancel contains an important tomb of Sir Richard Harewell who died in 1576. Note his effigy in alabaster with his Elizabethan dress. Look out also for the Sebright memorial.

TRAVEL By road, take the A4104 from Pershore towards Upton. After 2.5 miles, over bridge, turn right at signpost to Besford. Follow minor road 1 mile and turn left at 'village only' sign into Harewell Lane. Church is 400 yards down the lane. Church can also be reached by network of paths from Defford or Pershore. **PARK** Along wall by entrance gate, limited to a few cars and/or minibus.

OUTSIDE Rare timber framed church structure with stone chancel.

ACTIVITIES Services 2nd (9.00 am) and 3rd (10.00 am) Sundays each month.
Church will be open on 9th September.

SPECIAL Visitors welcome. Information about church key on notice board.

CONTACT Groups recommended to make prior arrangements with wardens (0386 556390 or 750776).

FOOD Pubs with food Defford and Pershore. Restaurants, shops in Pershore. Please feel free to picnic in churchyard. Picnic site at Eckington Bridge (3 miles on B4080).

VISIT Historic Pershore with Abbey and waterside, Bredon Hill, Eckington Bridge. Easy walk from Defford church.

Birlingham

St James

| 12th Century | Worcester |
| Victorian | |

The church was built in the 12th Century and dedicated to St James (a popular dedication in this district). The Norman chancel arch was in situ until 1872 when it was removed and incorporated in the modern lych-gate. The patronage remained with the Lords of Nafford until the 17th Century, passing through many patrons until Canon Duke presented it to the Dean and Chapter of Worcester. In the 15th Century a tower was built at the west end of the nave with resting places for the Rector's pigeons. Only eight such church dovecotes remain and two are in this district, the other one is in Overbury. The tower has six bells. The churchyard has foot stones and is noted for bulbs in the springtime.

TRAVEL Off the A4104. **PARK** Limited in the lane adjoining churchyard.

OUTSIDE The Norman chancel arch moved out of the church to form a lych-gate in 1872. Also the old stocks put in the pound in 1787 and stored in the church in 1926.

FOOD The Swan Inn: very small pub which does not serve food.

VISIT Manor House garden, open Thursdays in the summer. Pershore Abbey.

| Blakedown | SO 881 785 |

St James the Great

| 1860 | Worcester |
| Victorian Country Church | Grade 2 |

St James the Great was built in 1860 as a Chapel of Ease by the Parish of Hagley. It is a medium sized sandstone building with a timber framed Tower and Spire. The architect was the renowned G E Street who was responsible for many Victorian churches. The South Aisle and the Tower were later additions.

90

The interior of the church features beautifully carved Pew ends and Panelling together with a fine stone Reredos.

TRAVEL The church is situated at the upper end of the village on the A456 (main road from Birmingham to Kidderminster). Trains: good service from Birmingham New Street and Kidderminster (except Sundays). **PARK** On the two special weekends there will be space for cars to the rear of the church and also adjacent in the School Playground.

ACTIVITIES 3rd June, 2 pm - 5 pm: In the steps of St Wulfstan.
1st, 2nd July : Flower Festival. 10 am, Sunday morning Family Service to which visitors will be most welcome. 23rd, 24th September: Harvest Festival. A traditional Harvest Display. On each of these two weekends the church will be open from 9.30 am - 5.30 pm. **SPECIAL** There will be guides to welcome you and refreshments will be available.

FOOD Blakedown village has two good pubs which serve food: The Old House at Home and The Swan.

VILLAGE Blakedown is surrounded by a number of splendid lakes most of which are man-made and date from Medieval times. In the 19th Century the area was famous for Forges. There is still a working forge at Churchill (see Churchill entry).

VISIT St James the Great, Churchill and St Peters, Broome.

WORCESTERSHIRE

Bretforton 150/ SP 093 438

St Leonard

Reconsecrated 1295   Worcester
Transitional/Early English   Grade 1

The church is the oldest building in the village, set in the centre with the Manor, the Fleece Inn, and (much later) the school around it. Inside look for: a) The font, which is older than the building (it existed in 1206). The wooden font cover dates from 1721. b) Some splendid Victorian stained glass, and fragments of medieval glass: c) The boxed, "Squire's (Ashwin) Pew", used by the Ashwin family who owned the Manor for 400 years (until 1983). From it the Squire could see the people in church, the Vicar preach, but not the altar...

TRAVEL The church is situated in the centre of Bretforton, just off the B4035 3 miles east of Evesham. **PARK** In the public square (called the Cross). Coaches and minibuses are welcome.

ACTIVITIES 27th,28th,29th May, 10 am onwards: Flower Festival, refreshments available.
Sunday 4th June, 7 pm: Open Air service, in the Cross followed by Annual Asparagus Auction at the Fleece Inn.
17th, 18th June: Open gardens 17th June: Last night of the Proms style evening concert by Bretforton Silver Band and Pig Roast in The Manor gardens. Group parties welcome. **SPECIAL** Guided Tours.

CONTACT Will open by arrangement, contact Church Warden, Tel. 0386 831654.

FOOD The Fleece Inn, The Victoria Arms.

VISIT The Twyford Country Centre. Nearby Cotswold towns of Chipping Camden and Broadway, Evesham market town with its Abbey and Almonry, and riverside walks.

Bricklehampton   98 42

St Michael and All Angels

prior to 972   *Worcester*
Mediaeval/Victorian   *Grade 2*

Standing in a tranquil churchyard, partly a natural wildlife refuge, St Michael's features a saddleback tower. The splendid 12th Century south doorway is recessed in 2 orders, chevron ornamented and has side shafts with foliated capitals. Note the two remaining medieval windows. Within, the font, stoup and (near the altar) a piscina and remains of the sedilia from the 14th Century, are permanent reminders that this peaceful place has welcomed pilgrims for over 1000 years. There is good stained glass, particularly 5 excellent Kempe windows. The timbered roof is a gem, whilst memorials to local families show interesting heraldry. Enjoy your visit.

TRAVEL Take the A44 from Pershore towards Evesham. Three miles along turn right, marked "Elmley Castle and Bricklehampton". Turn right at the T-junction into village. The church is on the left approached through a lych-gate. **PARK** On side of road outside the church, sufficient space for minibus parking.

OUTSIDE Look at the south doorway. A 13th Century lancet on the north wall and, on the south wall a 14th Century window with one light and trefoiled head.

ACTIVITIES 9th September: Church will be open for the annual cycle ride and during harvest festival. Sunday 1st October, 10 am - 5 pm: Harvest Festival Thanksgiving Service at 6.30 pm.

CONTACT Open by arrangement. Tel. 0386 710602.

FOOD The New Inn on the A44, the Queen Elizabeth and The Old Mill public houses at Elmley Castle - all serve food. Picnic sites at Pershore beside river and at Tyddesley Wood.

VISIT The churches at Elmley Castle, Great and Little Comberton which, together with St Michael's complete the benefice. The market town of Pershore and its Abbey.

Broadway

St Michael and All Angels

1840   *Worcester*
Victorian

The Parish Church of St Michael was built in 1839-40. It occupies the site of a chapel of ease which was here from 1608. The ancient Church of St Edburgha (just over half a mile further along the Snowshill Road) was the parish church from the latter part of the 12th century. The stained glass and carved oak pulpit are worthy of note and the friendly atmosphere within.

TRAVEL The church is a little way along the Snowshill Road - turn at the village green. **PARK** Village car park adjacent to the church. Coach parking a short distance away.

OUTSIDE The church has a rather plain frontage.

ACTIVITIES 6th May, 10 am - 6 pm: Church open day.
18th June, 2 pm - 5 pm: Summer Party - (details on church notice board).
8th & 9th July, 11 am - 6 pm: Flower Festival.
12th August, 2 pm - 5 pm: Church Fete.
30th September, 7.30 pm: Cotswold Choir Concert.
1st October, 8 am, 9.45 am, 11 am: Harvest Festival.
SPECIAL At the moment we have no wheelchair access to St Michael's. St Edburgha's has easy access.

CONTACT Group visits can be arranged - contact the Vicarage - 0386 852352.

FOOD There are numerous pubs, restaurants, cafes and picnic places very close to the church.

VISIT St Edburgha's church. Snowshill Manor, Hidcote Gardens, Evesham, Pershore Abbey, Tewkesbury.

Callow End   835 494

St James

1888   *Worcester*

St James' Chapel of Ease was built at Callow End by the Sixth Earl of Beauchamp who resided at and owned the Madresfield Estate. Before the chapel was built evening services were held in the nearby school, also built by the Earl in 1870. The centenary of St James' coincided with the 150th anniversary of the coming of the nuns to close by Stanbrook Abbey in 1838. Improvements have been made over the years and the interior is well kept with the original benches. A lively active congregation creates a friendly atmosphere with a hearty welcome for visitors.

TRAVEL On the Upton road, B4424 in Callow End between the school and the Working Men's Club. **PARK** Space on the wide verge opposite the school.

OUTSIDE The memorial to Winsmore Hooper family.

ACTIVITIES 25th July, 10 am - 6pm: Patronal Festival of St James.
1st October, 10 am - 4pm: Harvest Festival.

FOOD The Old Bush and The Blue Bell. Pixham Ferry picnic area.

VISIT The parish church of St Peter's, Powick. Walks on the Old Hills and The Malverns.

Chaddesley Corbett   SO 89 74

Saint Cassian

Norman and later

Worcester
Grade 1

Set on the west side of the southern end of the village street, it is surrounded by a large churchyard with many important tombs. Built of sandstone, of attractive proportions and uncommonly large for a village church. It has a nave with north and south aisles, a lady chapel, tower and spire. The attractive interior houses a Saxon font, some ancient monuments, a notable organ, two effigies and the tower contains a peal of 8 bells.

TRAVEL Chaddesley Corbett village street leaves the A448 Kidderminster-Bromsgrove road, equidistant between Kidderminster and Bromsgrove. **PARK** In the village street.

OUTSIDE Ancient grammar school in churchyard. Architecture of village street.

ACTIVITIES Sunday services: 9.30 am and 6.30 pm. Wednesdays: 10 am Communion. **SPECIAL Wheelchair access.** School groups and history groups welcome.

FOOD 3 pubs in village: The Talbot, The Swan and The Fox.

VISIT Harvington Hall. Chaddesley Woods, Clent Hills, Avoncroft Musuem, Bewdley Safari Park, Droitwich Spa.

Church Lench   150/ 023 513

All Saints

1289   *Worcester*
Norman/Early English

Church Lench is one of the five Lench villages in the Vale of Evesham. The village of Church Lench has been in existence for over a thousand years and is mentioned in the Domesday Book. A Saxon church stood on the site of the present church but in the 12th Century a Norman church replaced the older Saxon building. Many alterations and additions were undertaken in the following centuries to create the church as it is today.

TRAVEL From the A435 in Harvington take the turn to 'The Lenches" and proceed to Church Lench. The Wychavon Way footpath passes beside the church. **PARK** There is parking available for cars, minibuses and a coach.

OUTSIDE A medieval font which has been made into a sundial can be found in the churchyard.

ACTIVITIES 3rd June: In the Steps of St Wulfstan 8th, 9th July: The flower festival.
The church will be opened and manned on Blossom Sunday (advertised in the press and on the radio).

CONTACT The church key can be obtained from the shop.

FOOD The Wheelbarrow and Castle, Radford. Annard Mill.

VISIT Evesham.

Churchill in Halfshire   **SO 879 794**

St James the Great

rebuilt 1868   *Worcester*
Architect W.J. Hopkins Victorian   *Grade 2*

Sandstone with plain clay tile roof; Nave with chancel at East end; Square tower at North/East end; South Porch; Vestry by tower. Pleasant churchyard surrounded by trees and standing in rural village surroundings.

TRAVEL Proceed from Kidderminster to Blakedown - A456. Go past the church and take the first turn on left across level crossing. Turn right at "T" over bridge and proceed 0.5 mile with church on right. **PARK** There is small church car park adjoining the church.

OUTSIDE Pleasant churchyard and surround. Note the yew tree as large tree in 1868 - pictures in church.

ACTIVITIES 3rd June, 2 pm - 5 pm: In the Steps of St Wulfstan.
1st, 2nd July, 1 pm - 7 pm: Garden opening for a number of gardens in the village. **SPECIAL** There will be central car park for the garden opening and teas will be available. The church will be open 1 pm - 7 pm on each day.

FOOD Old Wagon and Horses at Ismere on A451. Churchill Forge. This will be open on 1st/2nd July.

Cookhill   **581 056**

St Paul's

1876   *Worcester*
Victorian Gothic   *None*

St Paul's is set in a lovely area with a tidy churchyard of about an acre, with about a third of the ground taken up by graves. On entry you are greeted by a nice light country church, which looks even nicer when the sun is shining. On your left (west wall) is a large stained glass window in memory of Sarah Ann Foster, Kathleen Mary Foster, Mary Ann Wigan and William Foster, this was erected in 1933. On the wall opposite (north wall) will be found three windows two of which are stained glass, one in memory of the dead of the first World War, the other is in memory of Thomas and Alice Barber, Thomas being Treasurer of St Paul's, both were teachers of the local school. Also on the north side can be found the Organ and Vestry. Turning to the East Wall you will find another large stained glass window erected in 1919 in memory of Joseph and Mary Jane Moore of Cladswell. On the Lectern can be found the Holy Bible, this was presented for the use of St Paul's Chapel, by the Earl and Countess of Yarmouth on the 26th October 1876. The oak cover being carved by the Countess. In the centre of the church can be found a small Communion table in memory of Dorothy Chambers 1897-1987. Under some of the chairs can be found Kneelers that have been worked by the ladies of the church and of the village.

TRAVEL Situated on the A441 between Redditch and Evesham. In between the B4090 Alcester to Droitwich and the A422 Alcester to Worcester Roads. **PARK** Layby on the A441, also in Church Lane, both outside the church.

OUTSIDE The nice tidy churchyard and the glorious views over the local countryside.

ACTIVITIES Saturday 15th April,
Saturday 9th September.
Saturday 16th September All between 10 am and 4 pm.
16th April, 9.30 am: Easter Day Service.
17th September, 9.30 am: Harvest thanksgiving.

CONTACT The church can be opened by arrangement by ringing 0527 892248 or 0527 893111.

FOOD The Why Not and The Nevill Arms.
The Old Bull, Inkberrow (setting for Radio programme "The Archers").

VILLAGE There are lots of lovely walks and rambles to be taken through the lovely countryside.

VISIT The Jinny Ring Centre, Hanbury. Coughton Court. Ragley Hall.

Cowleigh (Malvern)　　　　**SO 769 475**

St Peter

1866　　　　　　　　　　　*Worcester*
13th Century style

St Peter's is built on an east-west slope of the Malvern hillside and was designed by George Street. From the outside it is clear that the church is wider than might be expected for its length because of the sloping ground. Inside, with low side aisles, it has the character of an ancient village church. The nave is lofty with clerestory windows. It has many "Street touches": the half clerestory windows which work so well in a small church; the plain round columns with deliberately simplified capitals and the pulpit with its semicircular railing of columns of varied coloured marbles.

TRAVEL By road from the B4219 Malvern to Storridge road, turn right down Cowleigh Bank at crossroads signposted Leigh Sinton. **PARK** On Cowleigh Bank and in St Peter's Road.

OUTSIDE Single bell, weather vane, Malvern stone walls, lych-gate, war memorial, interesting grave stones.

ACTIVITIES 3rd June: In the steps of St Wulfstan. 9th September: Sponsored Cycle Ride.

CONTACT Arrangements for access to the church can be made via the church wardens or the Team Vicar. Details are available on the notice board, or telephone 0684 574041.

FOOD The Cross Keys, Belmont Road. The Prince of Wales, Newtown Road.

VILLAGE The church is on the northern end of the Malvern Hills and many fine walks can start from Cowleigh Road, and the West Malvern Road which are close to the church. The Malvern Hills.

VISIT Malvern has many attractive churches, a museum, and entertainment complex as well as the extensive walking available. The Church of the Ascension can be reached by a short walk down Cowleigh Bank and right along Belmont Road.

Croome D'Abitot   SO 886 451

St Mary Magdalene

1763   *Worcester*
Late Georgian Neo-Gothic   *Grade 1*

A building of attractive yellow-buff Cotswold stone, erected as an eye catcher in Croome Park by the 6th Earl of Coventry, replacing the former medieval church. Designed, like nearby Croome Court by Capability Brown, the light and airy interior by Robert Adam. There is an imposing array of black and white marble Coventry monuments removed from the old church; also a series of later Coventry wall tablets. Much of the furniture is contemporary with the building, including an outstanding pulpit, with tester supported on delicately carved brackets. **Closed for regular worship in 1975 and now in the care of the Churches Conservation Trust.**

TRAVEL Crome is signposted from the A38 at Severn Stoke (through Kinnersley and High Green) and at Kempsey (opposite Baynall Garage). At T-junction approx. 1 mile beyond High Green, turn right. Church is reached by public footpath on right, signposted 'To the Church'. **PARK** None at Church. Park on side of road by signpost to church.

OUTSIDE Close to the church are tombs of members of the Coventry family. Splendid views across the fields to Croome Court (not open to the public).

ACTIVITIES Sunday 16th July: Croome Annual Service and Open Day
Saturday 9th September: Sponsored Bike Ride with church open 10 am - 6 pm.

> **See entry under Severn Stoke.**

Cropthorne   150/ 001 452

St Michael

1100   *Worcester*
Norman

This 12th Century church is set in a well kept churchyard behind a local stone wall at the north end of the main village street. The inside of the church has traces of an ancient wall painting and there are unusual large decorative tombs of the local family Dingley. The most interesting feature is the Saxon Cross head which was originally found embedded in the wall of the church. The intricate designs on the Choir Stalls were carved in 1896 by Daughters of Squire Holland, Lord of the Manor. The Font and old Pews are of some interest. The Tower has a peal of six bells and ringers are always welcome. A Guide to the Church is available.

TRAVEL The church is situated at the North end of the picturesque village of Cropthorne 3 miles distant from both Pershore and Evesham between the A44 and the B4084. **PARK** Village Hall car park, opposite the church.

OUTSIDE Gargoyles and Belfry openings. Unusual wooden cross near the gate.

ACTIVITIES 3rd June: In the Steps of St Wulfstan. On Bank Holiday Sunday and Monday in May the annual Cropthorne Walkabout (open gardens and Flower Festival) is held. **SPECIAL** Exhibitions, stalls, activities and refreshments.
9th September: Sponsored Cycle Ride

FOOD The New Inn and the Bell Inn situated on the A44. Picnic site and car park at Jubilee Bridge - quarter mile from Church.

VILLAGE Village Shop and Post Office. Holland House, Retreat Conference and Laity Centre.

VISIT Bredon Hill, Pershore Abbey, historic riverside town of Evesham. Charlton and Fladbury churches.

> **Holland House is also in Cropthorne**

| Crowle | 922 559 | Defford | 150/ SO 917 432 |

St John the Baptist

1884   *Worcester*
Victorian   *Grade 2**

12th Century origins, altered in 14th and 15th Century, demolished in 1881 and rebuilt 1882-5 by Preedy retaining some earlier features. Interior: 19th Century Rood Screen richly carved with overhanging vaulted cornice. Late 12th Century limestone lectern restored 1845 with scrolled vine design and kneeling figure at front. 15th Century Octagonal Font with finely detailed traceried panelling.

TRAVEL From east and north: A422 at Broughton Hackett - turning for Crowle village approx 1.5 miles. Church appears on left side. From south and west: follow signs for Crowle from roundabout on A4358 just south of J6 on M5. **PARK** In Bredicot Lane (South side of church). Minibuses welcome.

OUTSIDE Porch 14th Century re-used from older church. Stone coffin - medieval - Burford limestone.

ACTIVITIES 3rd June, 11.00 am - 4.30 pm: In the Steps of St Wulfstan.
10th June, 2.00 pm - 5.00 pm: Crowle Church Fete.
24th June, 11.00 am - 5.00 pm: Patronal Festival.
9th September, 10.00 am - 6.00 pm: Cycle Ride.
SPECIAL Level access for the disabled. Information on footpath walks.

FOOD Chequers Inn, Crowle Green, March Hare, Broughton Hackett.

St James

13th Century   *Worcester*
       Grade 2

The nave has 17th Century windows, chancel is Victorian. The west tower is 14th Century and now has a timber framed upper stage (visible for several miles). The church is set on an elevated small churchyard (the parish cemetery is some 100 yards away).

TRAVEL Turn off the A4104 Pershore - Upton road into Defford village; either turning right 2.5 miles from Pershore opposite garage then left, church is 100 yards, or 5 miles from Upton turn left at signpost, church is 800 yards. **PARK** On street parking around church.

OUTSIDE Ancient "queen's-head" keystone over the door.

ACTIVITIES Services on 1st (10.00 am), 2nd (Oct-Apr 6.00 pm) and 4th (9.00 am) Sundays. Church will be open 3rd June and 9th September.

CONTACT Visitors welcome. Information about key on notice board. Groups recommended to make prior arrangements (0386 750880 or 750203).

FOOD Along the main road (A4104) there are three pubs/restaurants - The Defford Arms (750378), The Railway (750309) and The Oak (750327).

VILLAGE Post office (opposite church) has leaflets and photographs, including 1 mile footpath walk to Besford Church.

VISIT Pershore (Abbey and shops), Eckington (church, bridge with picnic site), Bredon Hill (footpath from Eckington). Footpath (1 mile) to Besford Church.

Dodford SO 932 724

Holy Trinity and St Mary

1908   *Worcester*
Arts & Crafts   *Grade 2**

The church, the vicarage and the lodge (the latter now both private dwellings) were built by the first Vicar, the Revd. Walter Whinfield, at the beginning of this century. Integral with the church is a cloister enclosing a quadrangle and outside pulpit. The church is very light having little stained glass and this shows up very well all the decorative work done by the Bromsgrove Guild. Of special note is the woodcarving and the plaster panels on the ceiling arches.

TRAVEL Approaching from Bromsgrove turn right off the A448 Bromsgrove to Kidderminster road at Cross Roads Garage, take the first left into Priory Road. The church is on the right hand side, and is signposted in a quarter of a mile. **PARK** The church car park, up the drive is suitable for minibuses but not for coaches.

OUTSIDE Dodford is one of five Chartist villages in England, and was laid out as a planned settlement. All the cottages were the same and set in their own four acres of land. Many of the cottages are much altered, some beyond recognition, but a few remain as they were. The 12th Century moated Priory remains as a private house and can be seen from Priory Road but is not open to the public.

ACTIVITIES Regular: The church is open every Tuesday (except after Bank Holidays) from 11 am to 12 noon for private prayer.
Wednesday 19th April,
Monday 5th June,
Sunday 1st October (Harvest Festival service at 11.00 am). Open 11.00 am - 6.00 pm.

CONTACT Visits by arrangement: Tel. 0527 831197.

FOOD The Dodford Inn. The Gate, the Nailers Arms and the New Inn are in the adjacent village of Bournheath. The Park Gate lies off the Kidderminster Road, between Bromsgrove and Dodford. All will provide lunch. There is a picnic site below the Dodford Inn.

VILLAGE There are many delightful local footpaths. Maps are to be found in the church car park and at the village hall.

VISIT The Avoncroft Museum of Buildings at Stoke Heath, off the A38(T), grid ref. SO 953 685. Bromsgrove Museum, Birmingham Road, Bromsgrove. Harvington Hall, Chaddesley Corbett, off the A448, grid ref. SO 877 745.

Doverdale 150/ 661 861

St Mary

12th Century   *Worcester*
Early English   *Grade 2*

Doverdale is a peaceful little church surrounded by farm land. It serves a small parish mentioned in the Domesday Book - in 1086 there were some 46 parishioners and the situation is little changed today. The prizewinning churchyard is edged by a sandstone wall beyond which is a ditch or ha-ha. The church has a 4 sided turret of ornamented white oak capped by a square lead spire housing 3 bells. A 300 year old yew tree guards the door. Inside it is simple, though visitors can see a 15th Century stained glass window depicting Our Lady in the north wall.

TRAVEL Take the A449 between Kidderminster and Worcester. Turn East at the Jet garage signposted Doverdale. After approx. 1 mile take the first right turn to the church. **PARK** In front of the church.

OUTSIDE The prizewinning churchyard is edged by a sandstone wall beyond which is a ditch or ha-ha Look at the unusual turret.

ACTIVITIES 24th and 25th June: Floral Decoration.

FOOD The Ripperidge, Yew Tree House Garden.

VISIT River Severn, Ombersley Village, Gallery and Restaurant.

St Barnabas

1857   *Worcester*
Victorian

St Barnabas was originally built as a Chapel of Ease to serve the then small community and founded by the Rev. Richard Williamson, Vicar of Pershore. By 1923 it had come under the auspices of the Parish of Stoulton and is now known as the Parish of Stoulton with Drakes Broughton. The main point of interest is the great East Window depicting Simeon with the Christ-child. The window is dedicated to George Handy, Parish Clerk from 1892 to 1946. The church's steeple is a landmark and it is interesting to note that it blew down in the gales of Christmas Eve 1977. Within one year £11,000 was raised and a new steeple erected and dedicated on Ascension Day 1979.

TRAVEL The village lies about 7 miles south-east of the City of Worcester and 2 miles north-west of Pershore along the A44. It is well served with public transport from both directions. The church lies a few yards along Stonebow Road (off the main road) on the corner with Walcot lane. **PARK** Coach parking is available in the large lay-by on the A44 just east of Stonebow Road. Cars may be parked in the village hall car park at the rear of the church in Walcot Lane.

ACTIVITIES 3rd June: In the steps of St Wulfstan. 9th September: Cycle Day.

FOOD Meals are served at the Bird in Hand on the A44 one mile west of the village.

VISIT Stoulton church. The market town of Pershore is characterised by its beautiful Abbey. Adding to its charm is the River Avon with the town lock and picnic sites on its banks.

St Peter and St Paul

12th Century, on earlier site.   *Worcester*
Early English   *Grade 1*

This lovely old 12th century Norman foundation lies within the Teme Valley and situated by the old manor house and farm. Many interesting features to see, including reredos with 17th century richly carved panelling; rood loft stairway with incense lamp; leper window in chancel. Largely built of local travertine tufa stone. Many interesting memorials and two paintings: the arms of George I and George II, and a 17th or 18th century Crucifixion. The font dates back to the 12th century. The bell tower has four bells, dated 1663, 1665, 1699 and 1754, which are rung by local and visiting teams.

TRAVEL On A443 Worcester - Tenbury road, turn over small brick bridge 5 miles before Tenbury (signposted Eastham). On A456 Kidderminster - Tenbury road turn left 1.5 miles before Newnham bridge, then right and left over bridge at the bottom. On B4204 Worcester - Tenbury road via Clifton-on-Teme, turn right at Fox Inn, (signposted Hanley William initially). **PARK** Outside churchyard in farm area. Suitable for coaches by appointment.

OUTSIDE South doorway and carvings adjacent. Opposite door, remains of an ancient (possibly Saxon) preaching cross. Half-timbered cottage opposite was once the Rectory and before that part of a monastery. Also an ancient animal pound.

ACTIVITIES Sunday 19th March, 11 am - 4 pm: Daffodil Sunday in conjunction with nearby garden of 'Robins End' and Hanley William church. Teas. Sunday 25th June, 11 am - 5 pm: Patronal Festival ending with open air 'Songs of Praise'. All welcome to join us.
Sunday 22nd October, 11 am - 5pm: Church decorated for Harvest Festival. Service begins 5pm.

CONTACT Open by appointment to groups. Please telephone: 0584 781657.

FOOD Talbot Hotel, Newnham Bridge (1 mile); Fox Inn and Tally Ho, both on B4204 on Broadheath (3 miles). Picnic area at Eastham Bridge.

VISIT Garden Centre at Newnham Bridge. Tenbury Wells market town (5 miles).

> **Eastham, Hanley William, Kyre Wyard, Stoke Bliss, Rochford.**

WORCESTERSHIRE

Eckington SO 923414

Holy Trinity

c. 1100   *Worcester*
Heavily modified Norman   *Grade 2*

In the centre of busy and attractive village with many half-timbered houses. Built in several styles, the western end of the nave and the arcade to the South Aisle are 12th Century. The internal stone work is in its 'rough-hewn' condition. The 14th Century tower holds 8 fine bells.

TRAVEL From Pershore - 2.5 miles towards Upton-on-Severn and turn left along B4080, continue for 1.5 miles over ancient bridge into village. From south - 3 miles north of Bredon on B4080. **PARK** Small private car park opposite church, otherwise on side roads.

OUTSIDE The western Norman entrance was moved from South side in the 19th Century. There is a small priest door in the south wall of the Chancel. The churchyard has a number of interesting headstones - look out for the artist's palette.

ACTIVITIES Regular: Open on the first Saturday morning of each month.
6 - 8th May: VE Day, 24th June: Village fete, 9th September: Cycle Ride.
Services: Communion: 8 am on 1st, 3rd and 5th Sundays, 10 am on 2nd and 4th Sundays. Evening Ecumenical service: 6 pm on 1st Sunday.

CONTACT Arrangements for visiting, for individuals and groups, can be made with the vicar, Rev. Peter Thomas: 0386 750203.

FOOD 2 pubs with food within 200 yards of the church (Anchor - 0386 750356; Bell - 0386 750205); excellent picnic site at Eckington Bridge (half a mile north of church on B4080.

VILLAGE Medieval Eckington Bridge; footpaths along the side of the Avon; locks on the Avon; footpaths up Bredon Hill (visible for many miles and made famous by the poet A E Housman). Leaflets on the church and the village and cycle ride can be obtained from the Post Office (near Ancient Cross 50 yds from church).

VISIT Adjacent parishes of Defford and Besford and their historical churches are linked with Eckington. Historic Pershore (Abbey and shops); villages of Bredon and the Combertons.

Elmley Castle 150/ 893 410

St Mary the Virgin

11th Century   *Worcester*
From Saxon/Norman onwards   *Grade 2*

The churchyard's lush greens contrast naturally with the church's Cotswold stonework, the two being framed under the beauty of Bredon Hill. The church has a very interesting history, including ties with the old castle (now dismantled) from which Elmley gets its name. Visitors have described the church as 'refreshing', 'tranquil', 'You can almost hear the silence' and that it is a 'step back in time'. Look out for the famous Savage and Coventry memorials, which reflect historical craftsmanship and elegance. Our church offers a quiet sanctuary for individual renewal in the house where all are welcome.

TRAVEL 4 miles from Pershore. Leave Pershore for Evesham on the A44. On crossing the River Avon just outside Pershore, turn right for Elmley Castle. Follow the road through Little Comberton and on to Elmley Castle. The church is easily found at the far end of the village. **PARK** On street parking for cars.

OUTSIDE Two very impressive 16th Century sundials.

ACTIVITIES 24th and 25th June, 2 pm - 6 pm:

Elmley Entertains, open gardens and much more! 9th September, 10 am - 6 pm: Sponsored cycle ride.

FOOD Elmley has 2 pubs serving good food and a picnic site by the cricket ground.

VISIT Pershore and the Abbey. Plant Centre at the Pershore Horticultural College. Evesham - Almonry Museum.

Far Forest

Holy Trinity

1844   *Worcester*
Victorian

St Wulfstan would have welcomed the formation of this new parish in the mid-nineteenth century. The church was deliberately provided to give Christian focus for the scattered Forest population, notorious for their lawlessness. Today the building, made in the local stone, retains its original simplicity, offering peace and quiet in its edge-of-forest setting, while reflecting changing community needs. Recently carpeted - Kidderminster's best! - it is cosy and inviting in winter, yet light and airy, thanks to its unadorned walls and lofty ceiling. The windows include twentieth century stained glass of exceptional craftsmanship. A wooden cross on the chancel east wall commemorates links with a Ugandan pastor.

TRAVEL About five miles west of Bewdley off the A4117 Bewdley - Ludlow road in Church Lane. Coming from Bewdley enter the village past the Plough public house on your left and take second

right into Church Lane. Holy Trinity is about 300 yards on the left. **PARK** In the lane outside the church.

ACTIVITIES 21st May: Rogation Sunday - organised walks around the area.
1st October: Wyre Forest in autumn colours also Harvest Festival.
Also note Church Fete at local village school on Saturday 8th July.

FOOD The Plough about half a mile back in the village. The Horse and Jockey, Ludlow Road. The Duke William, Callow Hill. Alton Guest House, Callow Hill. Callow Hill Visitors Centre. All providing food. The Royal Forester, Callow Hill - no food.

VILLAGE The Bower Crystal shop in the village. Far Forest Stores in the village.

VISIT Forestry Comission - Callow Hill Visitors Centre. Wyre Forest - an ancient deciduous forest and an area of outstanding natural beauty with a thriving herd of fallow deer. Treacle Hall and Bancroft Garden Centres. Historic Bewdley - fine Georgian town. Wharton Park Golf Club - Bewdley. Little Lakes Golf Club - Lye Head. Fishing at various localities both lake and river. Severn Valley Railway - Kidderminster, Bewdley, Bridgnorth. Deer Museum - Button Oak. West Midlands Safari Park - Bewdley. Boating on the River Severn Bewdley and Stourport.

Mamble, Bayton, Rock and Heightington

Fladbury   SO 996 463

St John the Baptist

Worcester

Though there was a church here in Saxon times, the present building is largely 14th century, with a Norman tower, and much in Victorian times. Look for the Norman windows in the lower slopes of the Tower. The porch is 14th century. In the chancel is the 15th century de Montfort window, commemorating knights who fought in the Battle of Evesham, 1265.

WORCESTERSHIRE

Also discover the altar tomb to John and Eleanor Throckmorton (1445) now in the choir vestry below the tower, and several brasses.

TRAVEL Alongside the River Avon, between Evesham and Pershore off the A4084. **PARK** On road or round village green.

OUTSIDE 14th century piscina to the east of the vestry in the north wall of the chancel.

ACTIVITIES 2nd - 3rd September, 12 noon - 6 pm: Flower Festival and Village Walkabout, with crafts and local produce on sale, boat trips and other attractions.

FOOD The Chequers and The Anchor in the village. Tea Room at Craycombe Farm Craft Centre at Fladbury Cross, opposite Golf Club (A4084).

VISIT Pershore 3 miles, Evesham 3 miles. Many good walks on Bredon Hill.

Great Comberton   **150/ 955 421**

St Michael and All Angels

11th century ?   Worcester
15th Century   Grade 2

The village of Great Comberton is signalled from afar by the impressive tower of St Michael's. "That tower is too large for the church!", declared a noted clergyman of the district. Lichens, however, which can grow only in the purest air, thrive upon its stones. This beautiful Cotswold church, surrounded by Yews which nod in windless moonlight, has a charmingly simple white painted interior surmounted by a magnificent nave roof. Some of the pews are Jacobean, with wood twice as thick as we would use today. Other pews have been gouged by the horny hands of the smock-clad who, you imagine, stand among us on Sunday, their joys and sorrows identical to ours. God's Special Peace is in this church. All year round bright butterflies, emerge fluttering from the stained glass during a poignant pause in sermons. It's coincidence, of course; ... isn't it?

TRAVEL It is 2.5 miles from Pershore Centre. Turn first right on the A44 to Evesham just outside Pershore, ignoring Pensham, turn right twice more at the fork and subsequent 'T' junction. Second left, past the phone box will lead you to the church.
PARK No car park as such, so considerately, please. "Twenty is plenty" speed-wise.

OUTSIDE The Malvern Hills and the Worcestershire Beacon frowning across the Vale. A huge and very ancient Yew tree thought to have been planted in 1265 to commemorate the Battle of Evesham. What has it witnessed over the years?

ACTIVITIES Saturday 17th and Sunday 18th June, 2 pm - 6 pm: Open Gardens Weekend with displays in church.
Saturday 26th August, 10 am - 6 pm: Great Comberton Flower Show. This lovely village event attracts people from far and wide.
Saturday 9th September, 10 am - 6 pm: Sponsored cycle ride. "Blossom Trails" in the Spring.

FOOD The Queen's Head at Elmley Castle. Good restaurant. "The Old Mill" at Emley Castle has an impressive and varied menu. Two other hostelries are at Eckington, and a range of "Takeaways" and Pubs entice many tourists in Pershore. On the Evesham side of the A44 Avon Bridge is an extremely picturesque picnic site, with the original bridge as its centre piece. There are many beautiful walks in the area - 4 within 400 yards of the churchyard.

VILLAGE Great Comberton contains arguably the most beautiful thatched house in Worcestershire, and lies on the northern slopes of Bredon Hill, whose summit affords breathtaking views. Elmley Castle, Eckington and other hamlets are easily found on foot.

VISIT Pershore College of Horticulture (former Gold-of-Golds award winners at Chelsea Flower Show). There is produce for sale; also plants shrubs and trees in season.

Grimley	836 606

St Bartholomew

12th/13th Century,   *Worcester*
restored during Victorian era.

Small rural church close to the River Severn and situated within the heart of the small village of Grimley, though the parish extends away from the river to include the hamlets of Sinton Green and Monkwood Green. Some evidence of the church's 12th and 13th century origins can still be seen in the chancel and south wall. 15th century stained glass windows are to be found in the nave, that on the south wall, depicting the Annunciation, being of particular interest. The present tower dates from 1845 and extensive restoration took place in the 1880's when both the outside staircase to the bell-tower and the gallery were added. The church Tenor Bell dates from 1482 and is the third oldest medieval bell in the County made by the Worcester Foundry.

TRAVEL Grimley is clearly signposted from the A443 Tenbury road, approx. 2 miles from the outskirts of Worcester. The church can be seen on the left towards the end of the main street. **PARK** Car park at the side of church, opposite the school.

OUTSIDE The oldest part of the churchyard is that to the right of the main path, situated there are the tombs of Samuel Good, Esq., Surgeon in Ordinary to Prince Albert; Sir Samuel White Baker, who discovered the source of the White Nile; and a Preaching Cross which is an ancient listed monument.

ACTIVITIES 3rd June: In the steps of St Wulfstan.

FOOD The Wagon Wheel Italian Restaurant and Pub, and the Camp Inn, both situated on the banks of the River Severn. There are other pubs at Sinton Green and Monkwood Green.

VISIT Monkwood Nature Reserve, at the western end of the parish, for birds, rare butterflies and beautiful wild flowers and plants. Excellent woodland walks are signposted, and there is a car park, plus picnic space. It is also possible to walk along the banks of the river, north towards Holt and south, via Bevere Lock, towards Hallow. Grimley is within 2 miles of both the churches of Holt and of Hallow. Within a 5 mile radius are the ruins of Witley Court and church (further along the A443 Tenbury road) and the Elgar Birthplace Museum at Broadheath. St Martin at Holt.

Hanbury	SO 954 643

St Mary the Virgin

836 AD   *Worcester*
Medieval Gothic   *Grade 1*

Hill top site, magnificent views over unspoilt countryside. Norman, Medieval, local sandstone building. Dedicated in 836 AD. The tower was built in 1790 and contains 8 bells. The church has box pews, a gothic Regency gallery, a splendid ornate organ case (believed to be the work of Revd. Frederick Sutton). The ceilings were decorated by Victorian Architect Street. Magnificent East Window. 17th Century (Jacobean) Monument of Richard Vernon and his Wife d. 1627. The Vernon Transept contains splendid family monuments by sculptor Sir Francis Chantry and Roubiliac. North Aisle contains the original artist's models of the Nativity and Resurrection, panels for Reredos of Liverpool Cathedral. Look at 100 Tapestry kneelers of many different designs. This is an Archers Location: Phil Archer and Grace, David and Ruth, Elizabeth and Nigel were 'Married' here.

TRAVEL M5 junction 5 (Droitwich), then B4090 School Road (signposted Hanbury Hall). Turn opposite the school. The church is situated on a hill top one mile from Hanbury village. **PARK** 40 cars (one coach by appointment).

OUTSIDE See "Outside Trail Leaflet" (green). Herbage and wild flowers. Emma Vernon's grave (local heiress) beside coppice on the north side of the churchyard. Mass dial on south west buttress. Large hooded Norman SW window. 'Ogee' West entrance.

ACTIVITIES 3rd June: In the steps of St Wulfstan. Saturday 9th September, 10 am - 6 pm: Cycle Ride. Sunday 8th October, 11 am: Harvest Festival.

CONTACT By appointment. For times of church services please see notice board.

FOOD The Country Girl, Sharpway Gate, Stoke Prior, 01527 821790. The Gate Hangs Well (Holmes Lane) Wood Gate, Hanbury, 01527 821459. The Eagle and Sun, Hanbury Rd., Droitwich. 01905 770130. The Jinny Ring Craft Centre & Restaurant, Hanbury, Tel. 01527 821272.

VILLAGE Jinny Ring Craft Centre, Hanbury, Bromsgrove, 01527 821272. The Vernon Arms, Droitwich Rd., Hanbury, 01527 821236. Hanbury Hall (N.T.) Wren Style red Brick House 1701. Ceiling by Thornhill. Restored original 18th century gardens. Open April-Oct. Sat, Sun, Mon 2 pm- 6 pm.

VISIT Dodderhill Common, Medieval Woodland.

Hanley William	673 660

All Saints

c. 1150	*Worcester*
Norman	*Grade 2**

Set on high ground looking away to the beautiful hills of Shropshire, this was once the church for Hanley Court Estate. The tiny building has scarcely changed since the early Middle Ages and has one of the narrowest chancel arches in the country. Above the door is a 12th century stone carved Agnus Dei. The distinctive timber turret and shingled spire house a pre-Reformation bell. Inside, the windows and arches are faced with local tufa, quarried at Southstone Rock (access by footpath). Note the 12th century sandstone font, lovely East Window and the carved pulpit hewn from a single oak.

TRAVEL Signposted from the B4204 Tenbury - Clifton-on-Teme road, 6 miles east of Tenbury. The turning is opposite the Fox Inn. The church is approached by car through a field gate, or by a wicket gate from the road beside the church.**PARK** In meadow through labelled field gate west of church. Limited parking on road by wicket gate. Coaches by arrangement only.

OUTSIDE Magnificent views. Two fine old yews in old churchyard. Timber turret and spire. Hanley William Church retains its character serving a small and scattered rural community.

ACTIVITIES Sunday 19th March, 11 am - 4 pm: Daffodil Sunday, **in conjunction with Eastham Church and Robin's End garden.** Refreshments available - details in church.
Sunday 4th June: Village Fete.
Saturday 29th July, 10 am - 5 pm: **Open in conjunction with Stoke Bliss Church.** Refreshments available nearby.There are many other church-based activities - details in church. **Good disabled access via field gate - the church is all on the one level.** Coaches by arrangement only, please, due to narrow lanes.

CONTACT Telephone 0886 853 258.

FOOD The Fox Inn and Tally Ho Inn are both within 1 mile, on B4204.

VISITHanley Childe Church (2 miles), Kyre Park Gardens (6 miles - with tea rooms). T e n b u r y Wells (6 miles) - attractive market town. Eastham also open 19th March; Stoke Bliss also open 29th July.

> **Eastham, Hanley William, Kyre Wyard, Stoke Bliss, Rochford.**

Hartlebury	OF/SO 841 708

St James the Apostle

1269	*Worcester*
Commissioner's Gothic	*Grade 2*

A unique country church closely linked with the Bishops of Worcester, who have lived in Hartlebury Castle for 1,000 years. It is built from local sandstone on an ancient raised Saxon site, closely surrounded by historic village buildings. Five Bishops are buried in the churchyard and the coats of arms of 92 past Bishops are carved on the pew ends, including those of St Wulfstan. Between 1818 and 1837 the church was restored to the graceful designs of Thomas Rickman of Birmingham. The proximity of the Castle and the County Museum makes this a fascinating venue.

TRAVEL 4 miles south of Kidderminster on A449, turn right to Stourport on B4193 (sign County Museum). Church on left in village centre opposite White Hart Inn. From Worcester on A449 turn left into village, take turning to Stourport down Waresley Rd. and Quarry Bank, church on right. Regular bus service from Kidderminster and Worcester. **PARK** Limited to parking on roadside in Quarry Bank and Church Drive. The White Hart Inn opposite church.

ACTIVITIES 22nd , 23rd April, 2 pm - 5 pm: The Church and its people. Teas available.
3rd June, 10 am - 5 pm: In the steps of St Wulfstan. Teas available.
14th, 15th July, 10.30 am - 5 pm: Our Heritage

weekend, Exhibition, flowers, Village gardens open, Teas available.
16th August, 10.30 am - 3.30 pm: Children's Trail Day, "Follow the Bishops".
9th September, 10 am - 4 pm: Cycle ride day.
1st October: Harvest Festival 10.30 service, church open 2 pm - 4.30 pm. Teas available. Every Sunday 10.30 am service. **SPECIAL** Able to cater for group parties, disabled, children by appointment with guided tours.

CONTACT Numbers 01299 250375 or 01299 250736.

FOOD White Hart Inn, Talbot Inn, Old Worcester Rd.Little Chef on A449, Museum Tea Room and picnic site.

VILLAGE Hartlebury Castle staterooms and chapel, open 2 pm - 5 pm first Sunday in the month and Bank holidays from Easter to Sept. Wednesdays 2 pm - 4 pm Easter to August. County Museum. Hartlebury Common. Brindley's canals in Stourport.

VISIT Ombersley church was also designed by Thomas Rickman.

Thomas Rickman architect:
Ombersley and Hartlebury

Harvington   SP 057 488

St James

Unknown.   *Worcester*
Early English   *Grade 1*

St James' distinctive green spire can be seen from some miles away, as the church is built on a low hill overlooking the River Avon flood plain. Situated in the oldest part of a thriving village, it is surrounded by houses of all ages - from 16th century timber-framed buildings to modern family homes. Standing within an ancient graveyard, the small grey stone church is behind a wall, opposite the "Coach and Horses" public house. The area is renowned for coarse fishing, narrow boat holidays, fruit and vegetable growing (farm shops/PYO) and, in the spring the local "Blossom Trail".

WORCESTERSHIRE

TRAVEL Just off the B439, three miles north of Evesham. Buses from Stratford, Redditch, Alcester and Evesham. Access to/from River Avon, about one mile away. **PARK** Limited, unrestricted, on-street parking.

OUTSIDE Ancient ruined dovecote. Benchmark on the tower.

ACTIVITIES 3rd June: Exhibition in church.
8th, 9th July: Embroideries and Tapestries.
25th July: Patronal Festival Day.
1st - 3rd September: Festive Weekend.
9th September: Cycle Tour Day.
Ramp for wheelchairs. Clear access inside church.
SPECIAL Groups/refreshments/village walks by arrangement.

CONTACT Tel. 0386 871068.

FOOD The Mill at Harvington (hotel/restaurant). The Coach and Horses (pub).The Golden Cross (pub).

VISIT Ragley Hall; Evesham town; Bidford-upon-Avon.

Heightington

St Giles

                                    Worcester

Whether or not King John used this tiny Chapel in the hamlet of Heightington as a place of worship while hunting in the Wyre Forest - and the locals like to believe he did - there is no doubt of the Chapel's antiquity. The appointment of a Chaplain in 1325 is on record, and the dedication to St Giles is thought to come from an association with the Greek St Giles who lived in France during the Crusades. The small north window is 12th Century and there are two more from 13th Century. There are Tie-Beams, a dual manual Organ in the Balcony, a Bell dated 1736 and the walls have Frescos, although mostly covered by plaster at present.

TRAVEL Take the A451 from Stourport on Severn to Great Witley and turn right in Dunley signed Heightington 2 miles.

WORCESTERSHIRE

ACTIVITIES 21st May: Rogation Sunday
1st July: Rock Fete
1st October: Autumn in the countryside.

CONTACT Phone 0299 822733 or 0299 825232 for further information.

FOOD The Dog at Dunley and The Bliss Gate.

VILLAGE Walks along the Worcestershire Way and the ancient Salt Ways.

VISIT Wyre Forest with Information Centre & Picnic Areas; Deer Museum at Button Oak; Golf at Little Lakes and Wharton Park; Bewdley Safari Park and the Severn Valley Railway.

Bayton, Far Forest, Heightington, Mamble, Rock

Himbleton   150/ 946 588

St Mary Magdalene

Norman with later additions

Worcester
Grade 1

Small church in rural setting with oak shingle clad tower topped by black and white belfry. A medieval porch leads into the church. The interior has a fine barrel roof and several stained glass windows. The Chancel East window has a 13th Century figure of Mary Magdalene said to be the oldest piece of stained glass in the diocese. Over the East window of the Chancel is the Tudor Royal Arms.

TRAVEL From the Droitwich /Hanbury road (B4080) turn towards Worcester following

Himbleton signs. From M5, junction 6 take the A4538 (Evesham) 1st exit at the roundabout to Crowle and to Himbleton. Near to Wychavon Way - many signposts.

OUTSIDE Galton memorial in churchyard. Porch and Tower, Lych-gate.

ACTIVITIES 24th and 25th June: Flower Festival 10 am - 6 pm. Refreshments in the village hall. To conclude with Evensong at 6.30 pm on Sunday 25th. 9th September: Cycle Ride Day
SPECIAL Wheelchair access through Vestry.

CONTACT Church Contact: 0526 821782 or 0905 391609.

FOOD The Galton Arms in Himbleton Shell Ford

VISIT The Jinny Ring Craft Centre, Hanbury. Hanbury Hall (National Trust).

Hindlip   SO 880 586

St James the Great

1st Dedication 5th Century?
Victorian

Worcester
Grade 2*

The Hindlip estate, connected with the Gunpowder plot, and more recently the country seat of the Allsopp family, surrounds the hill on which the church stands. The house and grounds were acquired by the Worcestershire Police in 1946 and have now been developed as the West Mercia Constabulary Headquarters. Much of the land now forms part of the Worcestershire Agricultural College. The church was almost entirely rebuilt by Lord Hindlip in 1864; all that remains of the previous building is the tower. Enlargements in 1888 by the next Lord Hindlip included the South Aisle, Lady Chapel and Vestry. At that time the Hindlips were affluent and no expense was spared on the church. Nearly all the windows are of stained glass. There is a good collection of carved oak items, many of these show scenes from the Bible. There is also an extensive collection of brassware.

TRAVEL From Fernhill Heath (mid-way between Worcester and Droitwich on the A38), take the Blackpole turn then turn left in half a mile; follow

signs to West Mercia Constabulary Headquarters.
PARK On the road outside the church, or use the police car park.

OUTSIDE In the graveyard, the further section belongs to the Allsopp family, although it is no longer used. It contains some interesting memorials. The Gaunt memorial in the main churchyard is also worthy of note.

ACTIVITIES Saturday 3rd June, 10 am - 4 pm: In the steps of St Wulfstan.
Saturday 9th September, 10 am - 4 pm: Cycle Ride. Light refreshments may be provided on open days.

FOOD The Pear Tree at Smite or, at Fernhill Heath, the White Hart and Half-Way House. The Swan at Martin Hussingtree. Picnic site: there is a small nature reserve below Hindlip. Return the way you came, turning left at the farm buildings belonging to the College.

VILLAGE The nature reserve is on the left in about half a mile.

VISIT Salwarpe and Martin Hussingtree.

well loved and cared for. Includes some interesting features: "The chancel arch is of the early 12th century, is quite splendid and in good condition... There is a fine window of early 15th century date in the South wall of the side chapel with good original glass... The font is probably of early 12th century design and execution is really quite magnificent." (English Heritage description).

TRAVEL Holt Heath village is 6 miles north of Worcester off A443. Church is signed 1 mile Worcester side of Holt, off A443. Also signed off A4133 between Holt Fleet bridge and Holt Heath.
PARK Parking available along unadopted lane adjacent to church.

OUTSIDE Fine Norman doorways on north and south side of church. Lych-gate. Stone mounting block. Brick and stone wall around churchyard. Holt Castle nearby.

ACTIVITIES 24th, 25th June: Village Fete and Flower Festival, Church field.
9th September: Sponsored Cycle Ride. The Church is open every Saturday and Sunday.

FOOD Red Lion, Holt Heath. Holt Fleet. Wagon Wheel, Grimley. Crown and Sandys, Kings Arms, Ombersley.

VILLAGE Footpath to Grimley.

VISIT Broomfield Apples - Sept to May. Witley Court and Church, Great Witley. Worcester. Farmhouse Flora, Shrawley. Ombersley Galleries, Ombersley. Monkwood conservation area, Grimley. Grimley Lock.

Holt Heath   83 63

St Martin

1086   *Worcester*
Norman   *Grade 1*

A fine small Norman church built from local red sandstone. It is in a rural setting, adjacent to Holt Castle, a fortified manor house set above the River Severn. The church is in very good repair, obviously

Inkberrow   017 573

St Peter

Worcester
Perpendicular - Decorated   *Grade 1*

Set in partly walled quiet country churchyard. St Peter's dates from the 13th Century, but the font is probably 12th Century, having been in the Saxon church originally on the site. Built of local stone, additions have been carried out (details inside church). Fragments of medieval glass in some windows.

Dormston chapel, with Savage Tomb, dates from 17th Century. Evidence of Civil War activity from damage to tomb, and book of maps left in Old Vicarage opposite by Charles I in 1644. More comprehensive information is available in the church. Work is being carried out from summer 1994 to build a church schoolroom at rear of church to provide increased facilities for the church's work in the parish.

TRAVEL Off the A422 Stratford/Worcester Road. Behind village green and Old Bull Public House. **PARK** Limited parking immediately outside. Large car park down hill on right, walkway to churchyard. 18th Century Sundial Near Lych-gate.

ACTIVITIES 3rd June: Flower Festival and evening concert. **SPECIAL** Information pack available in church.

FOOD Old Bull, village green. Bull's Head, opposite village green. Picnic site on bend of A422 (Worcs side of the village) near turning to the Lenches.

VISIT St Paul's, Cookhill.

Kempsey   848 490

St Mary the Virgin

Early English & Decorated   *Worcester*
                                               Grade 1

The church stands on a hill overlooking the River Severn near to the site of a Bishop's Palace where Henry III was held prisoner in 1265 before the battle of Evesham: though the palace is no longer there the setting has not changed. The church developed from an aisleless 12th century cruciform church into a beautiful decorated gothic church with the tower rebuilt and heightened in the 15th century. The tower boasts a peal of 6 bells which are regularly rung. Whilst most of the windows contain good Victorian glass there are two 14th century stained glass windows in the chancel; nearby there is a recumbent effigy of St Edmund Wylde who died in 1620. A medieval cross may be found in the attractive churchyard.

TRAVEL Kempsey is on the A38 three miles from Worcester. St Mary's church is located at the end of Church Road which is a turning off the main road in the centre of the village. There is a bus service running from Worcester, Tewkesbury and Upton upon Severn which stops at the end of Church Road. Walkers would have no difficulty in finding the church as it is signposted on the main road. **PARK** A small car parking area is available by the church but there are no coach facilities.

OUTSIDE The church is situated in an area of great scenic beauty overlooking the River Severn and the Malvern Hills. There is a ford and an 18th century pedestrian bridge with walks along the river and some attractive thatched cottages and Georgian houses situated along the main road and within the village.

ACTIVITIES Regular: every Saturday in August, 2 pm - 4 pm: Displays of local crafts. Refreshments will be available.
1st July: Church fete and open day.

CONTACT Keys are obtainable from 0905 821213 or 0905 820074.

FOOD There are a number of public houses and eating places in the village but the nearest restaurants are the Walter de Cantelupe Inn and the Talbot Inn which are situated on the main road. There are plenty of areas along the river suitable for picnics.

VILLAGE Kempsey is an attractive unspoilt village with a number of signposted walks described in a booklet obtainable from the Post Office and Clarke's Stores.

VISIT Within a short distance there are extensive commons commanding views over the Malvern Hills and Worcester. The lovely village of Severn Stoke with its Norman church and battlement tower is three miles further along the river.

Knightwick (with Doddenham) 734 561

St Mary

1855   *Worcester*
"Decorated" Victorian Gothic

Built in 1855, the architect was Mr Perkins of Worcester. Ankerdine wall-stone was used for the building with facings of Bromyard Down and Broxhill stone for dressings and window tracery.

The total amount of the contract was £900. The chair seats on either side of the Chancel arch depict the old Church of St Mary, Knightwick and the Chapel of St Andrew's, Doddenham. The Altar rail kneelers dispaly local farming and wildlife interests. Some of the wood carvings were done by a local group at the end of the 19th Century. The organ was purchased in 1981 from the Abbey School, Malvern.

TRAVEL At the foot of Ankerdine Hill on the B4197. **PARK** Roadside or in the Talbot Hotel car park (100 yards).

OUTSIDE 1886 flood mark when the River Teme washed through the church door on the 14th May.

ACTIVITIES Regular: Sundays 14th May, 11th June, 9th July and 13th August: open 2 - 5 pm.
Spring Bank Holiday Flower Festival, Saturday 27th May 11 am - 5 pm
Sunday 28th May 2 pm - 5 pm (Songs of Praise, 3 pm - 4 pm)
Monday 29th May 11 am - 5 pm: refreshments available throughout the 3 days.
9 September: Sponsored Bicycle Ride.

CONTACT The church can be opened by prior arrangement with Ankerdine Farm, Knightwick. Tel. 0886 821288.

FOOD The Talbot Hotel, 14th Century. Meals inside or outside by the river, 100 yards from the church. This is a popular inn. Picnic may be eaten in church grounds.

VILLAGE For walkers the "Worcestershire Way" passes the door.

VISIT Within 5 miles on A44 towards Bromyard is Bringsty Common suitable for picnics, walking dogs and children. Drive onto the Common. The footbridge by the Hotel takes walkers over the R. Teme and past the Surgery. Cross the A44 into Suckley Road. (Ignore the Alfrick turn) The first lane on the left leads to the Cemetery Chapel built on the site of the ancient Knightwick Church. A very tranquil spot.

WORCESTERSHIRE

Kyre Wyard   **626 635**

St Mary

c.1150	*Worcester*
Early English	*Grade 2**

This lovely little church has been closely associated with the Kyre estate from early medieval times. It lies between the manor house, the tithe barn and the medieval dovecote. It is of Norman origin, retaining a simple Norman font and a tiny Norman window. The arches and other windows are 14th century with an early wall painting of a saint by a window in the chapel. Fine marble monuments to the Pytts family in the chancel and interesting and unusual Victorian windows.

TRAVEL Off the B4214, 4 miles from Tenbury, 7 miles from Bromyard, signposted Kyre Church (pronounced Kear). Several footpaths lead to the church, which is within the private grounds of Kyre Park. **PARK** Car Park. Coaches welcome by prior arrangement. Phone: 0885 410277.

OUTSIDE The surrounding private grounds of Kyre Park are often open to the public: admission by ticket. Note Baldwin-Childe memorials under East window. Carved oak porch and cloisters (1894). Stone clock on south gable under the wooden bell tower.

ACTIVITIES Easter Monday 17th April, 11 am - 4 pm: Display and talks from 2 pm on the archaeology of Kyre Church and its recent restoration.
Sunday 21st May, 11 am - 5 pm: **SPECIAL** You are invited to join the parish for Rogation Sunday, including a circular walk of about 5 miles starting from Kyre Church at 12 noon. Bring a picnic lunch; stout shoes and trousers recommended.
Saturday 19th August, 11 am - 5 pm: Display of local crafts here and in Stoke Bliss Church.

CONTACT Wheelchair access and groups of more than 10, please contact: 0885 410277 in advance.

FOOD Kyre Park tea rooms adjacent. Several pubs within 3 mile radius of church. Picnic site at Village Hall on B4214. Details within church.

VILLAGE Kyre Park Shrubbery and Fern Nursery.

VISIT 'Treasures' Gardens at Burford, Bromyard Downs, Berrington Hall, Lower Brockhampton.

WORCESTERSHIRE

Rochford also open on 17th April; Stoke Bliss also open 21st May and 19th August.

```
Eastham, Hanley William, Kyre Wyard,
        Stoke Bliss, Rochford.
```

Tithe Barn (13th Century) - largest full-cruck barn extant.

VISIT The Knapp & Ravenscroft Nature Reserves in Alfrick. Well signposted footpaths (map available in church.) Bransford, Alfrick and Suckley.

Leigh

St Edburga

1100   *Worcester*
Norman   *Grade 1*

St Edburga lies on the west bank of the Teme in the hamlet of Leigh, forming part of a classic medieval grouping of Church, Manor Farm and Tithe Barn. It is a large church, reflecting the size of the original parish, which once included Malvern Link as well as Bransford and Leigh Sinton. Notable features include a fine Transitional arcade, a painted 15th Century screen, imposing tombs to the Colles and Devereux families, 15th Century encaustic tiles, and a rare 12th Century effigy of Christ in Benediction, once in a niche above a Penitents' door in the North wall, now installed by the V & A in the Lady Chapel.

TRAVEL Four miles from Worcester on the Hereford (A4103) road. Turn right at The Bank House Hotel and then take right fork signposted 'Alfrick and Leigh Church'. Church is on right approx. 1 mile on. **PARK** Limited parking is possible on gravel verge-courtesy of Leigh Court Farm. Coaches able to turn.

OUTSIDE The churchyard has splendid yews, interesting tombstones, a Norman niche on North wall and a scratch sundial on the South wall of the Bell tower.

ACTIVITIES Holy Communion 11 am Sundays. 3rd June, 10 am - 6 pm: In the steps of St Wulfstan. 9th September: Sponsored cycle ride. **SPECIAL** The heraldry displayed on tombstones has been researched and detailed for visitors.

CONTACT Groups can be given conducted tours by arrangement. Tel. 0886 832350.

FOOD Bank House Hotel. The Fox Inn, Bransford.

VILLAGE Bransford Chapel - linked to St Edburga's - behind Bransford Golf Course. Leigh

Little Comberton   SO 428 967

St Peter

                                       Worcester
Norman with Victorian restoration

A beautiful Norman church in picturesque setting at the foot of Bredon Hill, the church contains many 12th century features - look out for traces of wall painting in the nave, early 12th century single light openings and Norman cable moulding. The south wall contains interesting fragments of 15th century glass in the windows. The Chancel, rebuilt towards the end of the 15th century contains a massive oak arch (1886) and six windows between the roof levels. The tower is early perpendicular and contains a ring of six bells. Major Victorian restoration in the Chancel aisles and transept with red and white stone give a warm glow to the church.

TRAVEL By road - turn right off A44 just over Pershore bridge at T - junction signed "Elmley Castle and the Combertons". Follow road to village, church on right through village. By signed footpath from Elmley Castle, Bricklehampton and Great Comberton. **PARK** On the verge by church or ample parking and turning space in the village hall car park - 200 yards from church.

OUTSIDE The churchyard, carpeted with flowers in the spring, is kept tidy by local volunteers and the view from the seat at the back of the church across the fields to the wooded slopes of Bredon Hill is one of the finest in the area. Look out for the outlines of hands cut in the stone benches of the porch, said to be those of newly married brides! Also the 'Ashlar' and 'Rubble' masonry.

FOOD Queen's Head, Elmley Castle - 1.5 miles. The Old Mill,

VISIT Elmley Castle. Bredon Hill, Pershore, Elmley Castle and the many churches around Bredon Hill.

Lower Broadheath	SO 811 573	Malvern Link

Christchurch

1904 — *Worcester*
Early English — *Grade 2*

A red sandstone church built in 1904 in the Early English style of a 13th Century parish church. It contains some excellent woodwork and good examples of turn-of-the-century stained glass windows.

TRAVEL Take the A443 Tenbury Road from Worcester then off left onto signposted B4204 Martley road. Look for the Bell Inn on the left hand side. Take the 3rd turning to the right after The Bell into Church Lane. The church is on the right hand corner. **PARK** The village hall car park is in Church Lane next to the churchyard.

OUTSIDE The Ship weather-vane.

ACTIVITIES Sunday 15th January, 6.30 pm: "Thine be the Glory" - Songs of Praise for St Wulfstan's Day.
Sunday 16th April: Easter services 9.30 am and 6.30 pm. Open 2.00 pm to 6.30 pm for the public viewing of the Floral Decorations
Saturday 3rd June, 10 am - 6 pm: Exhibition of old Maps showing St Wulfstan's locations.
23-25 June Flower Festival, Theme: 'Thine be the Glory', refreshments in the Village Hall. Friday 23rd June, 12 noon - 8 pm. Sat 24th, Sun 25th 10 am - 6 pm Sat 8th July, 10 am - 5 pm, Sun 9th July, 2 pm - 5 pm:Exhibition of Tapestries and Embroideries. Refreshments in Village Hall.
Sat 9th September: Sponsored Bike Ride.
Sun 1st October: Harvest Services 9.30 am and 6.30 pm. Open 2.00 pm to 6.30 pm for public viewing of Harvest decorations.

FOOD The Bell Inn, Martley Road and The Plough, Crown East Lane.

VILLAGE The Birthplace of Sir Edward Elgar in Crown East Lane, also reached from A44. Parking at The Plough.

Church of the Ascension

1903 — *Worcester*
Late Victorian — *Grade 2*

Standing tall and distinguished in well kept grounds with views of the Malvern Hills, the church built in memory of the Ven. Arthur Livingstone and designed by William Tapper is noted for its fine acoustics which has enabled the Aldwyn Consort and others to record and hold regular concerts. Twelve yew trees line the path to the church door. On entering, one is immediately struck by the simplicity of line, everything leads the eye up and towards the High Altar. Six banners designed by Ian Thompson and made by members of the congregation hang from the clerestory arcade.

TRAVEL From the M5, take the A449 into Malvern Link. 1st Traffic Lights turn right, then 2nd left, continue to junction with Newtown Road. The church is three-quarters of a mile on the right. **PARK** Street parking.

OUTSIDE Marvellous views of the Malvern Hills.

ACTIVITIES 3rd June: open all day.
16th-18th June: Music/Flower Festival.
8th/9th July: Embroideries and Tapestries Week.
6th August: Church Detectives.
9th September: Cycle Ride.
24th September, 4 pm: Annual Animal Service.
18th November: Plant a Tree.

WORCESTERSHIRE

CONTACT Key available within 60 yards. Access to kitchen and toilets in church hall. Catering can be arranged. Telephone: 0886 832555.

FOOD Prince of Wales, Newtown Road. Cafe, Malvern Link. It is possible to picnic in the church grounds.

VISIT The Malvern Hills. The Morgan Motor Company - groups by appointment. St Matthias, Malvern Link and St Peter's, Cowleigh.

Malvern Link	SO 784 487

Saint Matthias'

1846   *Worcester*
Victorian   *Grade 2*

Against the backdrop of the Malvern Hills, a large, attractive Malvern Stone church is set in a leafy churchyard. The 100ft. bell tower contains a fine peal of ten bells rung twice on Sundays. Particularly significant are stained glass windows by Kempe. Presence of the Reserved Sacrament reflects Anglo-Catholic tradition. Three mice indicate Thompson of Leyburn carved the Lady Chapel screen. A finely carved rood, with exquisitely painted panels, draws one toward the beautiful modern dossal. Recently modified, the Nicholson organ is of notable quality. The west end conversion to a parish room is an asset to the community.

TRAVEL Follow the A449 from Worcester into Malvern Link. Turn right at the cross-road with traffic lights along Richmond Road. Turn left at the T-junction with Church Road. The church is 150m on the left. **PARK** Parking on Church Road outside the church entrance.

OUTSIDE The "Link Stone", an ancient boundary marker and the oldest monument in the Link, has a central well for collection of dues and is sited near the south entrance of the churchyard.

ACTIVITIES Regular opening: Sundays 8 am - 12 noon; Thursdays 10 am - 12 noon (April to Sept) Coffee served.
21st Jan, 7.30 pm: Davenham Ensemble, (music for wind, string and piano).

20th May, 7.30 pm: Organ Recital by John Widerspin A.R.C.O.
3rd June: 'In the Steps of St Wulfstan'; All Day, Raduna of Bells. Lunch & tea.
8-9th July: 'Embroideries and Tapestries Week'; Display of Vestments on Sat. 10 am - 2 pm; Sun. 8 am - 5 pm Refreshments available.
20th August: 'Church Detectives'; 2 pm - 6 pm Children's Treasure Hunt; Refreshments
16th Sept, 7.30 pm: Hereford Police Choir.
Sun: Harvest Festival Services 8 am, 10 am, 6.30 pm. **SPECIAL** Guided tours available. **Toilets with facilities for disabled.**

CONTACT Opening by appointment through the churchwardens Tel: 0886-832460 or 0886-833647, or Rector Tel:0684-573834.

FOOD Picnic sites at Victoria Park and Link Common; pubs, cafes, shops and restaurants all 5 mins walk from church in the Link.

VISIT The Link Common. The Malvern Hills; The Old Hills; Great Malvern with Malvern Museum and the Winter Gardens; P.Y.O. fruit farms. St Peter's, Cowleigh and the Church of the Ascension at Newtown.

St. MATTHIAS' CHURCH, MALVERN LINK

Mamble 3688 2717	**North Piddle**

St John the Baptist

Worcester
Late 12th Century Grade 1

Mamble church spire is visible from all directions, the bells still call the people. Beneath the spire lies the original open timber framed structure of the bell tower that bears closer inspection inside. Enter by the South Porch door to discover the Crusader Door, enabling Knights on horseback to receive their blessing before a crusade. Imagine the village orchestra playing in the Minstrel's Gallery above. Then sit quietly and consider the skill of the mason who constructed the Chancel Archway, or the beauty of the East Window that simply depicts Christ.

TRAVEL Turn off A456 into Mamble village, take the lane to the left of the public house. Immediately turn left into Church Lane, church on right (on foot only). **PARK** Limited road parking in village in front of public house (the lane to the church is a no through road). There is a large car park at the rear of the pub available to patrons.

OUTSIDE The bell tower and spire; the church is built of local sandstone; contrasting with the 'brick' remains of the 16th century Blount Chapel.

ACTIVITIES 21st May: Rogation Sunday Walk. 24th June: Flower Festival.
1st October: Wyre Forest in Autumn Colours.
1st Saturday in December: Church Christmas Bazzar in Village Hall.

CONTACT For any further information or openings by arrangement; ring: 0299 832886.

FOOD The Sun and Slipper Public House, opposite Church Lane, offers lunchtime and evening meals. Picnic site available in lay-by off A456 just west of Mamble.

VISIT The Neen Hill Garden, Neen Sollars - open Wednesdays 12 noon - 5 pm Easter - October.
Towns of Tenbury Wells, Cleobury Mortimer and Bewdley.

Bayton, Mamble, Rock, Heightington and Far Forest.

St Michael and All Angels

1837 Worcester
Late rural Georgian

A small country church on a cul-de-sac in a peaceful, pretty setting.

TRAVEL Located 0.5 mile off the A422 at the North Piddle turn. Turn left at small crossroads. **PARK** Very limited. No coaches.

OUTSIDE Well maintained country churchyard.

CONTACT Ring 0905 381402.

FOOD 1 mile to Flyford Flavell: The Flyford Arms or the Boot (both excellent).

VISIT Coneybury Farm Shop & Garden Centre on A422. 10 miles Worcester. 16 miles Stratford.

Norton

St James the Great

1080? Worcester
Norman with Early English and Victorian additions.

The Church lies back from the road in the centre of the village, and is surrounded by a churchyard containing many memorials and headstones including those of the Worcestershire Regiment. The Norman North wall has an interesting loop window and an Early English lancet window. The Tower dates from around 1370 and contains three bells, the oldest of which was cast in 1450. The building was enlarged and restored in the 1870s and shortly afterwards the Norton Barracks was built for the Worcestershire Regiment whose colours can be seen hanging in the South Aisle.

TRAVEL From the A44 or the A38, follow signs for Norton, the village lies approximately 4 miles south of the City of Worcester. Contact Astons coaches (0905 820201) for times of buses. **PARK** Roadside parking, minibuses welcome, coaches may park in the Retreat Inn by prior arrangement (0905 820274).

OUTSIDE North Wall - look for the Norman doorway, loop and lancet windows. Ancient yew trees, one of which is thought to be 440 years old. Fine Oak Tree planted in 1935 to commemorate the Silver Jubilee of King George V and Queen Mary.

ACTIVITIES 3rd June, 10 am - 5 pm: In the steps of St Wulfstan.
9th September, 10 am - 5 pm: Sponsored Cycle Ride.
SPECIAL There will be a display of local photographs from the past of Norton and surrounding area. Tea, Coffee and biscuits will be available on both open days.

FOOD The Retreat Inn, Woodbury Lane, Norton (pub and restaurant). Picnics may be eaten in the churchyard.

VILLAGE St Peter's Garden Centre, Broomhall - refreshments available. Princes Stores, Orchard Grove, Littleworth. Norton Service Station - sweets, chocolates and cold drinks as well as full garage services.

VISIT Worcester City and Cathedral.

Norton (Evesham)   **SP 042 478**

St Egwin

1206   *Worcester*

Set back off the A435 in an acre and a half with views across farmland. The church was built in 1206. It was restored in 1840 but retains much of its 14th and 15th Century stonework, including the Biggs chapel in the North Transept, which houses fine tombs and memorials of the Biggs family, resident in Lenchwick in the late 16th and early 17th Centuries. In this chapel, there is an interesting plaque to the late Sir Christopher Ewart-Biggs, diplomat and descendant of the Lenchwick Biggs. The stone lectern is 12th Century, reputedly from Evesham Abbey.

TRAVEL The Church is situated on the A435, two miles north of Evesham. **PARK** There is a small car-park which can accomodate mini-coaches and a larger grassed area for parking in fine weather.

OUTSIDE The Boulter tomb is listed.

ACTIVITIES Open: 21st May, 11th June, 2nd July. 9th September, 10 am - 4 pm: Cycle ride.

CONTACT The church key is available from "Churchdene", next to the church. Groups can be catered for and a guided tour provided. Contact P.C.C. Secretary 0386 870416.

FOOD Norton Grange Hotel (bar meals) is situated half a mile away to the north on A435.

VILLAGE Cottage Garden, 1 Church Lane - adjacent to churchyard. Open on 21st May and 11th June.

VISIT Twyford Country Centre with field path walks to river, craft centre, children's playground and picnic area.

Oddingley   **914 590**

St James The Less

Norman   *Worcester*
15th Century   *Grade 2**

This small rural cruciform church, built of local blue lias limestone, is sited on rising ground overlooking open countryside, a canal and railway. It is noted for old painted glass in the East and North windows. In the east window are St Wulfstan and friends. There is also a Galton brass in the church. It is also noted for the murder of its Vicar in 1806, whose case made legal history.

TRAVEL Take the Worcester Road out of Droitwich - at the top of the hill fork left into Taewell Road. Follow this road for 3.5 miles until the sign for Oddingley Church is seen. **PARK** Small adjacent car park for 5 cars. Lane verge 100 yds away. No coach facilities.

OUTSIDE Old, interesting headstones including Reverend Parker's (murdered 1806) burial stone.

ACTIVITIES 24th June: Flower Festival
9th September: Cycle Ride

FOOD "The Firs", Dunhampstead.

VISIT Dunhampstead Marina, Hanbury Hall (National Trust), Jinny Ring Craft Centre, Hanbury, Brine Baths, Droitwich.

Offenham

Ombersley   SO 84 63

St Mary and St Milburgh

1861   *Worcester*
Decorated Style   *Grade 2**

The church retains a Medieval Tower from the 15th Century, while the rest was rebuilt in 1861. The Font predates the existing structure and the bell hanging is from the previous church with 6 bells. The organ has a moveable keyboard. The old Bible is dated 1847. The tapestry at the rear of the church is a reflection of the window at the east end (above the altar).

TRAVEL Follow the B4035 off the Evesham by pass towards Evesham and take the first right towards Offenham. Approx. 1 mile at the cross roads, turn left. Follow road through village, church is on left, British Legion on right. **PARK** There is ample parking opposite church. Coaches can turn at the Maypole at the end of the village.

OUTSIDE Ornamental Iron work over the gate. The Yew Tree to the west is 270 years old and a gravestone along the church path, dated 1620, has a rubbing of the inscription in the church. **The churchyard still in use, regularly appears in the Best Kept Churchyard competition.**

ACTIVITIES Saturday 10th June: Wake Day. 1st October: Harvest Festival. **SPECIAL** On these dates will be an exhibition on the Registers dated from 1538.

CONTACT The church can be opened by contacting The Vicar - on Evesham 0386 - 442096 or by calling at The Vicarage, next door to the church.

FOOD The Bridge Inn is within the village and has gardens by the River Avon. The Maypole.

VILLAGE The Long Thatch (the longest thatch roof on a row of cottages in Worcestershire). The River Avon flows through the village.

VISIT Twyford Craft and Garden Centre. We are a joint benefice with Bretforton three and a half miles away. Their church is a Grade 1 listed building 800 years old and the famous "Fleece Inn" owned by the National Trust is nearby.

St Andrews

1829   *Worcester*
George IV   *Grade 2*

Surrounded by the Court's park, (with 41 listed grade II dwellings) set in an equally interesting churchyard, the church stands as a masterpiece of the work of the architect Thomas Rickman FSA. Rickman(1776-1841)who was a revolutionary pioneering architect of nationwide fame built the church in 1829. His lofty, elegant, George IV estate church still preserves original fittings and furbishings; i.e. box pews; 3 galleries; manorial pew with open fireplace and curtain-rails. Organ case, matching the outline of pulpit and altar boards. Stove of ecclesiastical design. Classical Sandys' memorial tablets in black and white marble. Splendid colourful windows by the well known Regency glazier firm of Hardman.

TRAVEL In the centre of village on the Worcester/ Kidderminster A449 road. The Spire is obvious. Daily bus service to centre of village. Located near the route of the Wychavon Way. **PARK** Special parking will be arranged - cars and minibuses only.

OUTSIDE The churchyard has 14 listed grade II tombs, the medieval village cross and the chancel of a 13th century - 15th century parish church (presently the Sandys - Barons of Ombersley - mausoleum)

ACTIVITIES Open day Saturday 16th September 1995, 12 am - 4 pm. Next day Sunday Harvest Festival service.

CONTACT For any special arrangements, please tel. 0905 620846.

FOOD The Crown & Sandys' Hotel and Inn 0905 620252.The Kings Arms Inn 0905 620315.The Venture Inn Restaurant 0905 620552.The Gallery Restaurant and Tea Room 0905 620655.The Cross Keys Inn 0905 620588. (All within easy walking distance.)

VILLAGE Ombersley Gallery with selected crafts and paintings. Newsagent, The Gallies.

VISIT At Witley Court (English Heritage): Court and Baroque Church At Droitwich: Hanbury Hall - National Trust.

WORCESTERSHIRE

Pirton   SO 886 468

St Peter

972 AD   *Worcester*
Norman/Early English   *Grade 2**

This beautiful country church of simple nave and
chancel construction stands on ridge 1 mile SE of its
village, with magnificent views over Severn valley
to Malverns and to Bredon Hill. The stone church
has an impressive 14th Century half-timbered tower,
with its own side aisles, built on to the North Wall.
Two 12th Century doors with original ironwork.
Norman font set in medieval tiles. Saxon mass-dial
over tower door. Outstanding Norman chancel arch
with effigy reputed to be St Peter. 3 good Victorian
stained-glass windows: some unusual deeply stepped
and splayed windows in North Wall.

TRAVEL From A44: 5 miles South of Worcester
turn right (4 miles north of Pershore turn left)
signposted Wadborough. Straight through
Wadborough to T-junction, turn left and on over
level-crossing for 1 mile. Up hill bear left,church on
left round corner. From A38: approach via Severn
Stoke (follow signpost to Pirton). **PARK** Good
roadside parking on grass, North side of churchyard.

OUTSIDE Base of 14th Century preaching cross.
Unusual weathercock. Wild flowers, especially
snowdrops, primroses and cowslips. Fine trees,
including Catalpa bignonioides (Indian Bean Tree).

ACTIVITIES 3rd June: In steps of St Wulfstan.
10th September: Diocesan Cycle Ride. **SPECIAL**
Circular 2-mile walk from church to village.

CONTACT For information contact: 0905 371 271,
or 0905 821573 or 0905 840254.

FOOD Mason Arms, Wadborough. Organ-Grinder,
Stonehall Common.

VISIT Croome D'Abitot Church, 1 mile.
Other half timbered churches in Worcestershire:
Defford.

Powick   834 515

St Peter's

Medieval   *Worcester*
                                               Grade 1

St Peter's was most likely a wooden structure when it
was recorded in the Domesday Book. Then St Wulfstan
requested churches to be of stone and the stone
structure (started in Norman times) looks today very
much as it did when the Battle of Worcester was
fought in 1651. There are some four acres of ancient,
interesting and tranquil churchyard. Beautiful stained
glass windows, historical monuments and mid-
Victorian fittings show testimony to the church's
continuity of use as a place of prayer and worship
through the ages. In years gone by monks from
Worcester Cathedral regularly walked to services.

TRAVEL It is signposted in Powick at the junction
of the A449 and the B4424. There are bus stops on
the Malvern road and the Upton road just a few yards
from the signpost to the church. A ramped access
road opposite the post office and the butcher's shop
leads to a kissing gate into the churchyard. **PARK**
Cars and minibuses on the drive. Coaches at the side
of the B4424.

OUTSIDE Musketry and cannon scars on the church
walls made during the Civil War in 1651. The chest
tomb to Charles Wheeley Lea (listed grade 2) and 6
twentieth century war graves.

ACTIVITIES Easter Sunday, 10 am - 4 pm.
Pentecost Saturday and Sunday, 10 am - 6 pm.
3rd June, 10 am - 6 pm: In the steps of St Wulfstan.
29th June, 10 am - 6 pm: Patronal Festival of St Peter.
5th July, 10 am - 6 pm: Embroideries and Tapestries
9th September, 10 am - 6 pm: Sponsored Cycle Ride.
8th October,10 am - 4 pm: Harvest Festival.

FOOD The Red Lion at the junction of the A449 and B4424. The Vernon Arms and The Crown on the A449.

VISIT St James' chapel of ease, Callow End. Old Powick Bridge - the first battle of the Civil War, 1642. The church is on a waymarked footpath which connects with others around the area.The Malverns with superb scenic walks and drives.

Teme to Tenbury road, about 2 miles east of Tenbury.
PARK Good, but limited. No coaches, please.

OUTSIDE Norman features include original windows and North Door. Spring flowers in churchyard. **Best kept churchyard 1993**.A triangular walk from the church (1 mile) takes in the site of the old ferry.

ACTIVITIES Sunday 29th January, 12 noon - 3 pm: Snowdrops and 'Songs of Praise'.
Easter Monday 17th April, 11 am - 5 pm: Church decorated with traditional Easter lilies.
Saturday 23rd September, 11 am - 5 pm: Church decorated for patronal festival and harvest.
SPECIAL Light refreshments including hot drinks, available at church.

FOOD "Tally Ho" on B4204 at Broadheath (3 miles). Selection of pubs, tea rooms etc. in Tenbury Wells (2 miles).

VISIT 'Treasures' gardens at Burford (4 miles). Kyre Park gardens (4 miles). Kyre Wyard and Kyre Park gardens also open on 17th April.

Eastham, Hanley William, Kyre Wyard, Stoke Bliss, Rochford.

Rochford   629 685

St Michael

c. 1120   *Worcester*
Norman   *Grade 2**

Nestling by the River Teme, amongst hop yards and orchards, in unspoilt countryside, lies Rochford Church. The ford, in ages past, was defended by a timber fort: a large grassy motte marks the site. Nearby, remains of a Roman wall border the old Roman road to Tenbury. The North door, now blocked, is a particularly interesting Norman design. The Tree of Life motif above the door is the only example in Worcestershire. An outstandingly beautiful East Window is an early work by William Morris. January snowdrops are well worth seeing at this cherished place of worship. Best kept churchyard 1993.

TRAVEL Signposted from the B4204 Clifton-on-

Rock

St Peter and St Paul

Worcester
Norman

Rock village is 600 feet above sea level and the church is the most outstanding building. Ralph III de Tosney gave the church and part of Wyre Forest to the monks of St Evroul in Normandy as recompense for burning their town. This agreement was ended in the 100 Years War but left Rock with the largest Norman church in Worcestershire. The North doorway, the Chancel Arch and the Font are fine examples of Norman masonry. Marks of weapon sharpening and target practice are on walls outside, and the village stocks, whipping post and an ancient chest are kept inside.

TRAVEL Take the A456 from Bewdley to

WORCESTERSHIRE

Leominster and turn left in approx. 4 miles signed Rock. **PARK** At the side of the road.

OUTSIDE Evidence of Norman decoration and sculpture.

ACTIVITIES 21st May: Rogation Sunday.
1st July: Rock Fete.
1st October: Autumn in the countryside.

CONTACT Phone 0299 832202 or 0299 832214 for further information.

FOOD The Rock Cross, Colliers Arms and the Bliss Gate.

VILLAGE Walks along the Worcestershire Way and the ancient Salt Ways.

VISIT Wyre Forest Information Centre and Picnic areas; Deer Museum at Button Oak; Golf at Little Lakes and Golf and Coarse Fishing at Wharton Park; Bewdley Safari Park and Severn Valley Railway. Churches at Heightington, Far Forest, Mamble and Bayton.

| Heightington, Far Forest, Mamble, Bayton,Rock |

Romsley   **139/ 944 806**

St Kenelm

Not known   *Worcester*

Mainly 12th Century walling,
15th Century tower, 16th Century porch.   *Grade 1*

Tranquil setting on Eastern slope of the Clent Hills and built over the spring rising on the site of the murder of the boy King of Mercia, Kenelm, in the 9th Century. Site of 'lost' village of Kenelmstowe. 12th Century doorway with fine tympanum within partly timbered porch. Norman arch above tympanum has beak-head mould. East of porch is a small carved figure in the act of benediction. Angle gargoyles on tower. Consecration cross on North West buttress. Inside: Traces of wall painting on North wall. East window given by W.E. Gladstone. North Window depicts the legend of St Kenelm. South window possibly Burne-Jones. Students of literature may be interested to know that the Legend of St Kenelm is referred to in Chaucer's 'Canterbury Tales' and that St Kenelm's is thinly disguised as St Chad's Church in Francis Brett Young's novel "Portrait of Clare".

TRAVEL From Romsley village: from the 'Sun' pub follow St Kenelm's Road for approx. 1.5 miles. Turn left into Chapel Lane. Church on right in 50 yds. From Birmingham: Follow A456 for Kidderminster. 1 mile after junction with B4551 turn left into Uffmoor Lane, first right Chapel Lane, church on right in 50 yds. From Kidderminster: Follow A456 towards Birmingham, approx. 0.5 mile past Badger's Sett turn right at island into Hagley Wood lane. At T-junction turn left, church 200 yds. on left. On foot: Follow Walk No. 108 in 'No Through Road" - AA publication. **PARK** Limited, but adequate for coach or minibus.

OUTSIDE St Kenelm's Well and Spring garden. Base of old Market Cross; grave of John Read (first burial in churchyard). Grave of John Medlicott, Founder of Methodism in Romsley. Grave of Francis Alexander Barton, aviation pioneer.

ACTIVITIES Regular: Open Saturday afternoons (2 - 5 pm) from 1st April - 30th Sept. 3rd June: In the steps of St Wulfstan.
15th & 16th July: St Kenelm Patronal Festival Weekend with Flower Festival.
Regular Sunday Services at 8 am, 11 am, and 6.30 pm.

CONTACT The church can be opened with guided tours for groups (including schools and history groups) by prior arrangement by telephoning: 0562 710216, 0562 710395 or 0562 710407. **Access for disabled is difficult as there are 4 steps down into the church.**

FOOD The Sun Inn and Fighting Cocks Inn on B4551 in Romsley. Manchester Inn 1.5 miles south on B4551. The Vine and Fountain Inns in Clent. Badger's Sett and Travel Lodge on A456. Picnic sites, toilets and snacks at nearby car parks at Nimmings Wood and Walton Hill.

VILLAGE Post Office and shops in Romsley village. PYO Fruit Farm. Caravan and Camping Club site in Fielshouse Lane, Romsley.

VISIT Halesowen Abbey (Sundays only July & Aug). Hagley Hall. Waseley Country Park. Beechcroft Garden Centre. Uffmoor Wood (Woodland Trust).

Rous Lench

St Peters

Norman   *Worcester*

Small stone Norman church with belfry, surrounded by yew trees and graveyard. Village green in easy walking distance. There is a small annexe to the church housing Rous family marble memorials. These are extremely impressive and very well worth visiting. Restoration work will be finished by Christmas 1994. In the Lady Chapel there is a triptych behind the altar which is a copy of the one in Ghent Cathedral by Jan van Eyck 1432, entitled 'The Adoration of the Mystic Lamb'.

TRAVEL From Worcester take the A 422 towards Stratford. Fork right at Tolleys garage and go to Radford. Take right hand turn in Radford towards Evesham. Rous Lench is about half a mile along the road. Church on left hand side. From Evesham, go through Lenchwick and Church Lench to Rous Lench. **PARK** In bay on road outside church.

OUTSIDE Figure of Christ above entrance door. Walk right up church path and view the Court house through the trees.

ACTIVITIES 3rd June: In the steps of St Wulfstan. 24th and 25th June: Summer flower festival and Pig Roast on Village Green at St Peters Tide.

CONTACT Key with Church Warden. Please ring 0386 792827.

FOOD Pub Wheelebarrow Castle on the road to Stratford in Radford. Seat on the village green and also one in churchyard.

VISIT Evesham, Abbots Morton with tiny Norman country church. Church Lench with old church on hill.

Salwarpe   874 620

St Michael

13th Century   *Worcester*
14th Century   *Grade 1*

The church, on the edge of a wooded scarp, is approached through a lych-gate; in the churchyard are a number of tall evergreen trees (Thuja gigantea). It is a fine example of a plain, substantial, village church - initially quite small and of Norman origin but enlarged in the 14th Century. We know that in 1651 King Charles II summoned 30 able bodied men from Salwarpe to join in the battle of Worcester - no one knows if they came back but the church contains many memorials and effigies of local people.

TRAVEL The church is approached from the A38, just south of Droitwich Spa, turning into Copcut Lane by the 'Trotters Hall' pub. **PARK** The lane is a cul-de-sac and there is limited parking near the churchyard.

OUTSIDE Apart from the church there is no village centre. Adjacent to the Church is a fine half-timbered house, Salwarpe Court, visible from the road but in private ownership. Once owned by the Beauchamp family and Warwick the Kingmaker was born there.

ACTIVITIES Regular: Church open 1st Sunday of each month from March - October (inclusive), 2 pm - 4 pm.
Sat 3rd June, 10 am - 4 pm: 'In the steps of St Wulfstan'.
Sat 8th July, 2 pm - 5 pm: Embroidery and Tapestry Week.

WORCESTERSHIRE

Sat 19th August, 2 pm - 5 pm: Salwarpe Village Fete.
Sat 9th September, 11 am - 5 pm: Cycle Ride.
Sun 19th Nov, 12 noon - 3 pm: Tree Sunday.

CONTACT Access can usually be arranged at other times. Contact the Rector on 0905 778757.

FOOD Trotter Hall, Worcester Rd. or the Bowling Green, Hadley Heath.

VISIT Droitwich Canal and River Salwarpe. St James, Hindlip, St Michael's, Martin Hussingtree.

Sedgeberrow   **SP 025 385**

St Mary the Virgin

1331   *Worcester*
Medieval with Victorian restoration   *Grade 2*

This medieval church is situated in the middle of the village. It was superbly restored during the Victorian era by Butterfield. Particular notice should be taken of the tiles in the Chancel, the Screen, the Reredos and the hand-painted stained glass windows.

TRAVEL Enter the village from the A435 (Evesham - Cheltenham road) and follow the road round to the church. **PARK** On the road outside the church.

OUTSIDE Unusual clock tower and spire; clock with no face (chiming hours and quarter hours); the lych-gate.

ACTIVITIES 3rd, 4th June, 2 pm - 5 pm: Flower Display (Whit Sunday).
24th June, 10 am - 5 pm; 25th June, 12 pm - 5 pm: Flower and Craft Display.
23rd & 24th September, 2 pm - 5 pm: Flower Display (Harvest Festival).
1st and 3rd Sundays in month: 9 am service. 2nd and 4th Sundays in month: 10 am service. Children's Church Tuesdays at 3.30 pm in term time.

FOOD Queen's Head (in village, near church), picnic site: the village green (opposite the Queen's Head).

VISIT River Isbourne (only river flowing North). Bredon Hill, Evesham, Cheltenham, Broadway.

Severn Stoke   **SO 855 440**

St Denys

Worcester
Early English/Decorated with traces of Norman work
Grade 2*

The prominent battlement church tower catches the attention of travellers on the A38. The building mainly dates from the 14th Century, though traces of an earlier Norman church remain. In the chancel note the wall tablet commemorating John Somers, erected by his son, the famous Lord Chancellor Somers. During the Civil War Captain Somers took a pot shot at a preacher for bringing politics into religion! There are several memorials to the Coventry family, two of whom successively held the incumbency between 1833 and 1920. There are fragments of medieval glass in the side aisle windows.

TRAVEL Severn Stoke is on the A38 Worcester - Tewkesbury road 7 miles south of Worcester. The church can be seen to the west of the main road. At the War Memorial turn off towards the Rose & Crown; the church car park is just beyond. From Worcester or Upton Midland Red bus services 372 or 373 stop at War Memorial. **PARK** Car parking at churchyard gates for 20 cars.

OUTSIDE The churchyard has some interesting early gravestones, the oldest dated 1656, and the shaft of a medieval cross with a rare little niche where the pyx was placed for holy days processions.

ACTIVITIES Sunday 16th June: Friends of St Denys Annual Service with church open all day. Sunday 25th June: Open Air Family Service on Rose & Crown Green.

Saturday 9th September: Sponsored Bike Ride. Church open 10 am - 6 pm.

CONTACT Key available, see details in porch. Guided tours available by arrangement - Tel. 0905 371309.

FOOD Rose & Crown is adjacent. Boars Head and Old School House Hotel on main road through village.

VISIT The Church of St Mary Magdalene, Croome D'Abitot (see separate entry). Attractive small town of Upton-upon-Severn 3.5 miles distant. Croome D'Abitot and Kempsey.

Stoke Bliss	651 629

St Peter

c. 1150   *Worcester*
Early English   *Grade 2**

St Peter's is set dramatically on a knoll between two streams. The shingled spire can be seen from most of the parish. The Early English main doorway has carved heads on each side; beyond this is the simple Norman font. Separating the nave and the chancel is a 15th century rood screen with rose tipped tracery, with a modern head of Christ in the centre. Above the altar are Victorian angels, behind it is a distinctive modern stained glass window. Notice the carved dragons on the reading desk dedicated to Roger Osland in 1635.

TRAVEL On the B4214, 5 miles from Tenbury and 6 miles from Bromyard, Stoke Bliss is signposted. Follow the narrow lane about a mile, turn left (signposted) and the church is another 0.5 mile on. There is a good network of seldom used footpaths and bridleways. **PARK** Limited parking by the roadside, unsuitable for coaches.

OUTSIDE The churchyard is oval which implies great age: it may pre-date the present church. The views are extensive and picturesque. Notice the medieval manor house opposite.

ACTIVITIES Sunday 21st May, 11 am - 5 pm: **SPECIAL** You are also invited to join the parish for the circular Rogation Sunday Walk (5 miles). **See Kyre Wyard** Church for details.
Saturday 29th July, 12 pm - 5 pm: There will be short talks on the architecture of the church and its symbolism, 2 pm - 4.30 pm.
Saturday 19th August, 11 am - 5 pm: Display of local crafts here and in Kyre Wyard.

CONTACT Wheelchair access and groups of more than 10, please contact 0584 810732 in advance.

FOOD There are several pubs serving bar snacks and meals within a 3 mile radius. Picnic site at the Village Hall on the B4214.

VILLAGE Details within the church. Teas available.

VISIT Kyre Park shrubbery and fern nursery (+Tea Rooms). 'Treasures' Garden Centre, Bromyard Downs, Berrington Hall, Lower Brockhampton. Tenbury market town. **Kyre will also be open on 21st May and 19th August, Hanley William on 29th July.**

Eastham, Hanley William, Kyre Wyard, Stoke Bliss, Rochford.

Stone	SO 862 750

The Blessed Virgin Mary

1832   *Worcester*
Gothic revival   *Grade 2*

Site of Saxon?/early Norman church demolished in 1831. Present church built 1831-32 during incumbency of John Peel, later also Dean of Worcester. Chancel extended 1900. Of particular interest is the 20th century stained glass by the Bromsgrove Guild and Francis Skeat. The windows by Skeat depict St Guthlac, St Wulfstan who is shown on his journeys chanting the psalms, and a memorial to Peter Collins, the racing driver, who died in 1958. One window contains some medieval and early Flemish glass from the original church. There are several monuments, notably one for John Peel, and two 17th century brasses for the Spicer family.

TRAVEL A448 1.5 miles east of Kidderminster, 7 miles west of Bromsgrove. PARK In Church Lane, adequate turning for coaches.

OUTSIDE The churchyard cross, now a war memorial, is on the 15th century base. The black and white building, much altered from the 15th century, contains a rare example of a timber-framed chantry chapel. This can be viewed at the SE corner of the churchyard.

CONTACT For group visits, or opening by arrangement, and for enquiries telephone 0562 69438 (the Vicar).

FOOD Stone Manor Hotel. The Dog Inn, Harvington. The Plough Inn, Shenstone (all within 1 mile).

VILLAGE Stone House Cottage Gardens and Nursery (next to Stone church).

VISIT Harvington Hall (SO 877 745). Elizabethan house with Priest Holes. Footpaths to St Mary's R.C. church, Harvington (1825, predating Catholic Emancipation 1829) or via A448, A450.

Stoulton

St Edmund King and Martyr

c.1120	*Worcester*
Early Norman	*Grade 2**

A church of striking simplicity, inside and out. The few alterations or additions since it was built include three Early English windows, installed about 1320 together with the roof timberings; the timber north porch (1848); and the present tower (1936). Inside look for the Acton family tombs in the chancel and the large plain font in the nave.

TRAVEL Stoulton is on the A44 between Worcester and Pershore about midway between the two (2.5 miles from junction 7 of the M5). From Worcester direction turn left into Church Lane at cross-roads after petrol station on your right. From Pershore direction turn right at cross-roads which are at the top of the hill as you come into the village. The church is on the right. PARK For cars and minibuses, anywhere in Church Lane: but please do not obstruct driveways. Coaches by arrangement. Bus services between Worcester and Evesham via Pershore. Tel: 0345 125436 for information.

OUTSIDE Outside the Normans added some decorative arches over the north and south doorways ("blind arcading"). On the sides of the south doorway are scratch dials (home-made sundials). There is a blocked window high up in the west wall: what was it for?

ACTIVITIES 3rd June, 10 am - 6 pm: (St Wulfstan) We hope to combine this with a Street Fair. 3rd - 9th July: Embroideries and Tapestries, phone: 0905 841554. 9th September, 10 am - 6 pm: Sponsored cycle ride. Light lunches and teas will be available in the Village Hall on Special Days. SPECIAL Talks on the church and the village will be given on these Special Days. Illustrated talks about the church and village can be given to interested small parties.

CONTACT Please telephone the Rector on 0905 840528 for an appointment. There is a service in the church every Sunday. Please speak to the Rector if you would like to combine a visit with your worship.

FOOD Bird in Hand, Hawbridge, about 0.25 mile away offers meals and bar snacks. Turn left out of Church Lane then right at signpost in about 150 yards. Picnics: small groups are welcome to picnic on the grassed areas in front of the church.

VISIT Pershore market town and Abbey. Spetchley Gardens. Worcester and the Cathedral.

St Mary the Virgin

Hereford
Grade 2*

The church has a rectangular nave, rectangular 14th century chancel and square tower with bell chamber. The oldest part is the tower, mid 12th Century, with a late Saxon style upper south window. The nave and aisles suffered badly in a flood of 1770, all then being largely rebuilt. Monuments include the Acton Adams alabaster altar tomb of 1581, the Little Crusader of the mid 14th Century, and the Big Crusader, probably of the late 14th Century. Look for the squint in the north wall of the chancel. The vestry, organ chamber and the south porch are modern.

TRAVEL From the A456 cross the River Teme on Teme Street, at the fork of the B4204 (to Droitwich) to the left and Market Street/A4112 (to Leominster) to the right, take the right hand fork. Church Street is a little way on your right on the corner as the A4112 turns a bend to the left. The church is straight ahead in Church Street. Bus, from Ludlow Nos. 731, 732 or 726. These are Midland Red West or Go Whittle. Bus stop on Teme Street. Footpath from here to the church. **PARK** Limited at church. Use main car park, access from Teme Street or the B4204. Coaches can turn, but not park at church.

OUTSIDE The upper south window (as described above).

ACTIVITES Regular: Saturdays in June and July: open for visitors. **Disabled visitors welcome. Easy access to church, including tower base.**

FOOD Several pubs in Teme Street and Market Street. A non-smoking pub is the Fountain, one mile from St Mary's on A4112, towards Leominster. Country restaurant in Teme Street.

TOWN Children's play area by the main car park. River Teme: public access by the river to the right of Teme Street.

VISIT Burford House gardens and restaurant. By car: on A456 towards Ludlow, turn left.

St Peter Ad Vincula

1869   *Worcester*
Victorian

The church was rebuilt in 1868 on the site of a former 13th Century chapel. The flooring and altar rails include woodwork from the old chapel. Situated 200 feet above sea level on a circular piece of ground, the church overlooks local countryside. There is seating for 145 people within. The church is made of stone, and has a Chancel and Nave, a porch and bell turret. There is a shingled spire. Inside, the walls are brick lined. The Worcester coat of arms is depicted in one of the windows.

TRAVEL From Junction 6 of the M5. Follow the B4084 Evesham Road. At the first roundabout, turn left into Tibberton, then take the first lane on the left. No coaches unless by prior arrangement. **PARK** Parking on left side of lane.

OUTSIDE Position of Timber framed buildings (15th and 16th Century), near to the site.

ACTIVITIES 24th June, 10 am - 4 pm: Flower Festival
9th September, 10 am - 4 pm: Cycle ride

CONTACT Church Contact: 0905 345688.

FOOD The Bridge Inn, Plough Road. Speed the Plough, Plough Road.

VILLAGE Shop - Tibberton Post Office.
The Worcester/Birmingham canal. By arrangement: Eatons Farm Museum. There are many footpaths in the area.

VISIT Hanbury Hall, Droitwich. The Jinny Ring Centre, Hanbury. Open in conjunction with Oddingley (20 min by towpath).

Tibberton and Oddingley

WORCESTERSHIRE
Trimpley SO 789 788

Holy Trinity

1844 *Worcester*
Neo-Norman *Grade 2*

Clear evidence of a place of Christian worship at
Trimpley traces back to 1370. The present church
was consecrated in August 1844 as a Chapel of Ease
within the Parish of Kidderminster. The church,
designed by Harvey Eginton, comprises a nave with
western bell-cote and an aspidal chancel all in
neo-Norman style. Within, the west gallery houses
a small Nicholson organ below a rose window. The
nave roof has two king posts each with four curiously
carved heads. The sandstone corbels supporting the
intermediate roof trusses are carved to individual
tail-like designs, a characteristic Eginton signature
and typical of the detail in the stone carving
throughout the church. The apse is formed in stone
with rib-vaulting. The pulpit, entered from the
vestry lobby, is of stone corbelled into the south-east
corner of the nave. Opposite the pulpit stands a
remarkable ornately carved stone lectern. Below the
gallery is a sturdy stone font to match the lectern.

TRAVEL The church is on the north side of the road
to Trimpley Reservoir about 100 yards from its
junction with Wribbenhall (on B4190) to Shatterford
(on A442) unclassified road. From Kidderminster
the approach to Trimpley is via Habberley Lane and
Low Habberley. **PARK** There is parking for three
cars on the roadside near the churchyard entrance.
Additional parking space is available at Trimpley
Village Hall within 200 yards of the church.

OUTSIDE The churchyard is a haven of tranquility
overlooking the Severn Valley with distant views of
the Clee Hills and the Wrekin. It is a rich habitat for
birds and wild flowers. The churchyard is now all
but full for burials but a small extension is soon to be
provided across its northern margin. One of the
glories of the churchyard is the fine Cedar of Lebanon
to the west of the church.

ACTIVITIES 10th June, 10 am - 5 pm: Open Day.
9th September, 10 am - 5 pm: Cycle Ride.

CONTACT Church Contact: 0299 402557.

FOOD Trimpley Reservoir has picnic sites.

VILLAGE Footpaths leave the church in all
directions. There are lovely walks on field paths to
Bewdley, Wribbenhall and Franche.

VISIT Habberley Valley (1 mile south-east) is a
lovely hidden hollow carved into the red sandstone
of which there are amazing water-worn outcrops and
steep cliffs. The Worcestershire Way passes through
Eymore Wood within a mile of the church. Trimpley
Reservoir (2 miles west on road) has access to the
River Severn with riverside walks to Arley or Bewdley
and has the Severn Valley Railway running by.

Upton Snodsbury SO 943 544

St Kenelm's

9th Century *Worcester*
Norman *Grade 2**

Stone construction from Norman period of 13th
Century when the Nave, Chancel, and Bell Turret
were built. The South Aisle and Tower were added
in the 16th Century. The six bells were installed in
1703 and within the last 2 years have been recast. In
the South Aisle stands a late Tudor Font. The oak
screen between Nave and Chancel dates back to the
15th Century. The church stands among many old
gravestones and is set high overlooking the village.

TRAVEL Approx. 5 miles out of Worcester on the
A422. Turning right at the Red Lion Pub in the
village. **PARK** Small parking area opposite main
gate.

OUTSIDE Superb hedged archway leading to main
door.

ACTIVITIES Sunday 14th May: Flower Display
Saturday 15th July: St Kenelm's Day and Church Fete.
Saturday 9th September:Sponsored Bike Ride.

FOOD Three pubs in the village: Coventry Arms,
The Royal Oak and Red Lion.

Upton upon Severn　　　　SO 851 402

St Peter and St Paul

1879　　　　　　　　　　　*Worcester*
Gothic revival　　　　　　*Grade 2**

The present church, designed by Sir Arthur Blomfield, was built when the riverside church became too small. Only the 14th Century tower and graveyard remain on the old site. In 1773, spire was replaced by the cupola, or dome, giving the tower the appearance of a giant pepperpot, hence the name. Memorials and brasses from the riverside church were transferred to the present church: look out for the monument to Sir William Boteler, a Crusader Knight. The Boteler family are believed to have been founders of the original church. There is much fine stained glass: find the windows showing Christ with little children, Mary Magdalene anointing Christ's feet and Christ raising Lazarus from the dead. Do not miss the west window by Whall based on the Benedicite, a song of praise to God, with saints, animals and other scenes. Consider the modern Corona or "Crown" above the altar in the centre of the church, it represents eight winged 'spirit figures'.

TRAVEL 0.25 of a mile from river on Old Street, the A4104 to Welland. **PARK** Free public car park, 2 hour limit, opposite the church. Minibuses may park here; but coaches should use the large pay and display park near the bridge.

ACTIVITIES 8th July, 10 am - 6 pm.
9th July, 2 pm - 6 pm: Display of hand worked kneelers.
9th September, 10 am - 6 pm: Sponsored cycle ride.
SPECIAL Disabled access: 1 step at entrance, ramp available in porch, otherwise level.

CONTACT The church can be open at other times, phone the Rectory 0684 592148.

FOOD Several restaurants and pubs in Old Street, New Street, the High Street and by the riverside. Picnic area on east side of river near bridge.

VILLAGE Pepperpot Heritage and Tourist Information Centre (displays about Upton in the Civil War etc.), the Old Church Tower by the riverside, Tel: 0684 594200. Tudor House opposite the Pepperpot, exhibits of local interest, Tel: 0684 592447. Town trail and footpath leaflets from the

WORCESTERSHIRE

Map Shop, 15 High Street, Tel: 0684 593146. Severn Leisure: cruises along the River Severn, Tel: 0684 593112. Moorings and Marina, Tel: 0684 594287.

VISIT Malvern Hills Animal and Bird Gardens with miniature railway near Welland. Grid ref. SO 800 411, take A4104 to Welland then left on B4208 towards Malvern, Tel: 0684 310016.

Warndon Villages (Worcester)　150/ 887 569

St Nicholas

1542　　　　　　　　　　*Worcester*
Half Timbered Tower　　*Grade 1*

St Nicholas church until the late 1980's served a rural parish, but since then housing has slowly encroached from Worcester city. There is thought to have been a chapel on the site before 900 A.D., then it served the Saxon/Norman manor house, the whole surrounded by a moat. The church has white plastered stone walls (inside and outside), with a half timbered tower, standing in a churchyard containing two ancient Yew trees and the base of a stone cross. Inside there are named/numbered box pews, Jacobean altar furniture, encaustic tiles, some old stained glass and church bells dating back to 1440.

TRAVEL Follow the WARNDON sign off the M5 (junction 6), straight over first roundabout, turn left, then immediately left again (following St Nicholas signs). At the top of the hill turn right, through entrance gate into farm/church area. **PARK** By churchyard perimeter.

OUTSIDE Scratch dial, Norman door arch (south side). Old timbered porch, marked out position of door arch (east end).

ACTIVITIES Regular: The church will be open every weekend from 1st July to 27th August, Saturday, 11 am - 4 pm; Sunday, 2 pm - 4 pm
3rd June, 11 am - 4 pm.

CONTACT Open by arrangement: Tel. 0905 616109.

FOOD Poacher's Pocket.

VILLAGE Trotshill Lane, Ancient Woods within easy reach of church, walks guide available in church.

VISIT Worcester Cathedral, The Commandery.

Wick   SO 963 453

St Mary

c. 1300   *Worcester*
Norman

In a perfect setting for a church, on a hillside opposite the Manor House in a village of farms and cruck cottages, the lych-gate stands between the war memorial and a medieval preaching cross. Inside the church look for the perpendicular waggon roof, round Norman windows and doorway, the Norman font and Norman pillars and capitals - quite exceptionally supporting pointed arches. See also the Jacobean altar rail, the fine Victorian east end and several fine windows including two by Kempe. You can also see a beautiful head for the preaching cross, made and erected, but later removed for safety.

TRAVEL Off A44, one mile SE of Pershore, in centre of village. Waylands footpath from Pershore Bridge to village. **PARK** Limited car parking on road. Set down only for coaches.

OUTSIDE Medieval preaching cross, lych-gate, and war memorial in churchyard.

ACTIVITIES Saturday 2nd September: Church open and manned. Church and village fete 2.30 pm to 5 pm in Church Meadow. **SPECIAL** Teas on Manor House Lawn.

FOOD Many in Pershore. Picnic site at Pershore Bridge, beside the River Avon.

VILLAGE Pershore College of Horticulture, RHS Regional Centre and Plant Centre.

VISIT Historic town of Pershore and Pershore Abbey.

Wribbenhall   SO 793 756

All Saints'

1879   *Worcester*
Victorian Gothic   *Grade 2*

Built in the Victorian Gothic style in local Alveley red sandstone, All Saints' church lies back from the B4190 (formerly A456) Kidderminster to Bewdley road, on the south side. It is situated within a typical churchyard, part of which predates the construction of the church in 1879. The church was designed by Arthur Blomfield (later Sir) to blend in with its then mainly rural setting and has a distinctive Belfrey Tower and Steeple. All Saints' church contains many fine stained glass windows. Amongst its furnishings are items brought from Christchurch Wribbenhall (1701-1879) which closed upon the consecration of All Saints' in 1879. These include the Font and Altar. Look out for the delightful Lych-Gate (c. 1888) leading from Kidderminster road into the churchyard.

TRAVEL All Saints' church is readily visible from the B4190 road in Wribbenhall. Wribbenhall is located on the east (Kidderminster) side of the River Severn. The Midland Red 192/292 Birmingham to Ludlow/Hereford buses stop outside the church also local minibus services no.2B/2C. The Severn Valley Railway Station - Bewdley - is 0.5 mile away and is served by steam trains from Bridgnorth and Kidderminster during the railway's operating season - phone 0299 403816 for details. **PARK** Small car park for approx. 20 cars adjoining west end of churchyard. Parking for coaches and minibuses is available in Bewdley Town Centre (0.5 mile).

OUTSIDE Lych-gate and Octagonal Belfrey Steeple

ACTIVITIES Saturday 15th April 10.00 am - 4.00 Saturday 3rd June, 2 pm - 5 pm: In the steps of St Wulfstan. Saturday 16th September, 10.00 am - 4.00. pm:Special display. Sunday 17th September, 11.30 am - 4.30 pm: Special display.

FOOD 'The Great Western' pub, 250 yards on Bewdley side. 'The Old Wagon and Horses' pub, 300 yards on Kidderminster side. Picnic at Rhydd Covert adjacent to West Midlands Safari and Leisure Park.

VISIT West Midlands Safari Park, three-quarters of a mile. Severn Valley Railway - Bewdley station half a mile. Georgian Riverside Town of Bewdley, half a mile.

Wyre Piddle

SO 980 475

St Anne

Rededicated in 1989
Norman

Worcester

The church is situated on high ground above the River Avon with fine views out to Bredon Hill. The present church was originally built in the Norman period probably in the first two decades of the century. Major restoration work was carried out in 1989 when many Saxon objects were found. The stone altar slab is medieval. A typical 12th century pillar piscina with square bowl stands on the south side of the sanctuary. The west window contains some fine pieces of 15th century glass. The encaustic tiles are medieval and amongst the designs can be seen the popinjay and badge of the Talbot family.

TRAVEL About 500 yards down Church St. which is off A4084 by stone cross. **PARK** On road near church.

FOOD Anchor Inn on A4084 serves meals and has riverside gardens.

VISIT Church of St John the Baptist at Fladbury. Pershore which is 1 mile away and has fine Georgian Buildings, riverside walks and interesting shops. Evesham is 5 miles away. There are many fine walks on Bredon Hill.

NEWS FROM NEIGHBOURING DIOCESES

THE DIOCESE OF LICHFIELD

Within the Church of England the County of Shropshire is divided into two administrative areas. The northern part, including the county town of Shrewsbury, is a part of the Diocese of Lichfield. In 1995 this Diocese will be celebrating the 800th anniversary of the consecration of the Cathedral dedicated to St. Mary and St. Chad in Lichfield. During the Dedication Festival - 1-22nd October the Archbishop of Canterbury will rededicate the Cathedral to its work of:

Worshipping God

Supporting the Faithful

Serving the Community

Many country churches in the Diocese of Lichfield welcome visitors. For more information about the rededication Festival at the Cathedral and details of the special opening arrangements of churches in northern Shropshire contact: Canon A Barnard at the Lichfield Cathedral Visitors Study Centre on 0543 250300.

THE DIOCESE OF GLOUCESTER

Follow the church trails around the Diocese of Gloucester and discover the hidden treasures of the Parish Churches of rural Gloucestershire.

For more information contact:

The Secretary
Churches and Visitors Group
Church House
College Green
Gloucester GL1 2LY